Africa's Cities

Opening Doors to the World

Somik Vinay Lall

J. Vernon Henderson

Anthony J. Venables

With

Juliana Aguilar, Ana Aguilera, Sarah Antos, Paolo Avner,
Olivia D'Aoust, Chyi-Yun Huang, Patricia Jones,
Nancy Lozano Gracia, and Shohei Nakamura.

ISBN (paper): 978-1-4648-1044-2

ISBN (electronic): 978-1-4648-1045-9

DOI: 10.1596/978-1-4648-1044-2

Design and production by Zephyr
www.wearezephyr.com

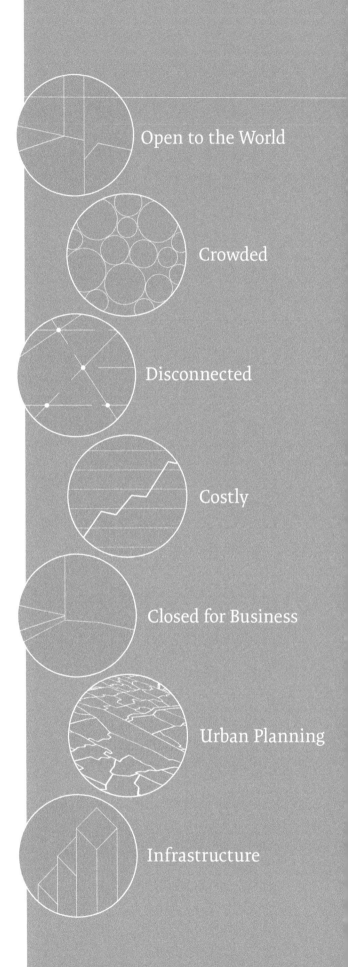

Open to the World

Crowded

Disconnected

Costly

Closed for Business

Urban Planning

Infrastructure

Contents

Figures

Maps

Tables

Boxes

Acknowledgments

This volume is part of the African Regional Studies Program, an initiative of the Africa Region Vice-Presidency at the World Bank. This series of studies aims to combine high levels of analytical rigor and policy relevance, and to apply them to various topics important for the social and economic development of Sub-Saharan Africa. The Office of the Chief Economist for the Africa Region provides quality control and oversight.

A team led by Somik V. Lall, together with J. Vernon Henderson and Antony J. Venables, prepared this report. Members of the core team included Juliana Aguilar, Ana Aguilera, Sarah Antos, Paolo Avner, Olivia D'Aoust, Chyi-Yun Huang, Patricia Jones, Nancy Lozano Gracia, and Shohei Nakamura. Neeraj Baruah, Louise Bernard, Julia Bird, John Felkner, Arti Grover Goswami, Rashmin Gunasekara, Rawaa Harati, and Dzhamilya Nigmatulina provided additional research inputs. Paul Collier, Indermit Gill and William Maloney were key advisors to the report team.

The main authors and contributors were:

- The Overview was written by Somik V. Lall.

- Chapter 1 (Crowded with People, Not Dense with Capital) was written by Nancy Lozano Gracia, J. Vernon Henderson, and Juliana Aguilar, with contributions from Ana Aguilera, Olivia D'Aoust, Somik V. Lall and Tvisha Nevatia.

- Chapter 2 (Disconnected Land, People and Jobs) was written by Paolo Avner, J. Vernon Henderson and Somik V. Lall, with contributions from Neeraj Baruah, Louise Bernard, Julia Bird, Olivia D'Aoust, Somik V. Lall and Dzhamilya Nigmatulina.

- Chapter 3 (Costly for Households, Costly for Firms) was written by Olivia D'Aoust, Patricia Jones, and Shohei Nakamura, with contributions from Rawaa Harati.

- Chapter 4 (Africa's Urban Development Trap) was written by Anthony J. Venables with contributions J. Vernon Henderson and Patricia Jones.

- Chapter 5 (Clarifying Property Rights and Strengthening Urban Planning) was written by Chyi-Yun Huang, Olivia D'Aoust, and Somik V. Lall, with contributions from Juliana Aguilar and Julia Bird.

- Chapter 6 (Scaling up and Coordinating Investments in Physical Structures and Infrastructure) was written by Olivia D'Aoust and Somik V. Lall, with contributions from Juliana Aguilar, John Felkner, J. Vernon Henderson, and Julia Bird.

The report draws on a set of over twenty-five research papers produced as part of a research program on Urbanization and Spatial Development in Developing Countries, conducted by the World Bank, Oxford University and the London School of Economics. The research has been supported by generous financial contributions from UK-Aid through the Multi-donor Trust Fund on Sustainable Urbanization at the World Bank.

The team received valuable comments from Richard Damania, Marianne Fay, Indermit Gill, William Maloney (peer reviewers), Souleymane Coulibaly, Eric Lancelot, Mark Lundell, and Roland White. The team thanks Francisco H. G. Ferreira for providing guidance to the team during his tenure as Africa Chief Economist for the World Bank. The team benefited from discussions with Abebaw Alemayehu, Andre Bald, Mapi M. Buitano, Meskerem Brhane, Punam Chuhan-Pole, Narae Choi, Dean Cira, Sateh Chafic El-Arnaout, Sylvie Debomy, Roger Gorham, Andre Herzog, Sheila Kamanyori, Michel Matera, Megha Mukim, Shomik Mehndiratta, Martin Onyach-Olaa, Dina Ranarifidy, Apurva Sanghi, Maria Angelica Sotomayor and Roland White. The team appreciates the opportunity to discuss the policy framework and findings at various forums including at the East and Central African Forum (Kampala), Habitat III (Quito), Johns Hopkins University (Washington DC), UN Habitat (Nairobi), TDLC Seminar on Land Use Planning & Spatial Development (Tokyo), UK DFID (London), and World Bank Sprig Meetings and workshops in Addis Ababa, Dar es Salaam, Nairobi, Pretoria, and Washington.

The report has been produced under the supervision of Sameh Wahba, Director for Urban and Territorial Development, and the overall direction of Albert Zeufack, Africa Chief Economist for the World Bank.

Nick Moschovakis and Bruce Ross-Larson, with a team at Communications Development, edited the report. Zephyr designed and typeset the report.

Africa's Cities: Opening Doors to the World

The low development trap
— Africa's urban economies are limited
to nontradable goods and services

Crowded, disconnected, and thus costly
— Africa's cities are limited to
nontradables by urban form

Out of service, closed for business:
The urgency of a new urban
development path for Africa

Springing cities from the low
development trap

Opening the doors

African cities are crowded, disconnected, and costly.

Typical African cities share three features that constrain urban development and create daily challenges for residents:

Crowded, not economically dense — investments in infrastructure, industrial and commercial structures have not kept pace with the concentration of people, nor have investments in affordable formal housing; congestion and its costs overwhelm the benefits of urban concentration.

Disconnected — cities have developed as collections of small and fragmented neighborhoods, lacking reliable transportation and limiting workers' job opportunities while preventing firms from reaping scale and agglomeration benefits.

Costly for households and for firms — high nominal wages and transaction costs deter investors and trading partners, especially in regionally and internationally tradable sectors; workers' high food, housing, and transport costs increase labor costs to firms and thus reduce expected returns on investment.

55%

African households face higher costs relative to their per capita GDP than do households in other regions — much of it accounted for by housing, which costs them a full 55 percent more in this comparison

In eight representative African cities, roads occupy far lower shares of urban land than in other cities around the world.

20%
African cities are 20 percent more fragmented than are Asian and Latin American ones.

In Harare, Zimbabwe, and Maputo, Mozambique, more than 30 percent of land within 5 kilometers of the central business district remains unbuilt.

472 million
Urban areas in Africa comprise 472 million people. That number will double over the next 25 years as more migrants are pushed to cities from the countryside. The largest cities grow as fast as 4 percent annually.

Africa's Cities: Opening Doors to the World

Cities in Sub-Saharan Africa are experiencing rapid population growth. Yet their economic growth has not kept pace. Why? One factor might be low capital investment, due in part to Africa's relative poverty: Other regions have reached similar stages of urbanization at higher per capita GDP. This study, however, identifies a deeper reason: African cities are closed to the world. Compared with other developing cities, cities in Africa produce few goods and services for trade on regional and international markets (figure 1).

To grow economically as they are growing in size, Africa's cities must open their doors to the world. They need to specialize in manufacturing, along with other regionally and globally tradable goods and services. And to attract global investment in tradables production, cities must develop scale economies, which are associated with successful urban economic development in other regions.

Such scale economies can arise in Africa, and they will — if city and country leaders make concerted efforts to bring agglomeration effects to urban areas. Today, potential urban investors and entrepreneurs look at Africa and see crowded, disconnected, and costly cities. Such cities inspire low expectations for the scale of urban production and for returns on invested capital. How can these cities become economically

dense — not merely crowded? How can they acquire efficient connections? And how can they draw firms and skilled workers with a more affordable, livable urban environment?

From a policy standpoint, the answer must be to address the structural problems affecting African cities. Foremost among these problems are institutional and regulatory constraints that misallocate land and labor, fragment physical development, and limit productivity. As long as African cities lack functioning land markets and regulations and early, coordinated infrastructure investments, they will remain local cities: closed to regional and global markets, trapped into producing only locally traded goods and services, and limited in their economic growth.

The low development trap — Africa's urban economies are limited to nontradable goods and services

How does the production of locally consumed, or nontradable, goods and services trap cities into low economic growth? Put simply, producing for local markets limits returns to scale. The consumer base of one city, however large, is much smaller than a regional or global market. Specializing in nontradables for local consumption leads to diminishing returns (both for technological reasons, and because prices are set locally and decline as supply increases). In contrast, export markets are key to a dynamic industrial sector.

Since the 1980s, much of the growth in developing countries has depended on the expansion of exports through industrial production and higher technology. Unlike nontradables, tradable goods and services face elastic global demand. They may also allow for agglomeration economies, which increase returns to employment (box 1). Rapidly growing cities require growth in employment — and the returns to expanding employment are highest in tradable sectors.

FIGURE 1

Share of firms in internationally traded and nontradable sectors, selected developing-country cities (latest post-2010 data)

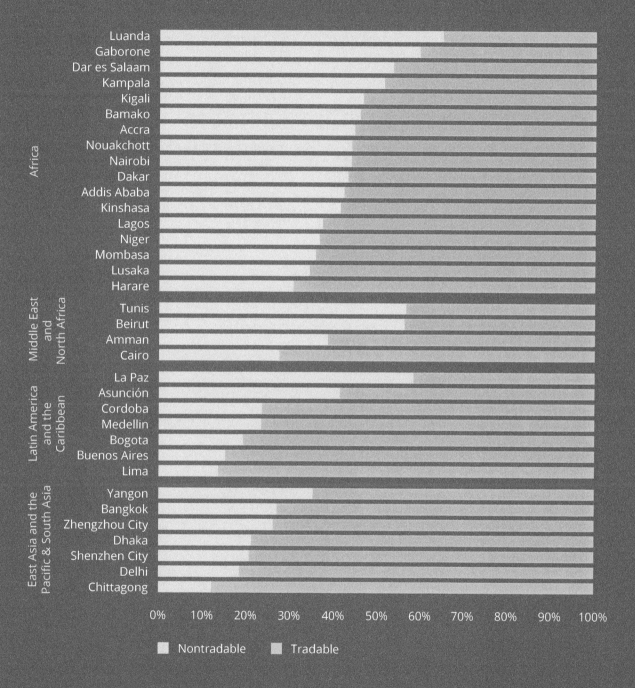

Source: Calculation based on the World Bank Enterprise (WBE) surveys.

Note: The data is from the latest WBE surveys post-2010 (with more than 15,000 firms in capital cities, or cities of at least one million inhabitants, and with at least 50 firms sampled). Only firms with five or more employees are interviewed. The sectoral specialization analyses used the UN International Standard Industrial Classification of All Economic Activities (3.1 revision). Manufacturing, wholesale and commission trade, and business services (such as travel agencies, transport, financial intermediation) are all tradable activities. By contrast, construction, local services, retail trade, health and social work, and other local activities are classified as nontradable.

Because of manufacturing's importance in entering regional and global markets, one can look at the share of manufacturing in GDP to see whether an urbanizing economy is opening its doors to the world — or closing them. For example, we compare the structures of non-African and African economies during periods when the urbanized share of the population rises to 60 percent. Based on a cross-section of African and non-African economies, the comparison shows that Africa's cities are indeed trapped in the production of nontradables for local markets. As the African economies attain 60 percent urbanization, their share of manufacturing in GDP stays flat (or somewhat falling) at about 10 percent. In contrast, the manufacturing share of the non-African economies rises from 10 percent to nearly 20 percent (falling back only when urbanization exceeds 60 percent).

Why have African urban economies remained local? Two reasons stand out. One, paradoxically, is natural resource development. Such development can create a high demand for nontradable goods and services. As growth in the natural resource sector raises factor prices, this sector crowds out others — notably manufacturing (figure 2). Countries that depend heavily on natural resource exports tend to sprout urban economies dominated by nontradable services ("consumption cities"). This syndrome is known as Dutch Disease.

Another reason for Africa's local urban economies is related to urban form: how cities are built and spatially organized. The findings in this report draw on spatial and economic analysis based on 64 cities covering large, medium, and small cities across Africa and shows that cities are growing under a patchwork of constraints — inefficient land markets,

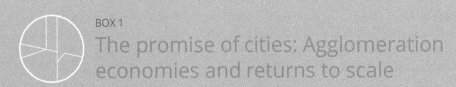

BOX 1

The promise of cities: Agglomeration economies and returns to scale

What is an urban agglomeration economy, and how does it arise from economic density? A simple case is the reduction of transport costs for goods: When suppliers are close to their customers, shipping costs decline. In the late nineteenth century, four fifths of Chicago's jobs were compactly located within four miles of State and Madison Streets — near residences and infrastructure (Grover and Lall 2015). And in the early 1900s, New York and London were manufacturing powerhouses because factories were built there to access customers and transport services. Many agglomeration benefits increase with scale: Each doubling of city size increases productivity by 5 percent, and the elasticity of income with respect to city population is between 3 percent and 8 percent (Rosenthal and Strange 2004).

Productivity gains are closely linked to urbanization through their ties to structural transformation and industrialization. As countries urbanize, workers move from rural to urban areas in search of better paid and more productive jobs. Similarly, entrepreneurs locate their firms in cities where agglomeration economies will increase their productivity. Close spatial proximity

has many benefits. Certain public goods — like infrastructure and basic services — are cheaper to provide when populations are large and densely packed together. Firms located near each other can share suppliers, lowering input costs. Thick labor markets reduce search costs, giving firms a larger pool of workers to choose from. And spatial proximity makes it easier for workers to share information and learn from each other. International evidence shows that knowledge spillovers play a key role in boosting the productivity of successful cities.

Evidence from East Asia (China, the Republic of Korea, Vietnam) points clearly to a close association between episodes of rapid urbanization and economic development. Unfortunately, these links appear weak in Sub-Saharan Africa. Cities in Africa are not delivering agglomeration economies or reaping urban productivity benefits; instead, they suffer from high costs for food, housing, and transport. These high costs — rising from coordination failures, poorly designed policies, weak property rights, and other factors that lower economic density — lock firms into producing nontradable goods and services.

overlapping property-rights regimes, suboptimal and ineffective zoning regulations — that hinder the drive toward dense concentrations of structures. More, the resulting scattered neighborhoods lack planned transport and infrastructure connections. Without either high physical density or adequate connective infrastructure, an urban area falls short of its potential: It cannot offer firms the cost efficiencies and job matching advantages that open a city's doors to regional and global trade.

Even if the symptoms of Dutch Disease are mitigated by falling commodity prices, the typical African city will remain bound by constraints related to its form. These physical constraints deter regional and global investment. And because they are likely to persist as the principal constraints on economic growth, addressing them is one of Africa's most urgent challenges today. This report combines recent findings

with original research and analysis to explain how the form of African cities is trapping them into local and nontradable production — and to point leaders toward policies that can spring the trap.

To be sure, urban form is not the only constraint on Africa's international competitiveness. Other important factors include business regulation; the lack of access to finance (for residential and commercial investments); the peculiarity of Africa's demographic transition; the absence of agricultural productivity gains; and, more generally, the macroeconomic context. These factors compound the risk that Africa's cities will remain unwelcoming to investment — that their development will continue along paths that preclude their entry into higher-productivity tradable goods sectors. And yet this threat of path dependency is itself closely, demonstrably related to the evolution of cities' physical form.

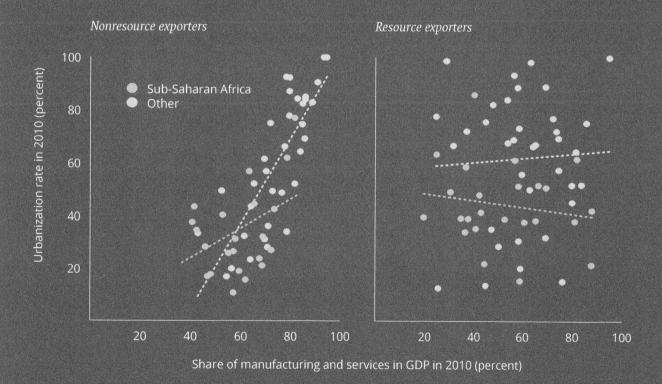

FIGURE 2

In resource exporting countries, urbanization is linked only weakly to the development of manufacturing and services

Source: Gollin, Jedwab, and Vollrath 2016.

Crowded, disconnected, and thus costly — Africa's cities are limited to nontradables by their urban form

Many Sub-Saharan African cities share three characteristics that constrain economic development and growth. Two appear directly in the cities' physical structures and spatial form: They are crowded with people and dwellings, and they are disconnected by a lack of transport and other infrastructure. Finally, and in Part because they are disconnected, cities are also costly. Indeed, they are among the costliest in the world, both for firms and for households — not least because of their inefficient spatial form.

Crowded cities

African cities are crowded in that they are packed with people who live in unplanned, informal downtown dwellings to be near jobs. Why? The immediate reason is that the urbanization of people is not accompanied by an urbanization of capital (box 2). Housing, infrastructures, and other capital investments are lacking. Across the region, housing investment lags urbanization by nine years (Dasgupta, Lall, and Lozano-Gracia 2014).

An underlying cause of this crowding is that African cities are not economically dense or efficient enough to promote scale economies and attract capital investment. In principle, cities should benefit businesses and people through increased economic density. Firms clustered in cities should be able to access a wider market of inputs and buyers, with reduced production costs thanks to scale economies.

Workers should consume more diverse products and services, pay less for what they consume, and enjoy easier commutes because of proximity to their jobs.

Africa's cities feel crowded precisely because they are not dense with economic activity, infrastructure, or housing and commercial structures. Without adequate formal housing in reach of jobs, and without transport systems to connect people living farther away, Africans forgo services and amenities to live in cramped quarters near their work. Often informal, these downtown districts are likely to lack adequate infrastructure and access to basic services. It is true that, within Africa as in other developing regions, population density is generally and strongly correlated with indicators of livability. For example, access to services is higher for African households in urban areas than in rural ones (Gollin, Kirchberger, and Lagakos 2016). But this relative advantage does not imply that cities are livable enough. Across Africa, 60 percent of the urban population is packed into slums — much higher than the 34 percent seen elsewhere (United Nations 2015a).

Related to the predominance of informal housing near African city centers is their relative lack of built-up area. For example, in both Harare, Zimbabwe and Maputo, Mozambique, more than 30 percent of land within five kilometers of the central business district remains unbuilt. This land near the core is not left unbuilt by design in African cities, as it can be in well-developed downtowns such as Paris (which reserves 14 percent of downtown land for green space, making densely populated districts more livable). Instead, outdated and poorly enforced city plans, along with dysfunctional property markets, create inefficient land use patterns that no one intended. The downtown lacks structures — despite being crowded.

3

Throughout Dar es Salaam, 28 percent of residents live at least three to a room

This figure rises to 50 percent in Abidjan

BOX 2

Low capital investment in Sub-Saharan African cities during a period of rapid urban growth

Africa's cities are crowded because they lack formal, planned housing that is connected to jobs and services. Without sufficient formal development, informal settlements that are relatively central and thus close to jobs — such as Kibera in Nairobi, and Tandale in Dar es Salaam — are constantly growing in population.

In Dar es Salaam, 28 percent of residents live at least three to a room; in Abidjan, 50 percent (World Bank 2015a, World Bank 2016). And in Lagos, Nigeria, two out of three people dwell in slums (World Bank 2015b).

One factor in the crowding of Africa's cities is their lack of capital investment, which for the past four decades has remained relatively low in the region, at around 20 percent of GDP. In contrast, urbanizing countries in East Asia — China, Japan, the Republic of Korea — stepped up capital investment during their periods of rapid urbanization. Between 1980 and 2011, China's capital investment (infrastructure, housing, and office buildings) rose from 35 percent of GDP to 48 percent, while the urban share of its population rose from 18 percent to 52 percent between 1978 and 2012. In East Asia as a whole, capital investment remained above 40 percent of GDP at the end of this period.

Housing investment in Africa has also lagged behind that in other low income and middle income economies. Between 2001 and 2011, African low income countries invested 4.9 percent of GDP in housing, compared with 5.5 percent elsewhere; and African middle income countries invested 6.5 percent of GDP in housing, compared with 9 percent elsewhere (Dasgupta, Lall, and Lozano-Gracia 2014).

These figures underline the fact that Africa is urbanizing while poor — indeed, strikingly poorer than other developing regions with similar urbanization levels. In 1968, when countries in the Middle East and North Africa region became 40 percent urban, their per capita GDP was $1,800 (2005 constant dollars). And in 1994, when countries in the East Asia and Pacific region surpassed the same threshold, their per capita GDP was $3,600. By contrast, Africa, with 40 percent urbanization, today has a per capita GDP of just $1,000 (box figure 2.1).

BOX FIGURE 2.1

Sub-Saharan Africa is urbanizing, but at lower levels of per capita GDP than other regions

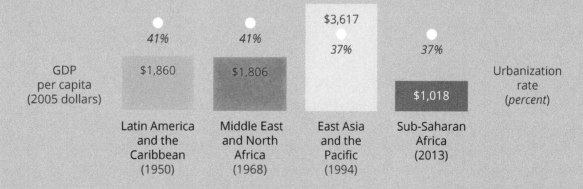

Source: Estimations using United Nations 2014 and WDI 2014 for the share of urban population, and WDI 2014 and Maddison Project to estimate GDP per capita.

Note: Years in parentheses are those with available data in which the region was closer to Sub-Saharan Africa's present urban share of about 40 percent. In 1950 urbanization in Latin America and the Caribbean was 41 percent; in 1968 urbanization in Middle East and North Africa was 41 percent; in 1994 urbanization in East Asia and the Pacific was 37 percent; in 2013 urbanization in Sub-Saharan Africa was 37 percent.

FIGURE 3

Connections among people as a function of population near the city center: Nairobi, Kenya is more fragmented and less well-connected than Pune, India

Nairobi (population 4.265 million)

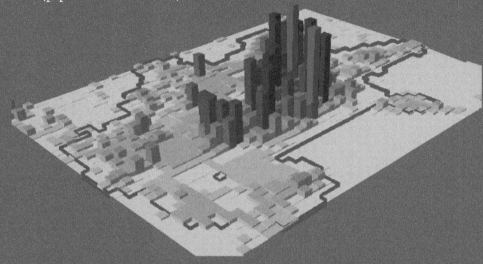

Pune (population 5.574 million)

⬜	0 - 364
⬜	365 - 103
⬜	1,033 - 22
⬜	2,295 - 40
⬜	4,042 - 67
⬜	6,735 - 97
⬜	9,777 - 13,984
⬜	13,985 - 19,534
⬜	19,535 - 27,747
⬛	27,748 - 39,955
⬛	39,956 - 53,912
⬛	53,913 - 71,973

Source: Henderson and Nigmatulina 2016.

Note: The blue bars show the highest densities in the city. While these peaks are concentrated in Pune, in Nairobi they are separated by lower densities.

Our analysis of imagery from satellites and geographic information systems (GIS) confirms that in African cities, capital investment not only appears low near the urban core, but rapidly declines outside it. A stark contrast emerges between patterns of downtown population density — in which Africa largely resembles other regions — and of economic density (as reflected in patterns visible from above that indicate capital investment). Africa's generally low levels of urban capital investment also appear in the assessed worth of building stock. For example, the total economic value of buildings in Dar es Salaam is estimated at around US$12 billion (Ishizawa and Gunasekera 2016), or just less than three times the city's share of GDP. Even lower are the estimated values for Nairobi, Kenya ($9 billion) and Kigali, Rwanda ($2 billion). Compared with cities in Central America, African cities have low replacement values for their built-up area, built-floor area, and population. Thus, Nairobi has the highest replacement value per square kilometer among the four African cities studied, yet it is just 60 percent of the value of Tegucigalpa, which has the lowest among six Central American cities.

Although the capital investment shortfall that makes African cities crowded appears across all building types, it is most severe in housing. In Nairobi, for example, commercial and industrial structures explain 55 percent of the total value of building stock — even though these structures occupy just 4 percent of the city's area. Residential development is urgently lacking.

Disconnected cities

While the lack of capital by itself might not always pose an obstacle to economic growth, African cities also are disconnected in that they are spatially dispersed. Structures are scattered in small neighborhoods. Without adequate roads or transport systems, commuting is slow and costly, denying workers access to jobs throughout the larger urban area. People and firms are separated from each other and from economic opportunity. And because urban form is determined by long-lived structures that shape the city for decades — if not centuries — cities that assume a disconnected form can easily become locked into it.

The lack of connections among neighborhoods means that African cities, compared with developed and developing cities elsewhere, show both lower exposure and higher fragmentation in connections among people living near the city center.

- Low exposure means that people are disconnected from each other. At a given distance (usually 10 kilometers), they cannot interact with as many people as in a city with higher exposure.

- High fragmentation means that within a specified area, population density varies widely: Its peaks are scattered, not clustered in a way that could promote scale economies. Fragmentation increases infrastructure costs, while it lengthens travel times among homes, job sites, and businesses.

According to a new study of 265 cities in 70 countries that controls for total population and per capita GDP, average exposure near the center is 37 percent lower in African cities than in Asian and Latin American cities, while African cities are 23 percent more fragmented (Henderson and Nigmatulina 2016). The contrast between Nairobi, Kenya and Pune, India illustrates these differences (figure 3).

One pattern that explains the low exposure and high fragmentation of African cities is their relative lack of new development near the center. New construction is not clustered to make capital more concentrated and increase economic density. Instead, it tends to push the boundaries of the city outward. In urban development language, this kind of building-out represents either expansion or leapfrog development; opposed to both is infill, which makes cities denser.

- Expansion development enlarges a city's footprint at the edge of the consolidated urban area.

- Leapfrog development also enlarges the footprint, but does so by establishing satellite areas — parcels of newly built land that do not border on or overlap existing development.

- Infill development is construction on unbuilt parcels surrounded by existing developments.

Among the three types of new development, infill is the best for economic exposure, or connections among people: It defragments the city and connects workers, jobs, and firms. Expansion and leapfrog development are the opposite: They are less likely to foster economic connections. Our analysis of GIS imagery for 21 African cities over 2000–2010 shows that, during this period, between 46 and 77 percent of new development occurred as expansion. The share of infill was typically much lower.

FIGURE 4

Leapfrog development: Undermining scale and agglomeration economies in African cities

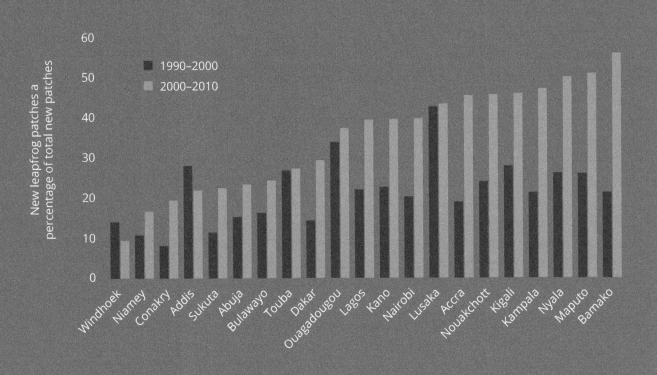

Source: Construction based on data in Baruah (2015).

Note: Leapfrog patches as a share of all new development patches, by city, 1990–2000 and 2000–2010. Leapfrog patches are defined as continuous built-up area that do not border or intersect with existing development.

An even greater concern than the preference for expansion over infill development is the increase in leapfrog development, which is now appearing outside various cities. In Bamako and Maputo, such leapfrog patches account for more than 50 percent of the change to the urban fabric over 2000–2010. In many other cities this share approaches or exceeds 40 percent (figure 4). The patches often being small, their isolation from existing development will undermine city governments' efforts to provide the networked services that require scale economies — and that undergird urban productivity.

The prevalence of expansion and especially leapfrog development is just one pattern that makes urban commuting challenging in African cities; another is deficient transport infrastructure. Traffic congestion can hobble the economy with long commuting times.

In Nairobi, the average journey-to-work time is one of the longest for 15 global cities studied (IBM 2011). Part of the reason is that walking accounts for a large share of commuting — in Nairobi about 41 percent (UNEP and FIA Foundation 2013). But even if more city dwellers could afford transport by car or minibus, commutes would remain impractical for lack of roads. In eight representative African cities, roads occupy far lower shares of urban land than in other cities around the world.

The deficiency of urban road infrastructure is made worse by its extreme concentration near the core of African cities, leaving outer areas disconnected. Our GIS study shows that in well-developed cities outside Africa, land allocated to roads declines only gradually as one looks out from the center toward the periphery: An example is Paris (figure 5). By contrast,

FIGURE 5

Paved roads occupy a smaller share of urban land in Africa than elsewhere — and usually drop off abruptly beyond the city center

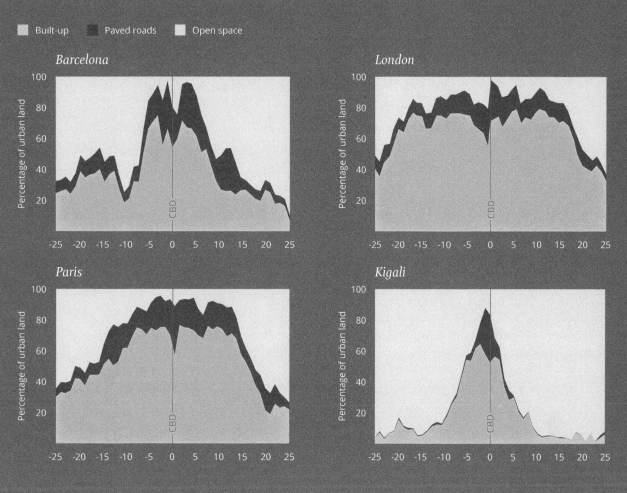

Africa's urban roads are disproportionately clustered near the center. In Addis Ababa, Dar es Salaam, Kigali, and Nairobi, paved roads drop off so abruptly outside the downtown area that they nearly disappear (Dakar being a notable exception to the African pattern). Households in African cities find it difficult to settle outside central business districts, as the lack of paved roads makes commuting from the periphery impractical (Felkner, Lall, and Lee 2016).

Considered as a whole, the average urban area in Africa is not strikingly less built-up than its counterparts in other regions (except in Asia, where cities are more densely built; Angel and others 2011). What is lacking is the economically dense concentration of capital and infrastructure investment that enables households to live decently and affordably near jobs. Because of this lack of economic

density, Africa's city centers remain dominated by a retail industry that does not benefit from economies of specialization: For example, in Kigali and Kampala many urban workers purvey food and beverages. The spatial fragmentation of Africa's cities prevents firms from reaping both scale and agglomeration benefits. It prevents scale economies by reducing workers' access to jobs, constraining firm size: Africa's urban firms employ 20 percent fewer workers on average than comparable firms elsewhere (Iacovone, Ramachandran, and Schmidt 2014). In addition, spatial fragmentation hinders agglomeration economies by preventing job market pooling and matching and the transfer of skills and knowledge — a special concern in light of African cities' low human capital endowments. Urban agglomeration economies thrive on knowledge spillovers, which presuppose a mix of specialized

FIGURE 5 *(cont.)*

Paved roads occupy a smaller share of urban land in Africa than elsewhere — and usually drop off abruptly beyond the city center

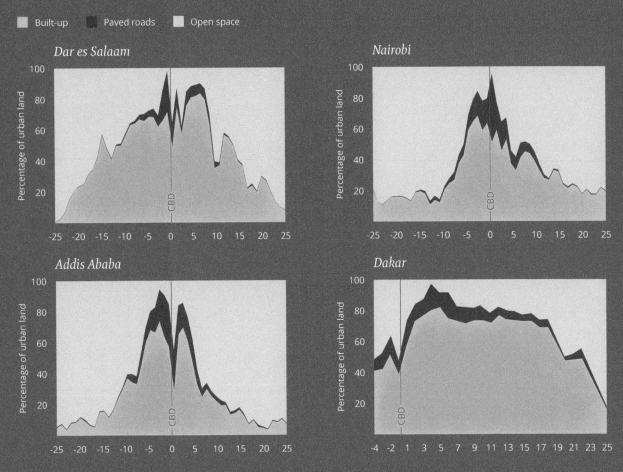

Source: Based on Antos, Lall, and Lozano-Gracia 2016 and Felkner, Lall, and Lee 2016.

Note: CBD = Central Business District. Data for European cities are from the European Environment Agency's Urban Atlas data layers. Data for African cities are from very high resolution (0.5 m) satellite images taken in 2013.

cognitive skills in the labor market. African urban workers are relatively poor in such skills, according to results from the first initiative to measure skills in low-income and middle-income countries (the World Bank STEP Skills Measurement Program). If workers are to sort by ability — as they should to generate agglomeration economies — then Africa's cities will need, among other things, to restructure their labor market by attracting and growing more specialized talent.

In sum, the ideal city can be viewed economically as an efficient labor market that matches employers and job seekers through connections (Bertaud 2014). The typical African city fails in this matchmaker role. A central reason for this failure — one that has not yet been sufficiently recognized — is that the city's land use is fragmented. Its transport infrastructure is insufficient, and too much of its development occurs through expansion rather than infill. While the underlying causes of these problems are regulatory and institutional, the effects of spatial fragmentation are material: It limits urban economies.

Costly cities

Fragmented urban forms impose high living costs on workers and households, resulting in indirect costs and other constraints for firms: In short, African cities are costly both to live in and to do business in.

FIGURE 6

A fragmented urban form is associated with higher urban costs

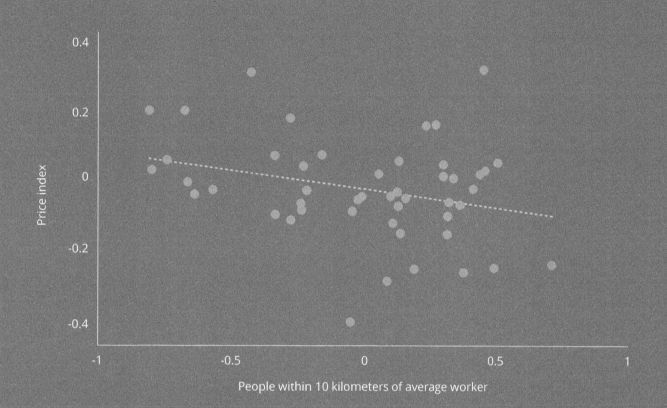

People within 10 kilometers of average worker

Source: Estimations using Nakamura et al. (2016) and Henderson and Nigmatulina (2016).

Note: The figure shows a residual-on-residual plot. The x-axis depicts the residuals from a regression of the Puga10 Index, log scale (based on Henderson and Nigmatulina, 2016) controlling for log GDP per capita, log population, a dummy for SSA, and percentage of urban population. The y-axis plots residuals of the adjusted price index, log scale (based on Nakamura et al., 2016), on the same controls. The lower the people within 10 km of the average worker, the higher the price index.

According to the new research underlying this report, the higher cost of living in African cities is related to their lack of dense spatial form and infrastructure connections (figure 6). Higher spatial densities appear to reduce costs: For example, a 1 percent reduction in spatial fragmentation measured by the Puga Index is associated with a 12 percent reduction in urban costs, controlling for income levels and city population.

While higher living costs directly affect workers, they ultimately are borne by urban firms. Higher wages mean lower returns — unless workers are more productive. And without the economic density that gives rise to efficiency, Africa's cities do not seem to increase worker productivity. The result is that investment expectations remain low for cities in the region.

Africa's higher urban living costs appear in rents, food prices, and prices for other goods and services. City dwellers pay around 35 percent more for food in Africa than in low-income and middle-income countries elsewhere: a premium that looms larger given the high share of African household incomes that goes to food. Even higher differentials apply to urban housing (55 percent higher in urban areas of African countries, relative to their income levels) and transport (42 percent higher in African cities than cities elsewhere, including vehicle prices and transport services). Overall, urban households pay 20 to 31 percent more for goods and services in African countries than in other developing countries (figure 7).

FIGURE 7

Urban living costs in Sub-Saharan African countries in 2011 exceeded costs elsewhere, relative to Africans' lower per capita GDP

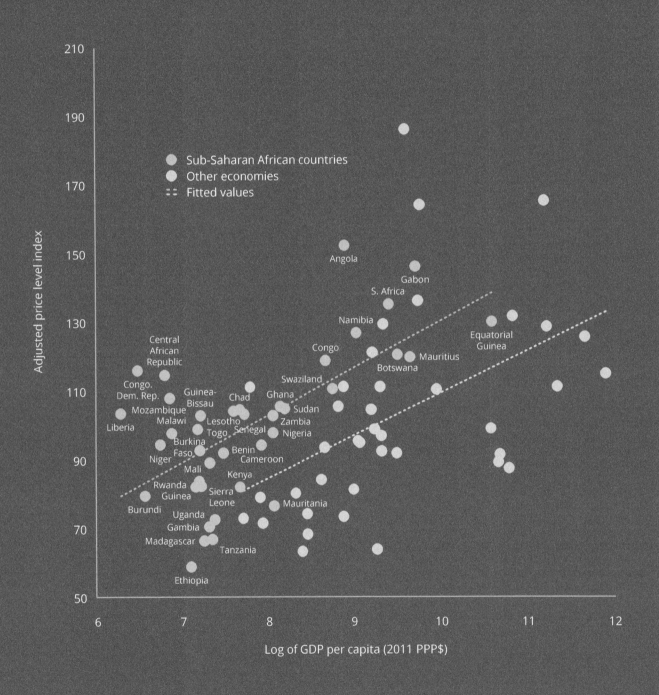

Source: Nakamura et al. 2016, based on data from the 2011 International Comparison Program (ICP) and WDI.

Note: The adjusted price level index (PLI) for household consumption excluding housing rent is standardized so that the average PLI equals to 100. PLIs for 15 Asian countries are inflated by 10 percent.

Urban workers in Africa incur high commuting costs — or they cannot afford to commute by vehicle at all, and must walk to work. The informal, often colorful minibus systems that dominate collective motorized transit in most African cities are far from cost-efficient: The buses' low load factor (passenger capacity) prevents them from realizing scale economies. For the poorest urban residents especially, the cost of vehicle transport in some cities is prohibitive, as measured in a study from 2008 (figure 8). The need to walk to work limits these residents' access to jobs.

The high cost of living affects not just households but also firms, which have to pay higher wages in cities where the cost of living is high. In addition, urban workers may need to be compensated for poorer living conditions in informal settlements with scarce amenities. Manufacturing firms in African cities pay higher nominal wages than urban firms in other countries at comparable development levels: unit labor costs are three times higher in Djiboutiville, Djibouti, than in Mumbai, India and 20 percent higher in Dar es Salaam, Tanzania than in Dhaka, Bangladesh.

Cities in Africa are costly for households, workers, and businesses. Because food and building costs are high, families can hardly remain healthy or afford decent housing. Because commuting by vehicle is not only slow but expensive, workers find it hard to take and keep jobs that match their skills. And the need for higher wages to pay higher living costs makes firms less productive and competitive, keeping them out of tradable sectors. As a result, African cities are avoided by potential regional and global investors and trading partners.

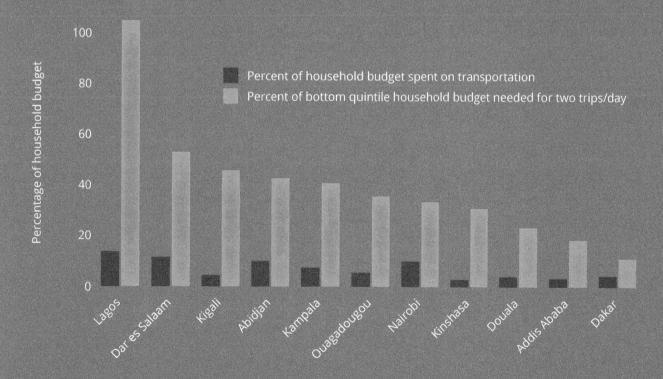

FIGURE 8

Share of urban household budgets spent or needed for transport in 11 Sub-Saharan African countries (analysis from 2008)

Source: Kumar and Barrett 2008.

25

Closed for business, out of service: The urgency of a new urban development path for Africa

African cities are crowded as well as disconnected, making them costly for firms and for residents (see figure 6). Potential investors and trading partners quickly see evidence of the physical and economic dysfunction that constrains public service provision, inhibits labor market pooling and matching, and prevents firms from reaping scale and agglomeration benefits. So these potential partners stay away, fearing lack of return on their investment.

The problem is not a simple one of underinvestment leading to low infrastructure, but a more complex one involving the interdependence of many investment decisions. Business investment decisions depend on the presence of other businesses — a firm's customers and its suppliers — and of workplaces that can be reached from residential areas. Investment will flow into housing if demand rises, driven by rising worker incomes. Infrastructure finance depends on revenues from a growing city. All these investments are interrelated, and in all of them expectations are crucial. Investors' low expectations become self-fulfilling when one investment fails to take place, reducing the expected return to others. The resulting vicious circle locks cities into a low development trap. (The underlying analytic framework describing such traps is presented in Chapter 4.)

Cities are "closed for business"

A firm's business decision to produce internationally tradable goods and services will depend on its input costs. Among these input costs are urban costs: the added costs that workers face when living in a city. Urban costs include rent, commuting costs, and the high price of many goods. To attract workers, firms must raise wages to offset (or partially offset) these costs. Yet even as nominal wages climb to reflect high or rapidly rising urban costs, real wages remain low (see chapter 4 for detailed discussion).

When urban costs drive nominal wages too high, firms will not be able to compete in the tradable sector and will produce only nontradables. The nontradable sector includes certain goods (beer and cement are examples), the construction trade, the retail trade, and many service sector activities, including informal sector employment. Demand for these goods and services comes from income generated within the city and its hinterland — but also from income transferred from outside, such as resource rents, tax revenues, and foreign aid.

The reason why a firm in the nontradable sector can afford to pay higher wages — while a firm in the tradable sector cannot — is that the nontradable producer can raise its prices citywide. By doing so, it passes its own cost increases on to consumers in the urban market. But such price hikes make the cost of living in a city even higher, contributing to the workers' urban costs. This sequence can become a vicious cycle that keeps African cities out of the tradable sector and limits their economic growth.

Often, proposed solutions to Africa's urban challenges focus simply on increased investments in structures or on reforming urban planning. These actions are necessary and urgent — but, by themselves, they are unlikely to lift cities out of the nontradables trap. Why? because coordination failures tend to inhibit the formation of new clusters of economic activity, which are necessary for efficient tradables production (see, among others, Henderson and Venables 2009).

Given the dynamics described above, no firm wants to be the first to enter the tradables sector. Yet many would become established if they could coordinate their entry. To enable coordination, a city needs a credible coordination agent: either a forward-looking group of firms that can harmonize their plans and make a move together, or a large-scale land developer or municipal government that can realize its vision through major infrastructure investment (Henderson and Venables 2009). Without such coordination the move into tradables will fail, leaving the city "closed for business."

Cities are "out of service"

More than 60 percent of African's urban population lives in areas with some combination of overcrowding, low-quality housing, and inadequate access to clean water and sanitation (United Nations 2015a). Why have cities in the region remained so deficient in housing and basic services?

A fundamental reason is that Africa's urban dysfunction is self-perpetuating: It lowers expectations, and low expectations deter the investments needed for improvement. Housing investment decisions shape urban form. Providing housing in the formal sector means deciding to sink costs in long-lived structures. And such decisions depend critically on expectations for a city's future prospects. Cities that inspire high expectations will attract greater investment in formal sector structures, including residential structures, which reduce urban costs and in turn attract more investment. In contrast, cities that seem likely to remain artisanal — based on low-value nontradables production — foster low expectations for the growth of land rents over time. With little incentive for investment in formal structures, a lack of capital investment keeps cities disconnected and urban costs high, perpetuating the cycle.

Alongside the general effect of low expected returns, specific features of the business and regulatory environment in African cities create further barriers to capital investment. These features include property law and land use regulations, along with the design and enforcement of urban plans.

Systems of property law and land ownership in Africa are often the first and most cumbersome regulatory burden weighing on urban development. For example, a majority of the land in Kampala, Uganda operates under a complex land tenure regime that recognizes independent rights over land and structures — giving rise to legal disputes and blocking investment (Muinde 2013). The problem takes a different form in Nigeria, where urban land transactions incur high costs, and inefficient regulations further bog down formal development. In Lagos and Port Harcourt, titling expenses alone can reach 30 percent of construction costs, while total transaction costs range from 12 to 36 percent of a property's value (World Bank 2015b). As a result, land is developed informally: In Ibadan in 2000, researchers found that 83 percent of homes violated city zoning rules (Arimah and Adeagbo 2000).

Urban plans are largely ineffective in Africa. One reason is that they are divorced from reality: They typically do not consider finances, market dynamics and interests, social diversity, or differences among income groups. Another reason is that, when enacted, regulations lack built-in implementation mechanisms. As a result, human capacity constraints and financial resource constraints preclude effective enforcement. More generally, the intentions and outcomes of urban plans are distorted by institutional failure and fragmentation (across sectors and levels); by political interference; and by lack of consideration of a city's political economy.

Inappropriate or unrealistic regulations and opaque guidelines, especially on land ownership, impede access to land and discourage the formal development of city centers. Political risk can make future rents even more unpredictable. As a result, the returns from construction in Africa's cities are intolerably uncertain — and cities remain "out of service."

Path dependence and interdependence

When a city appears "closed for business" and "out of service," potential partners stay away, fearing low to no returns. At present this vicious cycle of low expectations appears likely to keep Africa's urban economies undercapitalized, making the region's development all the more challenging.

Compounding this problem of low urban expectations is the reality of path dependence –identified in recent work as a central concern for policymakers. Cities that grow inefficiently, without any effective plans or incentives to integrate their physical form, are likely to be locked into the resulting disconnected forms. Urban structures share a "putty-clay" quality: Once built, they are difficult to modify and can stay in place for more than 150 years (Hallegatte 2009). In addition, infrastructure investment needs to be planned well in advance; if a growing city lacks a comprehensive, forward-thinking plan to provide basic infrastructure services — sewerage, drainage, electricity, clean water, and connectivity — it will have to add them later. That means adding them inefficiently and at far greater cost, and as afterthoughts and in response to piecemeal demand from individuals (Collier 2016).

As important as path dependence is interdependence among urban structures, infrastructure, and services. Much of a structure's value reflects complementarities with other structures in the neighborhood or city. For example, this report documents the benefits of road investments for private investments in residential and commercial structures (chapter 6). All social returns on public infrastructure depend on the proximity of housing and premises: Thus, a rapid transit system is more viable at higher densities. Policies need to leverage these complementarities, avoiding coordination failures and single-sector interventions that get in the way of economic density.

Cities that continue on inefficient development paths are growing, but in a counterproductive direction. Their physical structures and infrastructure will not keep up with their rising population. As they continue to amass sunk capital — while passing up opportunities for complementary investments that will never come again — they will sink deeper into the low development trap. And they might not dig themselves out. They could remain "out of service" and "closed for business" forever.

Springing cities from the low development trap

We now understand more about the low development trap in which African cities find themselves. They are crowded rather than economically dense, and they are physically disconnected; as a result, they are costly. High costs deter investors through low expected returns — while the city's unlivable appearance vividly corroborates these low expectations. As a result, the urbanization of capital in Africa is lagging far behind the urbanization of people. Migrants crowd into slums, simply to be near where the jobs are.

How can Africa's leaders and policymakers spring cities from this trap? Crucially, they must first realize that the problem does not begin with low capital investment and the lack of physical structures, or even with undersized infrastructure. To be sure, low investment in structures limits urban economic density; it exacerbates spatial fragmentation, and it precludes agglomeration economies. But the lack of investment results from low investor expectations, which result when cities are spatially dispersed and disconnected.

When potential investors and trading partners look at African cities, they see spatial fragmentation and a lack of connections. They know that such fragmentation constrains public service provision, inhibits labor market pooling and matching, and prevents firms from reaping scale and agglomeration benefits. So the key to freeing Africa's cities from their low development trap is to set them on a path toward physical and economic density, connecting them for higher efficiency and boosting expectations for the future.

The first priority is to reform land markets and land use planning — to promote the most efficient uses of urban land, and to develop land at scale.

Formalize land markets, clarify property rights, and institute effective urban planning

Informal land markets are not good enough for African cities. Urban land is a vital economic asset, and asset transactions are viable only where purchasers can rely on enduring extra-legal documentation of ownership. A formal market both offers purchasers the protection of the state and — because transactions are readily observable and recorded — generates the public good of accurate valuation.

Clear rights to urban land are a precondition for formal land markets. African cities struggle with overlapping and sometimes contradictory property-rights systems — formal, customary, and informal

(box 3). When these systems pose barriers to urban land access, they impede the consolidation of plots and the evolution of land use. Firms cannot readily buy downtown land to convert it from low-density residential use into higher-density apartments, or to build clusters of new commercial structures. Land transactions are long, costly, and complicated (World Bank 2015c). Such market constraints reduce the collateral value of structures, giving developers little incentive to invest in residential height — while tempting all parties to enter informal arrangements (Collier 2016).

Formalizing land markets is essential; so is making them work. Constraints on formal land markets contribute to the typical African city's spatial fragmentation and to the relatively low capital investment near its core. Not only will efficient land markets notably increase economic efficiency, they will also help African cities tap the potential of rising land values to finance infrastructure and other public goods. (But such financing strategies bear risk; they presuppose stable property rights and predictable law enforcement.)

While urban land markets need to work more efficiently, cities also must strengthen their urban plans and land use regulations. African cities today use planning models and regulatory codes that may be relics of colonial regimes, or that may be uncritically imported from developed countries (Goodfellow 2013). Urban planning documents do not give credible accounts of finance, market dynamics, or distributional impacts. Guidelines are not sufficiently articulated, granular, or transparent to support consistent and enforceable development planning. Capacity and resource constraints undermine implementation. City and country authorities will need to add urban planning capacity — and to make tough political decisions informed by technical evidence and assessments.

Land use regulations, such as zoning ordinances and building codes, are necessary to make urban plans into realities. Although planners may promote spatial density as a public good, the cost of investing in housing and commercial structures is borne by households and firms. (The benefits of economic density and exposure are an externality.) Because private actors on their own will not prevent market failures in the allocation and use of land, urban land use regulations must be clear and their enforcement predictable.

BOX 3

Urban land and property rights: A need for clarification

Unclear land rights are severely constraining urban land redevelopment throughout Africa, imposing high costs. Under the customary rules for land tenure that control much urban and peri-urban land, property rights depend on the consent of local chiefs or family elders. One example is Durban, South Africa. Other examples are in Ghana, Lesotho, Mozambique, and Zambia. Such cities often struggle with overlapping and conflicting tenure systems — formal, customary and informal.

Even where formal titles or clear land rights exist, basic mapping, geographic or ownership information is often inaccurate or land records maintained poorly, causing disputes. Applying for formal recognition can also be tedious and costly (Toulmin 2005). In Mozambique one can apply for concession to a land plot from the relevant municipal directorate or municipal cadaster services. But the application can involve as many as 103 administrative steps over several years (UN-Habitat 2008). The lack of a proper registration system prevents urban land markets from functioning well, and it creates obstacles to the raising of capital for development and investment — and to the raising of revenue by the local authority.

Across Africa, opaque and inadequate land databases and information systems distort land prices and availability. Finally, land administration systems (such as registries and cadaster records) are incomplete and underused for enforcing legal claims and landholders'

fiscal obligations, so lenders cannot always use land as collateral. In Sub-Saharan Africa, only 10 percent of total land is registered (Byamugisha 2013). In West Africa, only 2–3 percent of land is held with a government-registered title (Toulmin 2005).

The good news is that African countries are taking steps to clarify land rights. Botswana took the bold step of regularizing customary lands in 2008, partly because the Land Boards faced challenges to administering tribal land (Malope and Phirinyane 2016). Zambia passed a new planning bill in 2015, extending planning controls across state and customary land and designating all local authorities as planning authorities (Wesseling 2016). Namibia recognizes traditional leaders as part of the formal land system; they are designated by the president and their details published in the government gazette (United Nations 2015b).

Some countries and cities are developing hybrid regimes to make formal and customary administration more compatible. For example, in Nigerian states with largely Muslim populations, the emir's representatives subdivide and allocate land with the help of volunteer professionals from government: An example is the city of Rigasa, in the extreme west of Kaduna (Igabi, Local Government Area, Nigeria). Future Urban redevelopers in Africa may learn from the past successes of two approaches — land sharing and land readjustment — in several Asian cities.

The market pricing of land depends partly on other policies besides land use regulations. Taxes, charges, and subsidies can be used to complement regulations, creating financial incentives and disincentives. Revenues — land taxes, for example — can also be used to finance administration and infrastructure. And implementation tools such as capital investment, budget, and phasing plans can assist upstream planning.

Make early and coordinated infrastructure investments — allowing for interdependence among sites, structures, and basic services

Research conducted for this study supports the value of early investments in neighborhood infrastructure and services (chapter 6). But coordination among these investments is equally crucial, given that cities are both path-dependent and interdependent. Large

infrastructure projects carry high sunk costs: Like any large structures, they depreciate very slowly over decades or even centuries (Philibert 2007). And the costs of developing housing, infrastructure, and industrial premises depend on sequencing. Consider the relation of new transport systems and industrial zones. If not coordinated with one another, and with land markets and land use regulations, these projects can put cities on a counterproductive development path.

Such large investments, especially at scale, will require financing through new systems of revenue. Public infrastructure projects incur costs far in advance of their benefits to productivity and livability, and the large capital outlays required can appear daunting. The central government transfers on which African cities often rely will not suffice. City leaders, country authorities, and the international aid community

BOX 4

Leveraging land values to finance Africa's urban infrastructure

Making Africa's cities well connected and economically dense will entail huge infrastructure investments. Urban public finance in the region has traditionally relied on revenues from intergovernmental transfers. Future investments should leverage the value of city assets — mainly land — to finance infrastructure and provide public goods and services.

Land-based infrastructure financing will bring the biggest payoff where cities are growing rapidly. Rapid growth drives swift increases in land prices and creates large revenue opportunities. Yet it also magnifies infrastructure investment needs, requiring major sources of development finance. Land-based financing has funded large leaps in the scale of urban investment in France, Japan, and the United States.

Taxes on land can fund investments while also promoting more efficient land use — giving landowners an incentive to develop the land to its most profitable use given the market value of their property. Valuable downtown land will become more densely developed, attracting investment in residential and commercial structures. And land taxes are nondistortionary. (Appreciated land values are economic rents for a scarce resource, not a return on the economic activity of the owner — so, unlike in production, no owner behavior exists to be distorted.)

Higher revenues from land and real estate can come through:

- Improved valuation of land and properties closer to their market value, deepening the tax base.

- Improved enforcement of land and property taxes on a larger number of owners, broadening the tax base.

- Monetization of underused public land.

Devising systems of land and real estate taxation that promote economic density is not easy. Strong institutions are needed to clearly define property rights; to ensure standardized and objective methods of land valuation; and to support and oversee land management, land sales, and tax collection. For pure real estate taxes, policymakers should realize that property values generally respond more slowly than other taxable wealth to annual changes in economic activity — while "property areas" respond still more slowly.

should therefore study various financing options. One is to leverage land values (box 4) — although many cities in Sub-Saharan Africa are not currently allowed to raise revenues from land (World Bank 2015c), and their weak fiscal cadaster records and capacities pose a further challenge.

Unregulated markets are unlikely to solve the problems of coordination, path dependence, and interdependence. Public policy and planning are needed to get urban structures "right." This imperative is especially challenging in Africa, where fragmented urban development may already be locking cities into high-cost paths. And since the low expectations that come with high costs are self-fulfilling — expectations affect investments, which in turn affect expectations — cities that lack durable capital today may have an even harder time financing its acquisition tomorrow.

Even if developers expect an African city to grow, they might not know where growth is likely to occur — a type of coordination failure. One mechanism for overcoming such failures is a sunk investment made by the government or a group of investors. Sunk investments can have long-run effects, sending a strong signal to other potential investors. It has been argued that "investments sunk historically, even small ones that have now depreciated completely, might serve as a mechanism to coordinate contemporary investment" (Bleakley 2012).

Decisions about a city's growth pattern, based on underlying transport investment choices, will strongly influence future greenhouse gas emissions and environmental sustainability. Scholars have proven the impact of urban form on driving behaviors, modal choices, transport-related energy consumption, and carbon dioxide emissions (Newman and Kenworthy 1989). African cities now enjoy a unique opportunity to avoid carbon-intensive urban transportation trajectories. Getting these choices right the first time — while urbanization is still in its early stages — is critical. Given the path dependence of urban settlements, polluting now and cleaning up later is not an option.

In coordinating land use policies with infrastructure plans, it is finally important to consider risk from natural hazards. While 70 percent of high-income countries integrate land use with the management of natural-hazard risk, only about 15 percent of low-income countries do so (World Bank 2012a). Yet cities in these low-income countries are more vulnerable to natural hazards, including the floods that are now so destructive in many parts of the world. Coordinating land use planning with the management of natural resources, including water resources

and water supply, is essential (World Bank 2012b). Swakopmund, Namibia, a city of 42,000 surrounded by environmentally sensitive areas, limits development to zoned "townlands" and has protected watersheds with integrated environmental, sector, and land use planning.

Opening the doors

That African cities are crowded is apparent from the ground — both in the growth of informal settlements, and in the traffic that snarls urban roads. That the same cities are disconnected can be seen from satellite images showing land use. And that these cities are costly appears in price and wage data, as interpreted by economic analysis.

This report explains the high costs of living and doing business in African cities as consequences of their inefficient urban form. Distortions in factor and product markets leave cities without adequate

housing, commercial structures, or connective infrastructure. Such cities are not just difficult and costly to live in, but costly to do business in — they scatter firms, prevent labor market pooling, and limit specialization across settlements. The urban economy is restricted to nontradable, as opposed to tradable, activity.

So long as Africa's cities are in evident disarray, with fragmented forms and dysfunctional markets, they will continue to signal low expectations and stay in this low development trap. At best, they will proceed farther

BOX 5

Building dense, connected, and efficient cities: Two models of success

One model of successful urbanization is the Republic of Korea, where urban planning and land management institutions evolved to meet challenges at each stage of urbanization. Land development programs were established first, followed by a land use regulation system. Then came comprehensive urban planning, with guidelines for mandatory 20-year visions, zoning decisions, and planning facilities. Downtown development projects systematically adhered to phased scenarios under the comprehensive plans. Later, in the 1990s and 2000s, Korea integrated separate laws regulating urban and nonurban areas, and in 2000 it instituted metropolitan city-regional planning (between the city and the county or province). Meanwhile, the government initiated large-scale apartment construction projects that solved Korea's most serious urban housing problems. Multiple transport modes were developed. Road projects over time have included urban highways and pavement projects as well as a network of expressways. And the nation's rail network includes urban subway lines alongside traditional railroads and

high-speed rail — the bullet trains that have shrunk Korea into a half-day travel zone.

A different sort of success story is that of Bangkok, where less restricted land markets were able to adapt to growing demographic and economic pressures and climbing costs. Over 1974-88, when growth was rapid and land and housing construction prices on the rise, developers responded by increasing the density of their housing projects. Average units per hectare rose from 35 to 56. Multifamily housing increased from less than 2 percent of new construction in 1986 to 43 percent in 1990. With these shifts, developers were able to profit through the construction of affordable housing (Dowall 1992). Over 1986-90, almost half the growth in Bangkok housing stock was from private development, while informally produced housing composed a mere 3 percent of the total. In other cities with highly constrained land markets, informally produced housing composed 20-80 percent of the total (Dowall 1998).

along the inefficient path of slow and inadequate land development and infrastructure investment.

Fortunately, the need for more efficient cities is easy to see and impossible to ignore. Africa's urban areas are quickly gaining in population: Home to 472 million people now, they will be twice as large in 25 years. The most populous cities are growing as fast as 4 percent annually. Productive jobs, affordable housing, and effective infrastructure will be urgently needed for residents and newcomers alike.

In urgency lies opportunity. Leaders can still set their cities onto more efficient development paths if they act swiftly — and if they can resist flashy projects, steadfastly pursuing two main goals in order of priority:

- First, formalize land markets, clarify property rights, and institute effective urban planning.

- Second, make early and coordinated infrastructure investments that allow for interdependence among sites, structures, and basic services.

A third goal is to improve urban transport and additional services. But this must not come ahead of the two goals listed above — nor can it be achieved unless those are met first.

Models of success from other regions may offer illuminating analogies and contrasts with African cities, while exemplifying what leaders can achieve through coordinated and sustained action (box 5). Of course, political economy must be considered in designing and implementing policies. Leaders need to foresee policy impacts (opportunities, winners, and losers) and anticipate challenges to enforcement.

City growth will be central to development in Africa, as it has been elsewhere. By starting with reforms to land markets and regulations, then making early and coordinated infrastructure investments, governments can take control of urbanization and build more connected and productive African cities: cities that open their doors to the world.

Annex: Coverage of African cities used in the analysis

Small cities (<800,000)

Country	City
Benin	Abomey-Calavi
Burundi	Bujumbura
CAR	Bangui
Côte d'Ivoire	Bouake
Namibia	Windhoek
Nigeria	Maiduguri
Nigeria	Nnewi
Somalia	Hargeysa
South Africa	Soshanguve
Sudan	Nyala
Zimbabwe	Bulawayo

Intermediate cities (800,000-2 million)

Angola	Huambo
Congo	Pointe-Noire
DRC	Bukavu
DRC	Kananga
DRC	Kisangani
Eritrea	Asmara
Guinea	Conakry
Kenya	Mombasa
Liberia	Monrovia
Malawi	Blantyre-Limbe
Malawi	Lilongwe
Mauritania	Nouakchott
Mozambique	Maputo
Niger	Niamey
Nigeria	Benin City
Nigeria	Ilorin
Nigeria	Jos
Nigeria	Kaduna
Nigeria	Uyo
Rwanda	Kigali
Sierra Leone	Freetown
Tanzania	Mwanza
Togo	Lomé
Uganda	Kampala
Zimbabwe	Harare

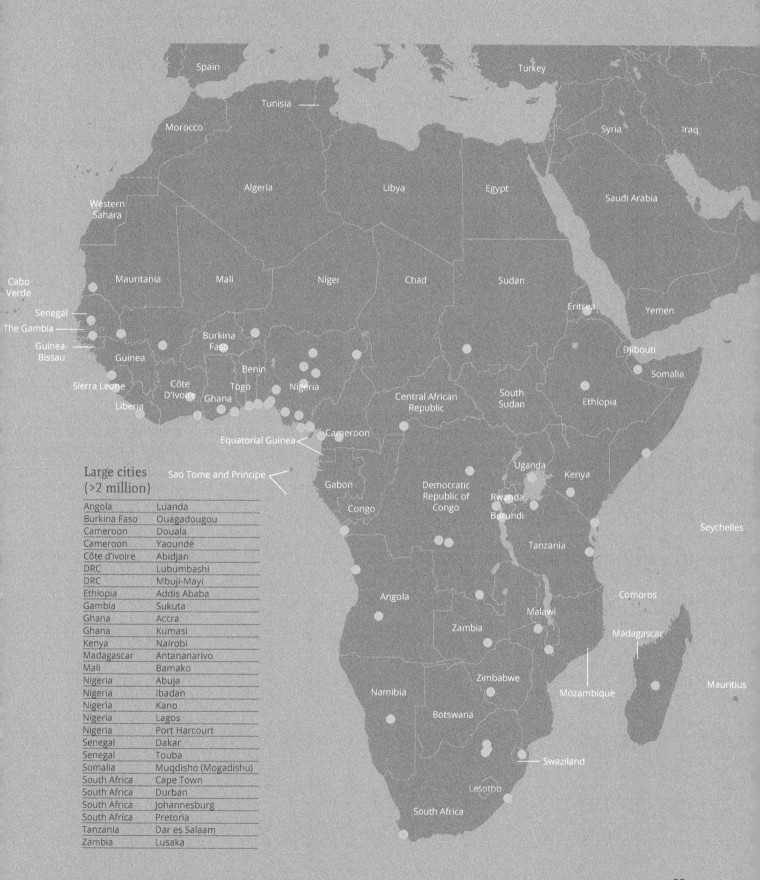

Large cities (>2 million)

Angola	Luanda
Burkina Faso	Ouagadougou
Cameroon	Douala
Cameroon	Yaoundé
Côte d'Ivoire	Abidjan
DRC	Lubumbashi
DRC	Mbuji-Mayi
Ethiopia	Addis Ababa
Gambia	Sukuta
Ghana	Accra
Ghana	Kumasi
Kenya	Nairobi
Madagascar	Antananarivo
Mali	Bamako
Nigeria	Abuja
Nigeria	Ibadan
Nigeria	Kano
Nigeria	Lagos
Nigeria	Port Harcourt
Senegal	Dakar
Senegal	Touba
Somalia	Muqdisho (Mogadishu)
South Africa	Cape Town
South Africa	Durban
South Africa	Johannesburg
South Africa	Pretoria
Tanzania	Dar es Salaam
Zambia	Lusaka

References

Angel, Shlomo, Jason Parent, Daniel L. Civco, and Alejandro M. Blei. 2011. *Making Room for a Planet of Cities.* Policy Focus Report, Lincoln Institute of Land Policy, Cambridge, MA.

Antos, Sarah E., Nancy Lozano-Gracia, and Somik V. Lall. 2016. "The Morphology of African Cities." Draft. World Bank, Washington, DC.

Arimah, C. B., and D. Adeagbo. 2000. "Compliance with Urban Development and Planning Regulations in Ibadan, Nigeria." *Habitat International* 24: 279–94.

Baruah, Neeraj. 2015. "Splintered and Segmented? Fragmentation of African Cities' Footprints." Presentation at the Spatial Development of African Cities Workshop, World Bank, Washington, DC, December 16–17.

Bertaud, Alain. 2014. "Cities as Labor Markets." Working Paper 2, Marron Institute on Cities and the Urban Environment, New York University, New York.

Bleakley, H., and J. Lin. 2012. "Portage and Path Dependence." *Quarterly Journal of Economics* 127 (2): 587–644.

Byamugisha, F. 2013. *Securing Africa's Land for Shared Prosperity.* World Bank, Washington, DC.

Collier, Paul. 2016. *African Urbanization: An Analytic Policy Guide.* Fourth Seminar in TICAD Seminar Series, "Land Use Planning and Spatial Development for Smart Growth in African Cities," World Bank Tokyo.

Dasgupta, B., S. V. Lall, and N. Lozano-Gracia. 2014. "Urbanization and Household Investment." Policy Research Working Paper 7170, World Bank, Washington, DC.

Dowall, D. E. 1992. "A Second Look at the Bangkok Land and Housing Market." *Urban Studies* 29 (1): 25–37.

———. 1998. "Making Urban Land Markets Work: Issues and Policy Options." Prepared for seminar on Strategy on Urban Development and Local Governments, World Bank, Washington, DC.

Felkner, John S., Somik V. Lall, and Hyun Lee. 2016. "Synchronizing Public and Private Investment in Cities: Evidence from Addis Ababa, Dar es Salaam, Kigali and Nairobi." World Bank, Washington, DC.

Gollin, Douglas, Remi Jedwab, and Dietrich Vollrath. 2016. "Urbanization with and without Industrialization." *Journal of Economic Growth* 21 (1): 35–70.

Gollin, Douglas, Martina Kirchberger, and David Lagakos. 2016. "Living Standards across Space: Evidence from Sub-Saharan Africa." March 31. Available at https://collaboration.worldbank.org/docs/DOC-20505.

Goodfellow, Tom. 2013. "Planning and Development Regulation amid Rapid Urban Growth: Explaining Divergent Trajectories in Africa." *Geoforum* 48: 83–93.

Grover Goswami, A., and S. V. Lall. 2016. "Jobs and Land Use within Cities: A Survey of Theory, Evidence, and Policy." Policy Research Working Paper 7453, World Bank, Washington, DC.

Hallegatte, Stephane. 2009. "Strategies to Adapt to an Uncertain Climate Change." *Global Environmental Change* 19 (2): 240–47.

Henderson, J. V., and A. J. Venables. 2009. "The Dynamics of City Formation." Review of Economic Dynamics 12 (2): 233–254.

Henderson, J. V., T. Regan, and A. J. Venables. 2016. "Building the City: Sunk Capital, Sequencing, and Institutional Frictions." Draft, March 23.

Henderson, Vernon, and Dzhamilya Nigmatulina. 2016. "The Fabric of African Cities: How to Think about Density and Land Use." Draft, April 20, London School of Economics.

Iacovone, L., V. Ramachandran, and M. Schmidt. 2014. "Stunted Growth: Why Don't African Firms Create More Jobs?" Working Paper 353, Center for Global Development, Washington, DC.

IBM. 2011. "Global Commuter Pain Survey: Traffic Congestion Down, Pain Way Up." http://www-03.ibm.com/press/us/en/pressrelease/35359.wss.

Ishizawa, O., and R. Gunasekera. 2016. "Economic Values of Buildings in Four African Cities." Background paper for this report.

Kumar, Ajay, and Fanny Barrett. 2008. "Stuck in Traffic: Urban Transport in Africa." AICD Background Paper.

Malope P., and M. Phirinyane.2016. "Enhancing Property Rights through Land Tenure Regularization in Botswana." Paper prepared for presentation at the 2016 World Bank Conference on Land and Poverty. World Bank, Washington, DC.

Muinde, Damaris Kathini. 2013. "Assessing the Effects of Land Tenure on Urban Developments in Kampala." March.

Nakamura, S., R. Harati, S. Lall, Y. Dikhanov, N. Hamadeh, W. V. Oliver, M. O. Rissanen, and M. Yamanaka. 2016. "Is Living in African Cities Expensive?" Policy Research Working Paper 7641, World Bank, Washington, DC.

Newman, P. W., and J. R. Kenworthy. 1989. "Gasoline Consumption and Cities." *Journal of the American Planning Association* 55 (1): 24–37.

Philibert, Cédric. 2007. "Technology Penetration and Capital Stock Turnover: Lessons from IEA Scenario Analysis." International Energy Agency, Paris.

Rosenthal, Stuart S., and William C. Strange. 2004. "Chapter 49 Evidence on the Nature and Sources of Agglomeration Economies." In *Handbook of Regional and Urban Economics* 4: 2119–71. Amsterdam: Elsevier.

Toulmin, C. 2005. *Securing Land and Property Rights in Sub-Saharan Africa: The Role of Local Institutions.* Geneva: World Economic Forum.

United Nations. 2014. *World Urban Prospects: The 2014 Revision.* New York: United Nations.

———. 2015a. Millenium Development Goals Indicators. Indicator 7.10 Proportion of Urban Population Living in Slums. http://mdgs.un.org/unsd/mdg/seriesdetail.aspx?srid=710.

———. 2015b. Thirteenth to Fifteenth International Convention on the Elimination of All Forms of Racial Discrimination (ICERD) Periodic Report by Namibia. United Nations International Convention on the Elimination of All Forms of Racial Discrimination.

UNEP (United Nations Environmental Program), and FIA Foundation. 2013. *Share the Road: Design Guidelines for Non Motorised Transport in Africa.* United Nations Environmental Program.

UN-Habitat. 2008. *Mozambique Urban Sector Profile.* Nairobi: UN-Habitat.

Venables, A. J. 2016. "Breaking into Tradables: Urban Form and Urban Function in a Developing City." University of Oxford, United Kingdom.

WDI (World Development Indicators). 2015. http://data.worldbank.org/data-catalog/world-development-indicators.

Wesseling, T. 2016. *New Approaches to Physical Planning in Zambia.* Royal Haskoning DHV. http://www.royalhaskoningdhv.com/en-gb/innovation/world-cities-day/new-approaches-to-physical-planning-in-zambia.

World Bank. 2012a. *Inclusive Green Growth: The Pathway to Sustainable Development.* Washington, DC: World Bank.

———. 2012b. *The Future of Water in African Cities: Why Waste Water?* Washington, DC: World Bank.

———. 2015a. *Measuring Living Standards within Cities. Households Surveys: Dar es Salaam and Durban.* Washington, DC: World Bank.

———. 2015b. *Nigeria Urbanization Review: From Oil to Cities: Nigeria's Next Transformation.* Washington DC: World Bank.

———. 2015c. *Stocktaking of the Housing Sector in Sub-Saharan Africa: Challenges and Opportunities.* Washington, DC: World Bank.

———. 2016. *Cote d'Ivoire Urbanization Review. Diversified Urbanization.* Washington, DC: World Bank.

Part 1

Crowded and Disconnected African Cities

Chapter 1

Crowded with people, not dense with capital

Crowded with people

Not dense with physical capital

Not dense with human capital

Chapter 2

Disconnected land, people and jobs

Disconnected land

People not connected to people:
High fragmentation, low exposure,
little potential for interaction

People not connected to jobs

When well managed, city growth can spur economic growth and productivity in two ways. First, it can boost incentives for investment through higher economic density and proximity, which support clusters of firms and increase connectivity among workers. Second, it can make cities more livable for poor and middle-class residents, by providing affordable services, amenities, and housing. Through both channels, a successfully developed city offers firms the incentives of agglomeration and high returns on investment.

Africa's cities share neither of these attributes. They are predominantly local, lacking global or even regional reach. They are unsuccessful because they have developed along a different trajectory — one that imposes heavy costs on residents and firms and locks them in a low-growth poverty trap.

Africa is far poorer than other developing regions were when they reached similar levels of urbanization. Urbanizing while poor means that cities lack the means to invest in physical capital, such as infrastructure. They have fewer resources for public services, such as schooling, and lack human capital, which hinders efficient administration and improvement of existing institutions.

Successful cities are economically dense and connected. Africa's cities are crowded but not dense, and they are disconnected. Investments in infrastructure, industrial and commercial structures, and affordable formal housing have not kept pace with the concentration of people. Congestion and its costs overwhelm the benefits of urban concentration. Cities have developed as collections of small and fragmented neighborhoods. The lack of connectivity, particularly the absence of reliable transportation, limits job opportunities for workers and prevents firms from reaping scale and agglomeration benefits. Chapters 1 and 2 examine each of these themes, describing the symptoms of Africa's unsustainable urban development path.

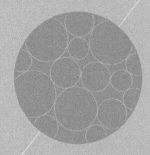

Chapter 1

Urbanization benefits people and businesses by increasing economic density. A worker in an economically dense area can commute more easily and consume a broader range of products. Firms clustered in cities can access a wider market of inputs and buyers. Scale economies reduce firms' production costs — in turn benefiting consumers.

Population density is indeed strongly correlated with indicators of livability — in Sub-Saharan Africa as elsewhere (Gollin, Kirchberger, and Lagakos 2016). Yet Africa's cities are not economically dense or efficient. They are crowded and unlivable. Most urban residents are packed into low-rise, informal settlements without adequate infrastructure or access to basic services. Two of every three people in Lagos, Nigeria dwell in slums (World Bank 2015b). Thus, even though households in densely populated areas of Africa are better supplied with services than rural households, the mere fact of higher population density does not imply a livable environment.

Why do a majority of people in Africa's cities live in slums? The immediate explanation is that the urbanization of people has not been accompanied by the urbanization of capital. Housing, infrastructure, and other capital investments are lacking, especially outside the city center. Urban building stocks have low replacement values. Across Africa, housing investment lags urbanization by nine years (Dasgupta, Lall, and Lozano-Gracia 2014).

The population density of African cities is similar to that of many cities elsewhere. What is holding these cities back is their low economic density — the lack of thriving urban markets that depend on adequate infrastructure and conveniently connected clusters of residential and commercial structures. A dearth of capital and capital investment keeps Africa's cities inefficient and less productive than they should be, limiting firms and workers to the production of goods and services for small and local hinterland markets locking them out of much more lucrative regional and international markets.

Crowded with people

Many of Africa's urban workers live in crowded quarters near the city center. In Dar es Salaam, Tanzania, 28 percent of residents are living at least three to a room (World Bank 2015c); in Abidjan, Côte d'Ivoire, the figure is 50 percent (World Bank 2016).

The reason for this crowding is that most people must live near the downtown district or industrial zones if they hope to work. They cannot conveniently commute from outlying areas, because little or no affordable transportation is available.

Africa's cities also suffer from a lack of adequate formal housing around the urban core. Consequently, people settle in relatively central informal settlements that are densely populated, ill served by urban infrastructure, and, by many measures, unlivable. Paradoxically, Africa's cities are sparsely built and laid out but feel crowded.

Slums: Workers' only option when urban economic density is low but highly concentrated

The crowdedness of African cities is most apparent in their slums. On average, 60 percent of Africa's urban population is packed into slums — a far larger share than the average 34 percent seen in other developing countries (United Nations 2015).

During 1960–72, Sub-Saharan Africa and Latin America had similar incidences of slums and squatter settlements (table 1.1). More recently, slum levels in Sub-Saharan Africa (62 percent) and Latin America (24 percent) diverged. South Asia's levels (35 percent) are similar to its historical levels, although some cities have experienced large increases in slum proportions.

Table 1.1 Slum population as percentage of total urban population in selected cities, historically and in 2014

Region/country	City	Share of city population living in slums	Share of national population living in slums in 2014
Sub-Saharan Africa			
Cameroon	Douala Yaoundé	80 (1970) 90 (1970)	37.8
Côte d'Ivoire	Abidjan	60 (1964)	56.0
Ethiopia	Addis Ababa	90 (1970)	73.9
Ghana	Accra	53 (1968)	37.9
Kenya	Nairobi Mombasa	33 (1970) 66 (1970)	56.0

Table 1.1 Slum population as percentage of total urban population in selected cities, historically and in 2014

Region/country	City	Share of city population living in slums	Share of national population living in slums in 2014
Liberia	Monrovia	50 (1970)	65.7
Madagascar	Tananarive	33 (1969)	77.2
Malawi	Blantyre	56 (1966)	66.7
Nigeria	Ibadan	75 (1971)	50.2
Senegal	Dakar	60 (1971)	39.4
Somalia	Mogadishu	77 (1967)	73.6
Sudan	Port Sudan	55 (1971)	91.6
Tanzania	Dar es Salaam	50 (1970)	50.7
Togo	Lomé	75 (1970)	51.2
Burkina Faso	Ouagadougou	70 (1966)	65.8
Zaire	Kinshasa	60 (1969)	74.8
Zambia	Lusaka	48 (1969)	54.0
Low-income Asia			
Afghanistan	Kabul	21 (1971)	62.7
India	Calcutta Bombay Delhi Madras Baroda	33 (1971) 25 (1971) 30 (1971) 25 (1971) 19 (1971)	24.0
Indonesia	Jakarta Bandung Makassar	26 (1972) 27 (1972) 33 (1972)	21.8
Nepal	Katmandu	22 (1961)	54.3
Pakistan	Karachi	23 (1970)	45.5
Sri Lanka	Colombo	43 (1968)	24.8 (1990)
Latin America and the Caribbean			
Brazil	Rio de Janeiro Belo Horizonte Recife Porto Alegre Brasilia	30 (1970) 14 (1970) 50 (1970) 13 (1970) 41 (1970)	22.3
Chile	Santiago	25 (1970)	9.0 (2005)
Colombia	Bogotá Cali Buenaventura	60 (1969) 30 (1969) 80 (1969)	13.1
Ecuador	Guayaquil	49 (1969)	36.0
Guatemala	Guatemala City	30 (1971)	34.5
Honduras	Tegucigalpa	25 (1970)	27.5
Mexico	Mexico City	46 (1970)	11.1
Panama	Panama City	17 (1970)	25.8
Peru	Lima Arequipa Chimbote	40 (1970) 40 (1970) 67 (1970)	34.2
Venezuela	Caracas Maracaíbo Barquisimeto Cíudad Guayana	40 (1969) 50 (1969) 41 (1969) 40 (1969)	32.0 (2005)

Source: City data are from Linn 1979; national data are from the United Nations' Millennium Development Goals database.

Note: A slum household is defined as a group of individuals living under the same roof in a dwelling that lacks one or more of the following conditions: access to improved water, access to improved sanitation, sufficient living area, durability. Figures in parentheses are years of the statistic.

FIGURE 1.1

Very high proportions of city dwellers live in slums in Africa

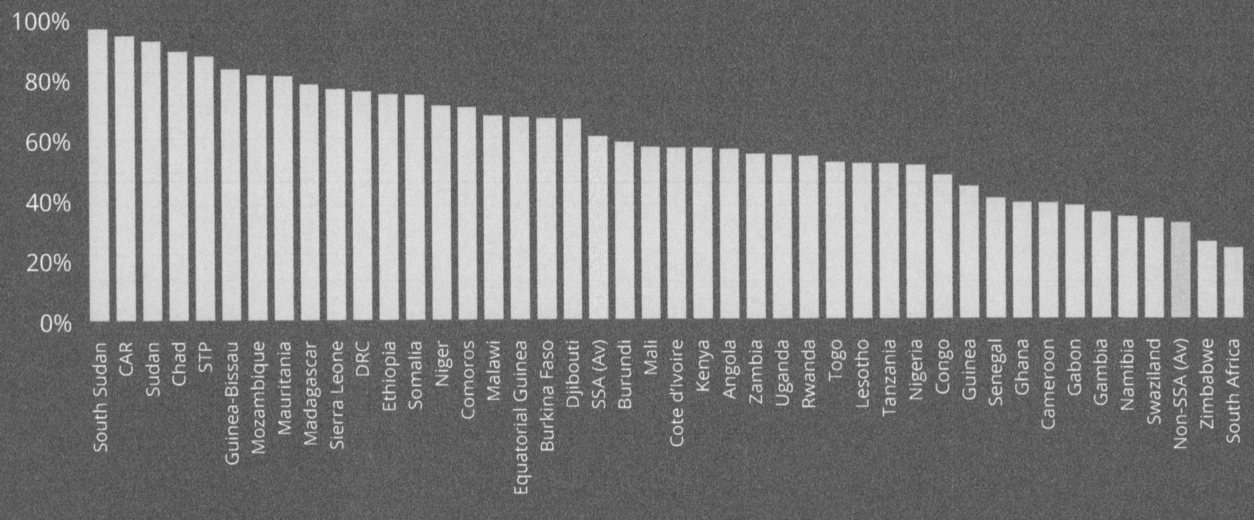

Source: United Nations 2015.   Note: Data are latest available for each country.

FIGURE 1.2

Population density in African cities is lower than in some other regions

Source: Data from Demographia 2015.

High rates of slum living within urban areas are characteristic of most African countries. Only two countries, Zimbabwe and South Africa, fall below the non-African average (figure 1.1). The proportion of Africans living in slums is not high because Africa has higher urban population densities than other countries. The average population density of African cities tracks the global average; it ranks third among seven global regions (figure 1.2).[1]

High population density at the city's core, rapid tapering on the outskirts

Africa does not stand out in a list of the world's 50 densest cities (only 6 African cities make the list, most of them in the Democratic Republic of Congo). And although peak population density is higher in Africa than elsewhere, the difference is not statistically significant. Using a sample of 265 cities in 3 regions, Henderson and Nigmatulina (2016) estimate that peak urban population densities are higher in Africa (57,600 people per square kilometer) than in Latin American (37,700) or Asia (50,900). In a sample of 39 cities in developing and developed countries, Henderson and Nigmatulina (2016) finds peak densities of 55,700 people per square kilometer in Africa and 50,800 in other regions. In most African cities, population and economic densities are higher near the city center and then fall steeply as one moves away. One kilometer away from the city center, average ambient population density falls 7 percent in African cities — a much more rapid rate of decline than the 4 percent in cities elsewhere. Economic activity as measured by nighttime light intensity falls at a rate of 15 percent in African cities, compared with 11 percent in non-African cities. In most African cities, the rate of decay of density gradients is above the sample median. Further, while most peak economic densities are below the median, most peak population densities are above the median.

People are clustering in downtown locations not because of the amenities or decent jobs they can access in central locations. These patterns reflect broader dysfunctionalities in land markets as well as limited investments in transport infrastructure, limiting the choices that people can make on where to live and how to access jobs (see chapter 5). For example in Nairobi, the current patterns of informal land use in centrally located settlements impose an economic loss of over $1.8 billion (Henderson, Venables, and Regan, 2016). And in Dar es Salaam, poor residents face squalid living conditions alongside low earning potential in downtown informal settlements (box 1.1).

Not dense with capital

Capital investment in Africa over the past 40 years has averaged about 20 percent of GDP. In contrast, urbanizing countries in East Asia — China, Japan, the Republic of Korea — stepped up capital investment during their periods of rapid urbanization. Between 1980 and 2011, China's capital investment (infrastructure, housing, and office buildings) rose from 35 percent of GDP to 48 percent; during roughly the same period (1978–2012), the urban share of its population rose from 18 percent to 52 percent. In East Asia as a whole, capital investment remained above 40 percent of GDP at the end of this period, helping the region become very dense economically.

These contrasts underline the fact that Africa is urbanizing when poor — indeed, strikingly poorer than other developing regions with similar urbanization levels. In 1968, when countries in the Middle East and North Africa region became 40 percent urban, their per capita GDP was $1,800 (in 2005 constant dollars). In 1994, when countries in the East Asia and Pacific region hit the 40 percent urbanization mark, their per capita GDP averaged $3,600. By contrast, per capita GDP in Africa is just $1,000.

Supporting rising population densities in African cities will require investments in buildings, and complementary physical infrastructure: roads, drainage, street lighting, electricity, water, and sewerage, together with policing, waste disposal, and health care. In the absence of higher levels of capital investment at around Asian levels, the potential benefits of Africa's cities are being overwhelmed by crime, disease, and squalor.

Overcrowding increases exposure to communicable diseases. Inadequate drainage increases the risk of malaria, and lack of sanitation raises the risk of dengue (Sclar, Garau, and Carolini 2005). Lack of access to clean water is a leading cause of diarrhea, which is responsible for an estimated 21 percent of deaths among children under five in developing countries — 2.5 million deaths a year (J-PAL 2012).

Evidence from a randomized evaluation of a Mexican housing program shows how improving floor quality in cities reduced the incidence of intestinal parasites, diarrhea, and anemia among young children while improving their cognitive development and their

BOX 1.1

Life in Africa's cities is often miserable: An urban migrant's story

In 1989, Fatma and her husband, Peter, sought to escape poverty by moving from rural Mbeya to Dar es Salaam. In many ways Dar es Salaam is better: Work is sometimes available, and services exist. But in some ways life is more hazardous than it was in Mbeya.

Despite savings, Fatma and Peter could not afford formal housing. To be close to work opportunities, they settled in a hazardous slum. Since then, rising housing costs or eviction have forced them to move more than a dozen times.

Today they live in Tandale, one of the city's largest slums. Built on a dumpsite just a few meters from the choked and contaminated river, their home sinks into the garbage a few inches every year. They share an open toilet with their neighbors and live in extreme poverty.

Why do they live in such conditions? Peter cannot afford transportation, so he walks wherever he goes. He leaves home every morning at 5 o'clock, walking to the city center, where he seeks day jobs as a mason. If there is no work — and often there is not — his family goes hungry. But if the family were living farther from the downtown, Peter would struggle to find work at all.

Fatma stays at home taking care of the couple's six children. She would like all of them to attend school, but only one does, because places for the others are lacking.

Despite low wages and high unemployment (estimated at 22 percent of the active labor force in 2014), Dar es Salaam is a relatively expensive city.

A meal costs twice as much as in Bangkok — even though average income in Bangkok is 23 times higher. Most of Fatma and Peter's income goes to food. Transportation, education, and health care are unaffordable.

Like millions of Africans, Fatma and Peter have had to give up livability in their quest for opportunity. The only central location they can afford is full of dangers. When Fatma and Peter migrated to the city, Dar es Salaam was about one-third of its size today. It now has more than 4.3 million residents, and it is projected to reach 10 million or more by the early 2030s, making it a "megacity." Many more families like Fatma's may soon be living in Dar es Salaam.

Source: World Bank 2015c.

To avoid a future in which Fatma and Peter's experience is the normal one, African governments must work with urban planners and development specialists to answer two key questions:

- How can the city ensure housing and transportation for the urban poor, allowing them to work without living in danger?

- How can high costs for people and businesses be reduced, making African cities kinder to their residents, enabling businesses to break into world markets, and lifting people like Fatma and her family out of poverty?

mothers' mental health and happiness (Cattaneo and others 2009). The program was associated with a 20 percent reduction in the presence of intestinal worms, a 13 percent reduction in the prevalence of diarrhea, and a 20 percent decline in the prevalence of anemia. Children 12- to 30-months-old scored 30 percent higher than controls on a communicative development test.

Further, improved access to piped water in urban areas has been shown to decrease infant mortality. Galiani, Gertler, and Schardrogsky (2005) show that the privatization of water services in Greater Buenos Aires improved young children's health outcomes by improving service quality and access to safe water, especially in the poorest areas, which benefited most from service expansion. Child mortality from infectious diseases dropped about 8 percent in areas that privatized the services, with the largest decline (26 percent) in the poorest areas. Gamper-Rabindran, Khan, and Timmins (2010) show that infant mortality in urban areas in Brazil declines as living standards improve.

In urban Morocco, connecting houses to water had no sizable effect on health outcomes, but convenient access to water improved household welfare by freeing up the time usually spent to fetch water. Tensions over water-related issues (such as shortages) decreased, and people reported spending more time on leisure and social activities. The program increased reported happiness and improved social integration (Devoto and others 2012).

Improved access to electricity improves health outcomes by reducing the inhalation of kerosene fumes and the risk of kerosene-related accidents, a frequent cause of burns. It also allows children to study after dark (see Wu, Borghans and Dupuy 2010 on Indonesia; Spalding-Fecher 2005 on South Africa; and UNDESA 2014).

Not dense with buildings

Evidence of overcrowding and low levels of capital investment appear in the value of building stocks. Disaster risk profiles were developed for four African cities. This methodology estimates the economic value of building stock and its distribution across the city at 1 square kilometer resolution. The total economic value of buildings in Dar es Salaam is estimated at about $12 billion — about five times the city's contribution to GDP. Even lower are the estimated

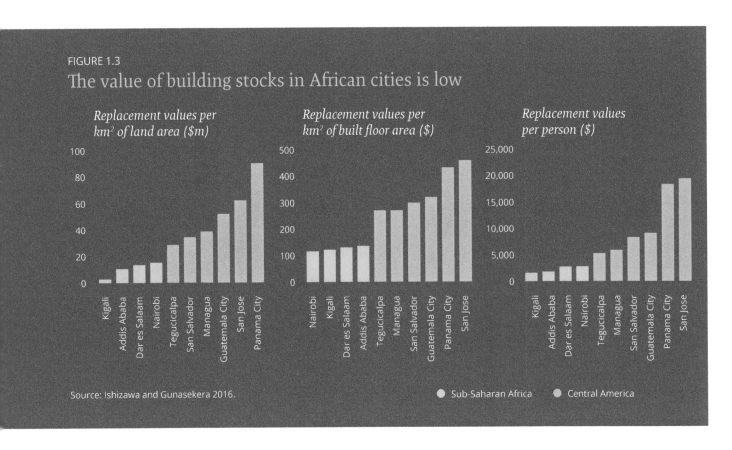

FIGURE 1.3
The value of building stocks in African cities is low

Replacement values per km² of land area ($m)

Replacement values per km² of built floor area ($)

Replacement values per person ($)

Source: Ishizawa and Gunasekera 2016.

● Sub-Saharan Africa   ● Central America

values for Nairobi, Kenya ($9 billion); Addis Ababa, Ethiopia ($6 billion); and Kigali, Rwanda ($2 billion) (Ishizawa and Gunasekera 2016).

The value of urban building stocks is much lower in Africa than in Central America (figure 1.3). The value per square kilometer in the four African cities studied ranges between $2.7 million (in Kigali) and $15.6 million (in Nairobi). In contrast, the range in Central America is $27.8–$90.4. The results are similar when other measures or value are compares. As elsewhere in the world, residential and commercial buildings are concentrated downtown (box 1.2).

Not dense with amenities, not livable

In most of the developing world — from India and Vietnam to Brazil and Colombia — large cities usually have better living standards than smaller cities. In countries where governments are still struggling to bring water and sanitation to most of the population, large cities usually fare better. In Brazil, where access to piped water is converging toward universal coverage, smaller cities lag behind metropolitan areas, with less than 90 percent coverage. In India, coverage levels reach 70 percent of the population in the largest cities reach but less than 50 percent in the smallest cities.

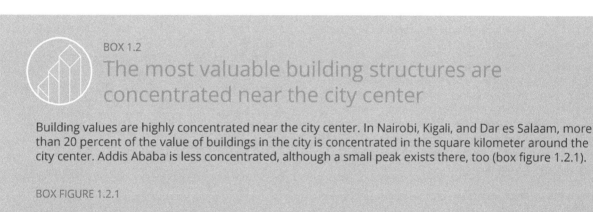

BOX 1.2

The most valuable building structures are concentrated near the city center

Building values are highly concentrated near the city center. In Nairobi, Kigali, and Dar es Salaam, more than 20 percent of the value of buildings in the city is concentrated in the square kilometer around the city center. Addis Ababa is less concentrated, although a small peak exists there, too (box figure 1.2.1).

BOX FIGURE 1.2.1

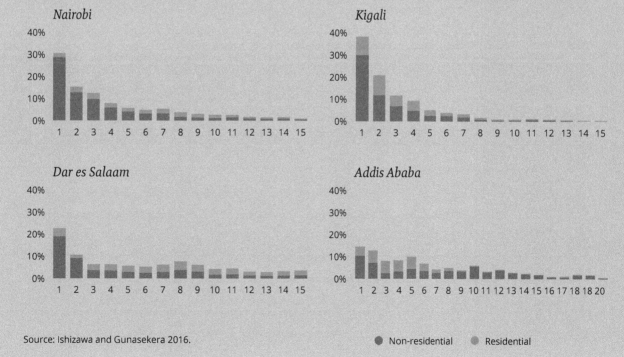

Source: Ishizawa and Gunasekera 2016.

● Non-residential   ● Residential

Coverage in Africa is lower — and it is not, on average, higher in larger cities. In Uganda, for example, coverage hovers around 20 percent for large, medium, and small cities (World Bank 2013).

Two patterns of living standards (measured by household durable assets, housing conditions, and infant survival rates) are evident in Africa (Gollin, Kirchberger, and Lagakos 2016):

• A wide variation of living standards is observed within countries, with urban areas ranking consistently higher across indicators.

• The links between density and living standards are strong in African countries, with a significant and positive correlation found consistently across countries.[7]

Although population density and living standards are correlated, higher population density does not imply a livable environment.

Access to electricity increases as density rises in all 20 of the Sub-Saharan African countries studied. The cost to provide piped water in dense urban areas is an estimated $0.70–$0.80 per cubic meter — far less than the $2 per cubic meter in sparsely populated areas (Kariuki and Schwartz 2005). Data for Colombia suggest that the operating costs for solid waste disposal services in large and dense metropolitan areas can be one-third to one-half the cost in smaller, less dense cities (Trojanis and Lozano-Gracia 2016).

At the national level, density and livability seem to be correlated in Africa. But within cities, the relationship is not straightforward. Although households in denser areas are better off than households in other areas of the country, living standards drop when crowding supplants density.

Population densities are rising and cities expanding rapidly in Africa: The largest cities are growing by as much 4 percent a year (United Nations 2014). Infrastructure investments have remained low, however, making density look a lot like crowding. African cities have failed to absorb large increases in population successfully because of lack of basic services, limited budgets in expensive cities, and limited connective infrastructure.

During the mid-1970s, the share of the population with access to water supply and sewage disposal was similar in Saharan Africa and South Asia. Since then, the gap between the two regions has widened dramatically (table 1.2). In urban areas in 2015, 88 percent of residents in South Asia but just 64 percent in Sub-Saharan Africa had access to improved water. The gap was even larger for improved sanitation, which reached 71 percent of urban residents in South Asia but just 46 percent of urban residents in Sub-Saharan Africa.

Table 1.2 Percent of population with access to water and sanitation, by region

| Region | Mid-1970s | | | | 2015 | | | |
| | Access to water | | Access to sewage disposal | | Access to improved water | | Access to improved sanitation | |
	Urban	Rural	Urban	Rural	Urban	Rural	Urban	Rural
Sub-Saharan Africa	66	10	70	14	89	64	46	27
South Asia	66	17	67	3	93	88	71	55
East Asia and Pacific	58	10	67	15	96	87	85	69
Latin America and the Caribbean	78	35	80	25	97	89	88	77

Source: Data for 1970s are from Linn 1979. Current data are from World Development Indicators 2016.

Note: Access to an improved water source refers to the percentage of the population using an improved drinking water source (including piped water on premises (piped household water connection located inside the user's dwelling, plot or yard), and other improved drinking water sources (public taps or standpipes, tube wells or boreholes, protected dug wells, protected springs, and rainwater collection). Access to improved sanitation facilities refers to the percentage of the population using improved sanitation facilities, that is, likely to ensure hygienic separation of human excreta from human contact. They include flush/pour flush (to piped sewer system, septic tank, pit latrine), ventilated improved pit (VIP) latrine, pit latrine with slab, and composting toilet.

Analysis of low- and lower-middle-income countries shows how urban areas of Sub-Saharan Africa perform with respect to other regions. The analysis compares three measures: improved water, improved sanitation, and mortality caused by road traffic injury. The empirical estimation is specified as follows:

$$WDI = \theta_1 1 \text{ } Regdummy + \theta_2 \log gdppc + \theta_3 \log landarea + \theta_4 \text{ \%urban} + \varepsilon_i$$

where WDI is the World Development Indicator measure; Regdummy is a dummy taking a value of 1 if the worker lives in South Asia (the base case) and different values for other regions; log *gdppc* denotes the log value of GDP per capita in the country, adjusted for purchasing power parity; log *landarea* gives the log value of the country's land area in square kilometers; and % urban denotes the percentage of population residing in urban areas.

The results indicate that South Asia (the base case) has more than 15 times greater access to improved sanitation than Sub-Saharan Africa and much lower mortality from traffic congestion. Europe and Central Asia and the Middle East and North Africa have much better access to improved sanitation than South Asia. Even controlling for poverty and urbanization levels, Sub-Saharan Africa lags other developing regions in these urban development indicators.

Research based on household surveys for 20 countries suggests that across Sub-Saharan Africa the proportion of households with shelter and infrastructure amenities varies not only by population density but also by amenity type, urban area type, and household expenditure quintile (table 1.3).

Table 1.3 Housing amenities in Sub-Saharan Africa, by type of area and expenditure quintile (percent of all households)

Variable	All areas	Type of area			Expenditure quintile	
		Largest city	Other urban	Rural	Bottom	Top
Shelter amenities						
Roof	16.1	18.6	19.6	13.7	15.4	18.0
Walls	65.8	90.3	80.0	53.0	58.7	72.1
Floor	52.8	91.4	77.0	35.2	40.7	65.8
Housing infrastructure						
Electricity	31.6	69.4	49.5	13.4	20.1	43.0
Toilet	27.6	48.8	38.3	17.6	19.6	35.5
Water	38.2	77.3	61.0	17.8	30.5	45.1
Other						
Home ownership	70.6	40.8	53.0	85.5	78.1	61.5
Lack at least one shelter amenity	92.5	85.3	87.6	96.6	94.9	89.2
Lack at least one shelter infrastructure structure	89.9	70.1	82.4	98.0	89.2	83.7
Overcrowded	17.6	17.8	16.0	18.4	30.4	7.4

Source: Lozano-Gracia and Young 2014.

Note: Figures are the means taken across all countries' reported percentages of housing amenities. For example, the percentage of households that have a permanent roof was calculated by country (and broken down by urban areas and quintiles); the figures shown are the mean percentages of households with a roof, where each observation is one country. This method prevents biasing the percentages toward countries with larger samples.

Amenities are poor across all areas and income quintiles. Only 16 percent of urban households in Africa have permanent roofs — and access is even lower in rural areas. Between 70 percent (in the largest cities) and 98 percent (in rural areas) of all Africans lack access to electricity, a toilet, or water.

The differences between the proportions of households that have access to housing amenities also varies significantly across expenditure quintiles. They are statistically significant at the 1 percent level for all amenities and infrastructure, indicating the stark difference between housing for the richest and the poorest households in Sub-Saharan Africa.

Housing conditions in Sub-Saharan Africa vary by subregion, country, and type of urban area. Shortages are less acute in Middle Africa than in Eastern and Western Africa (map 1.1). Eastern Africa has the largest share of households in overcrowded conditions, the smallest share of households with permanent floors and access to toilets, and the largest percentage of households with electricity connections. Middle Africa has the smallest share of households with electricity connections but the smallest share of people facing housing shortages. Western Africa has the greatest housing deficiencies and the largest proportion of households facing housing shortages.

16%

of urban households in Africa
have permanent roofs

Between 70 percent (in the largest cities) and
98 percent (in rural areas) of all Africans lack
access to electricity, a toilet, or water.

MAP 1.1

Housing conditions and shortages in Sub-Saharan Africa

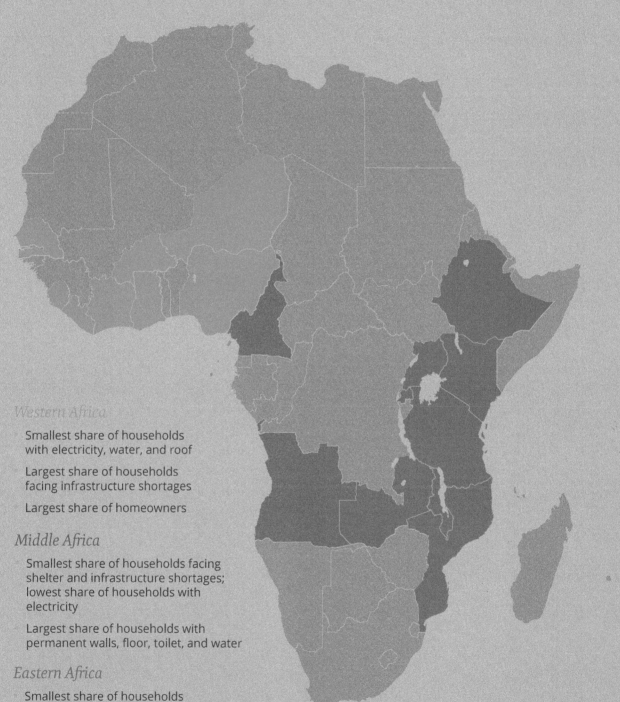

Western Africa

Smallest share of households
with electricity, water, and roof

Largest share of households
facing infrastructure shortages

Largest share of homeowners

Middle Africa

Smallest share of households facing
shelter and infrastructure shortages;
lowest share of households with
electricity

Largest share of households with
permanent walls, floor, toilet, and water

Eastern Africa

Smallest share of households
with nondirt floors and toilets

Largest share of households
with electricity

Largest share of households
living in overcrowded housing

Note: Subregional classifications are
adopted from the United Nations.

Source: Lozano-Gracia and Young 2014.

Case studies

Living standards also vary widely within cities, as recent surveys of Dar es Salaam and Durban reveal.

Dar es Salaam, Tanzania

About two-thirds of households in Dar es Salaam share their toilet facilities, and there is some indication that access rates are relapsing: Of the households in the survey that do not currently have access to sanitation, 15 percent said that they had access in a house they previously lived in, in Dar es Salaam. The most common form of improved sanitation is an improved pit latrine; other forms of improved sanitation are rare. Pit latrines are the most common form of unimproved sanitation (figure 1.4).

Access to water and sanitation is very limited throughout the city. It is slightly higher in peripheral areas than in central areas (figure 1.5). Households in the city's core rely mainly on improved pit latrines or pour flush to pit as their main toilets. The distribution of households by type of toilet remains similar across city areas, except in shanty areas, where a larger share of the population uses unimproved sanitation. Flush toilets connected to a septic tank are more common on the periphery.

FIGURE 1.4

Large shares of the population in Dar es Salaam lack access to basic sanitation and water services

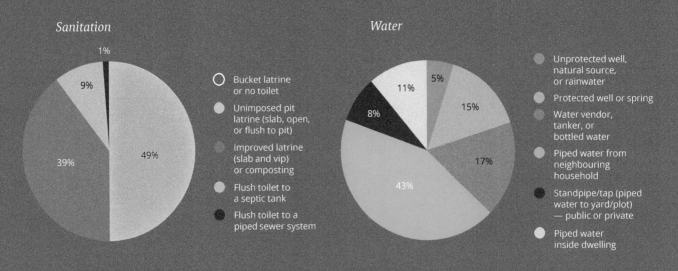

Source: World Bank 2015c.

Note: Improved latrine combines 33 percent slab latrine and 6 percent VIP latrine; unimproved sanitation includes 26 percent unimproved, 16 percent open slab, and 7 percent pour flush to pit.

Access to piped water is also very limited throughout the city, with only 17 percent of households in the city center and 14 percent on the periphery having piped water. In the city as a whole, only 11 percent of households report piped water as their main source of drinking water. The shares are much lower for households in shanty areas in the center (9.5 percent) and in the consolidated city (7.7 percent).

Access to electricity is much better toward the city center, where more than 70 percent of households (including households in shanty areas) have access. Access decreases with distance from the city center, with less than 45 percent of households on the periphery connected to the grid. Despite the high connection rate, the majority of households use charcoal as their main fuel for cooking.

Residents of Dar es Salaam seem to be benefiting to some extent from being closer to one another: More than 40 percent of households report using piped water from a neighboring household as their main source of water (figure 1.6). The share is much higher in shanty areas (51 percent of households).

While more than 60 percent of households in the city center and 80 percent in shanty areas report sharing their toilet facilities, only 36 percent of households on the periphery do so. When asked about the main constraint of not having piped water in their homes, more than 20 percent of households in all areas identified connection cost as the main hurdle. Half of all households indicated that they lacked access because their home was rented.

Even people with access to piped water in their homes face challenges related to service quality. On average, households reported having fewer than 5 days and 14 hours a day of service in the previous 7 days. Low quality forces more affluent households and businesses to rely on private boreholes, leading to saltwater intrusion (Mtoni and Walraevens 2010; Jones and others 2016).

FIGURE 1.5

Access to improved water and sanitation in Dar es Salaam tends to rise with distance from the center

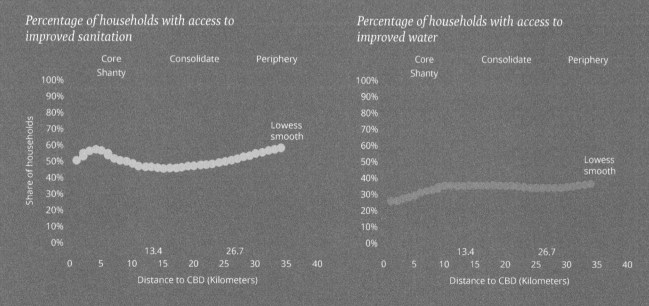

Source: World Bank 2015c.   Note: Smooth lines are based on locally weighted regressions.

FIGURE 1.6

Access to improved sanitation and piped water at home is low across Dar es Salaam

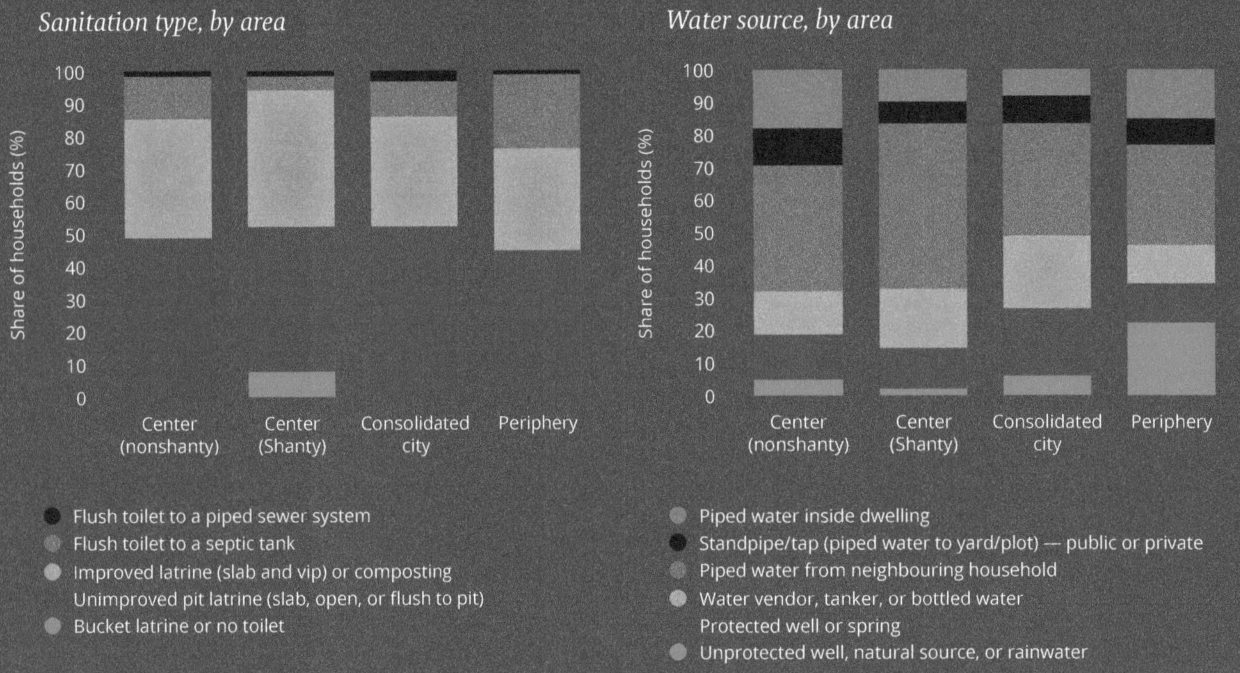

Sanitation type, by area

Water source, by area

Flush toilet to a piped sewer system
Flush toilet to a septic tank
Improved latrine (slab and vip) or composting
Unimproved pit latrine (slab, open, or flush to pit)
Bucket latrine or no toilet

Piped water inside dwelling
Standpipe/tap (piped water to yard/plot) — public or private
Piped water from neighbouring household
Water vendor, tanker, or bottled water
Protected well or spring
Unprotected well, natural source, or rainwater

Source: World Bank 2015c.

Durban, South Africa

The story is quite different in Durban, where more than two-thirds of households have access to piped water (against 14–17 percent in Dar es Salaam). Within-city variations in access are wide, however. Almost 87 percent of households in the urban core have piped water in their dwelling, but less than 20 percent on the outskirts of the city and less than 15 percent in shanty areas do. In shanty areas, households rely less on neighbors than in Dar es Salaam: Less than 5 percent of households in shanty areas and less than 8 percent of households in rural areas cite their neighbors' dwelling as their main source for drinking water. Almost 42 percent of households in shanty areas and 52 in rural areas rely on yard taps. Street standpipes are also an important source in shanty areas, with 36 percent of households relying on them for drinking water.

Durban is also far ahead of Dar es Salaam on sanitation. Variations in access are wide, however: Almost 92 percent of households in the urban core are connected to the sewerage system, but only 19 percent in the outskirts of the city and 45 in shanty areas are. In shanty areas, which in Durban are not very far from the city's core, 44 percent of households still rely on pit latrines as their main form of sanitation, against 15 percent in peri-urban formal areas and 76 percent in rural areas on the outskirts of the city.

Access to piped water and a flush toilet in the house fall with distance from the city center (figure 1.7). The average increase beyond 35 kilometers from the city center should be interpreted with care, however, because it is driven by the greater access in peri-urban areas farther from the city center. (Further exploration using a local polynomial estimation suggests some over-smoothing is happening that hides these low access values in rural areas.)

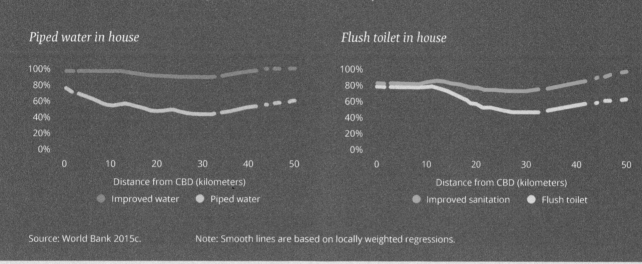

FIGURE 1.7

Durban: Some challenges are met, but many remain

Piped water in house

Flush toilet in house

Source: World Bank 2015c.   Note: Smooth lines are based on locally weighted regressions.

Migrants who arrived in Durban between 1960 and 2000 enjoyed improvements in access to basic services relative to their previous residence. Migrants today face a deterioration in living standards (figure 1.8). They sacrifice living standards in search of the opportunities the city offers.

FIGURE 1.8

Moving to Durban improved migrants' access to basic services before but not after 2000

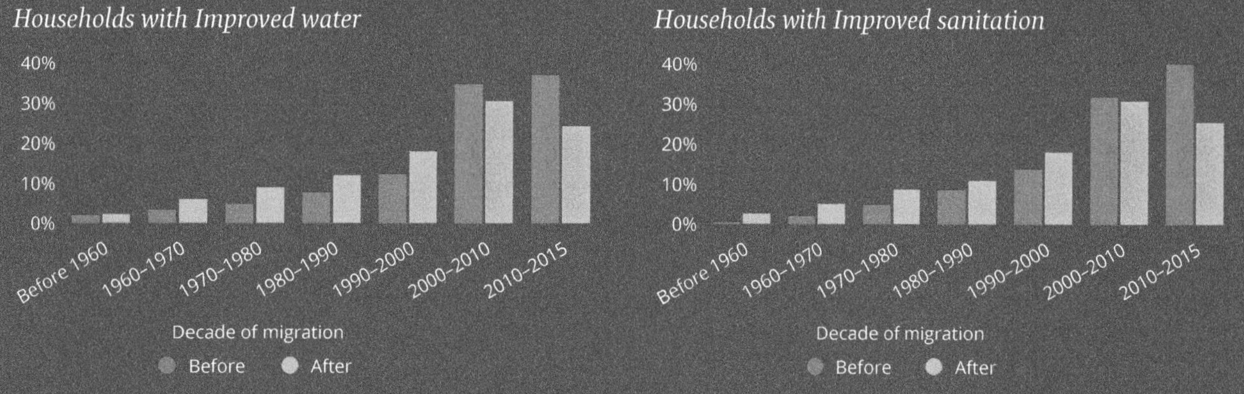

Households with Improved water

Households with Improved sanitation

Source: World Bank 2015c.

Household moves within the city reflect a similar trend. Before 1980, about 31 percent of within-city moves were from a house that did not have access to improved sanitation to one that did. These figures fell to 18.8 percent for 1980–2000 and 10.6 percent for 2000–15 (figure 1.9).

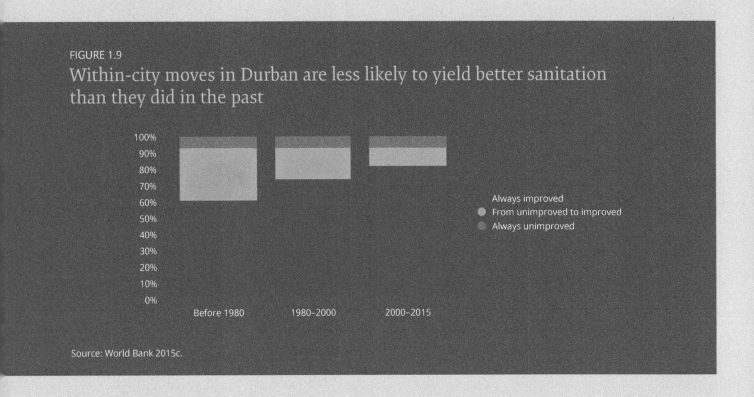

FIGURE 1.9

Within-city moves in Durban are less likely to yield better sanitation than they did in the past

Source: World Bank 2015c.

Elsewhere in Africa

Infrastructure and public services are concentrated in central areas and formal neighborhoods in Africa's cities, where access to water and electricity expanded between 1997 and 2013. Access to services declines rapidly once one leaves the center, however; peri-urban areas and informal neighborhoods have limited access to basic services.

The pressing challenges observed in Dar es Salaam and Durban are not unique to those cities. In Côte d'Ivoire, urban audits in 2013 showed that although infrastructure and public services are adequate in central areas and formal neighborhoods, they are lacking in peri-urban and informal neighborhoods, where basic infrastructure has failed to keep up with population growth. In San Pédro, for example, a city of about a quarter million people, informal neighborhoods with limited access to basic services cover about a third of the urban landscape. In Bouaké,

a city with more than half a million people, peri-urban neighborhoods are growing without access to water and electricity (formal neighborhoods in the center also have inadequate infrastructure) (World Bank 2016). In the communes (municipalities) of Abidjan where urban audits were conducted (particularly Yopougon, the largest), more than half the residential neighborhoods have limited access to public services and infrastructure.

In Ghana, access to piped water, waste disposal, and toilet facilities in Accra and Kumasi decreases rapidly as distance to the city center increases (World Bank 2015d). In Maputo, Mozambique, access to basic services is strongly concentrated in the city center, dropping off rapidly outside the center (figure 1.10). In Kinshasa, the Democratic Republic of Congo, access to piped water and septic tanks remains relatively low and declines with distance from the center (figure 1.11).

FIGURE 1.10

Access to piped water, septic tanks, and electricity improved in Maputo, Mozambique between 1997 and 2013

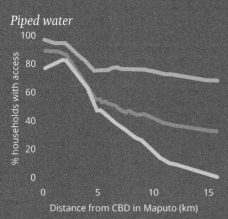

Piped water

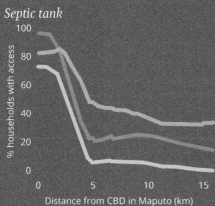

Septic tank

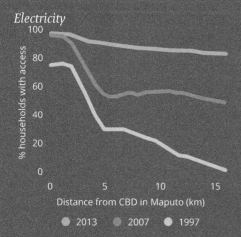

Electricity

● 2013 ● 2007 ● 1997

Source: Nakamura 2016.

Note: Smooth lines are based on locally weighted regressions.

FIGURE 1.11

Access to piped water, septic tanks, and electricity improved in Kinshasa, Democratic Republic of Congo between 2007 and 2013

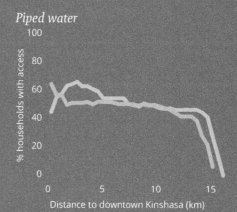

Piped water

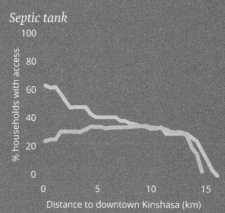

Septic tank

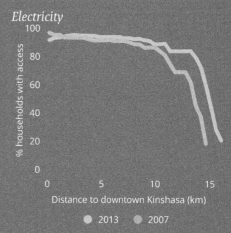

Electricity

● 2013 ● 2007

Source: Data from Demographic and Health surveys conducted in 2007 and 2013/2014.

Note: Distance is measured from Gombe. Smooth lines are based on locally weighted regression.

In Nigeria, only Lagos and Abuja have sewerage systems, and even in those cities the majority of households are not connected: Just 6 percent of urban households have a pour/flush toilet connected to a piped sewerage system (World Bank 2005). In Ethiopia, only Addis Ababa has a sewerage system — and the system serves only 10 percent of the population. In 2012, only 44 percent of the population of Addis Ababa has access to safe water; full coverage of 100 liters per person per day would require a two- to threefold increase in the water supply (World Bank 2015a). In other urban areas, access to water is even lower and even waste collection is limited: For Sub-Saharan Africa as a whole, only 45–82 percent of locally generated waste in urban areas is collected.

The lack of basic services puts further pressures on household budgets. Alternative sources of water are almost always far more expensive than piped water. In Lagos, the cost of buying informal water and garbage pickup is 1.3–3 times greater than the tariffs charged by the state (World Bank 2015b). In Accra, the cost of water from small-scale water sources, such as bottles and water "sachets," is typically five to seven times higher than piped water (World Bank 2015d). In Bouaké, Côte d'Ivoire, most taps are broken, forcing residents to buy potable water from informal water vendors, who can price hikes and sell unsafe or illegally sourced water (World Bank 2016).

Low human capital

For urban areas to be productive better human capital is needed. Workers bring to the workplace a bundle of skills that affect their productivity. Cognitive skills have long been recognized as an important determinant of productivity and wages. A growing body of evidence documents that, at least in the developed world, larger cities reward educated workers more than smaller cities do—one reason larger cities tend to attract higher-skilled workers.

Labor force participation rates in Sub-Saharan Africa do not lag other developing areas. But, on average, people in Sub-Saharan Africa are less educated and have worse health than people in other regions, adversely influencing the overall quality of the urban labor supply.

In attainment of education and literacy, Sub-Saharan Africa lags behind other developing regions of the world and has done so historically. South Asia is one exception which had poorer literacy than Sub-Saharan Africa in the 1990s, but over time overtook the latter. Sub-Saharan Africa, which has surging youth population levels, has the lowest levels of youth literacy today (tables 1.4 and 1.5).

Table 1.4 Adult literacy rate, population 15+ years

Region	1990	2000	2010
East Asia and Pacific	79.7	90.8	94.5
Latin America and Caribbean	85.2	88.6	91.5
Middle East and North Africa	56	68	77.9
South Asia	46.5	58	66.7
Sub-Saharan Africa	52.5	57	60.3

Source: UNESCO Institute for Statistics.

Note: Percentage of the population age 15 and above who can, with understanding, read and write a short, simple statement on their everyday life. Generally, 'literacy' also encompasses 'numeracy', the ability to make simple arithmetic calculations. This indicator is calculated by dividing the number of literates aged 15 years and over by the corresponding age group population and multiplying the result by 100.

Source: UNESCO Institute for Statistics.

Table 1.5 Youth literacy rate, population 15–24 years, both sexes (%)

Region	1990	2000	2010
East Asia and Pacific	93.6	97.9	98.8
Latin America and Caribbean	92.9	96.0	97.5
Middle East and North Africa	76.2	86.1	91.8
South Asia	59.1	72.6	83.4
Sub-Saharan Africa	64.7	68.2	70.8

Source: UNESCO Institute for Statistics.

Note: Number of people age 15 to 24 years who can both read and write with understanding a short simple statement on their everyday life, divided by the population in that age group. Generally, 'literacy' also encompasses 'numeracy', the ability to make simple arithmetic calculations. Divide the number of people aged 15 to 24 years who are literate by the total population in the same age group and multiply the result by 100.

Source: UNESCO Institute for Statistics.

Larger cities also pay a wage premium to workers with better social skills (Bacolod, Blum, and Strange 2009). This finding is unsurprising given that cities are often modeled as "interactive systems" in which the urban structure reflects the net benefits of interactions (that is, the value of interactions net of transportation costs) (see Fugita and Thisse 2002, among others). In France, human capital externalities increase earnings via greater communication in the workplace. This effect is larger in bigger and more educated cities (Charlot and Duranton 2004).

The World Bank's STEP (Skills towards Employment and Productivity) Skills Measurement Program is the first initiative to develop a consistent measure of skills — cognitive and social — in low- and middle-income countries. It integrates unique modules in household surveys to directly gauge the soft skills of respondents. The STEP survey incudes questions that directly assess reading, writing, and computer skills (cognitive skills) as well as questions assessing decision making, personality, and behavior (social skills). It also asks questions on whether physical skills are used at work (table 1.6).

The STEP survey was used to analyze skills premiums in the capital relative to other urban areas in two African countries (Ghana and Kenya) and five comparators (Armenia, Colombia, Georgia, and Vietnam). The skill indexes were constructed for each respondent using factor analysis.

Table 1.6 Skills assessed in the STEP survey

Index	Measure
Cognitive skill index (at and outside work)	• Read (forms, bills, financial statements, newspapers or magazines, instruction manuals, books, reports, and so forth); length of readings
	• Write at work; length of writings
	• Show numeracy (measure of size, weight, distances, price calculation, more advanced mathematics, and so forth)
	• Use a computer; type of software used
	• Show thinking and show learning
Social skill index	• Interact with others (clients, public, colleagues)
	• Make a formal presentation
	• Supervise the work of others
	Responses to questions about personality and behavior (answers are almost always, most of the time, some of the time, and almost never).
	• Are you talkative?
	• Do you like to keep your opinions to yourself? Do you prefer to keep quiet when you have an opinion?
	• Are you outgoing and sociable — for example, do you make friends very easily?
	• Do you like to share your thoughts and opinions with other people, even if you don't know them very well?
	• Do you ask for help when you don't understand something?
	• Do you think about how the things you do will affect others?
Physical skill index	• Operate or work with any heavy machines or industrial equipment
	• Regularly have to lift or pull anything weighing at least 50 pounds
	• Have a physically demanding job

Figure 1.12 (overleaf) shows the standardized distribution of skills between the capital and other urban areas in each country. Across countries, the left-tail density is higher than the right-tail density, indicating that most urban workers are poorly endowed with these skills. In most countries, the distribution of cognitive skills in the capital city is denser, because workers with higher cognitive skills prefer to work in larger cities. This pattern is not as pronounced in Ghana and Kenya, however, suggesting that such sorting is not as important in Africa as it is elsewhere.

BOX 1.3

The contribution of cognitive and noncognitive skills to urban performance

The empirical estimation is specified as follows

$$\log w_i = \theta_1 cc_i + S'_i \theta_2 + (cc_i \times S'_i)\theta_3 + + X'_i \beta + \varepsilon_i$$

where w_i is the nominal wage of worker i; cc_i is a dummy taking a value of 1 if the worker lives in the capital city; S'_i denotes a worker's cognitive, social, and physical skills; and X'_i is a vector comprising the worker characteristics, including educational attainment, the size of the firm, the number of hours worked, and the number of tasks assigned. Occupation and industry fixed effects are accounted for. ε_i is the error term.

Box table 1.3.1 shows the skills premium and the interaction effects capturing the effect of agglomeration associated with more cognitive, social, and physical skills. In all countries, workers with more cognitive skills earn more. On average, a one standard deviation increase in the cognitive skills index is associated with a 20 percent increase in the nominal wage.[1] Social skills also tend to be positively associated with wages, albeit to a lesser extent. Agglomeration does not seem to reinforce the positive effect of soft skills on wages in these countries studied.

Box table 1.3.1 Ordinary least squares estimates of the effect of agglomeration and soft skills

	African countries			Comparator countries		
Item	Kenya	Ghana	Vietnam	Colombia	Armenia	Georgia
Capital city	0.018	0.022	0.133**	0.018	0.225***	0.316***
	(0.052)	(0.116)	(0.052)	(0.060)	(0.063)	(0.062)
Cognitive skills index	0.224***	0.193	0.180***	0.216***	0.133***	0.198***
	(0.039)	(0.125)	(0.044)	(0.042)	(0.047)	(0.050)
Cognitive skills × capital	0.043	0.040	0.021	–0.068	–0.072	–0.025
	(0.061)	(0.114)	(0.050)	(0.060)	(0.053)	(0.078)
Social skills index	0.096***	–0.008	0.098***	0.052	0.080*	0.039
	(0.031)	(0.069)	(0.031)	(0.036)	(0.046)	(0.046)
Social skills × capital	0.044	0.142	–0.059	0.034	–0.134*	–0.015
	(0.055)	(0.122)	(0.046)	(0.057)	(0.068)	(0.061)
Physical skills index	–0.032	0.036	–0.043	–0.052	0.008	–0.082
	(0.031)	(0.078)	(0.032)	(0.039)	(0.041)	(0.054)
Physical skills × capital	0.020	0.070	0.050	–0.023	–0.076	0.060
	(0.045)	(0.102)	(0.039)	(0.063)	(0.065)	(0.073)
Years of education	0.021***	0.012	0.045***	0.014	0.005	0.027**
	(0.007)	(0.024)	(0.008)	(0.010)	(0.013)	(0.012)
Constant	6.789***	0.221	3.851***	10.316***	0.880*	0.064
	(0.697)	(0.673)	(0.495)	(0.348)	(0.453)	(0.711)
Occupation dummies	Yes	Yes	Yes	Yes	Yes	Yes
Industry dummies	Yes	Yes	Yes	Yes	Yes	Yes
Observations	2108	763	2102	1635	895	634
R^2	0.44	0.36	0.34	0.43	0.37	0.61

Source: Based on the World Bank STEP Skills Measurement Program.

Note: The dependent variable is the log of weekly earnings. Standard errors are clustered by worker. All regressions control for gender, age and its square, marital status, firm size, and the number of tasks performed. Robust standard errors are in parentheses.

*** statistically significant at the 1 percent level, ** statistically significant 5 percent, * statistically significant at the 10 percent level.

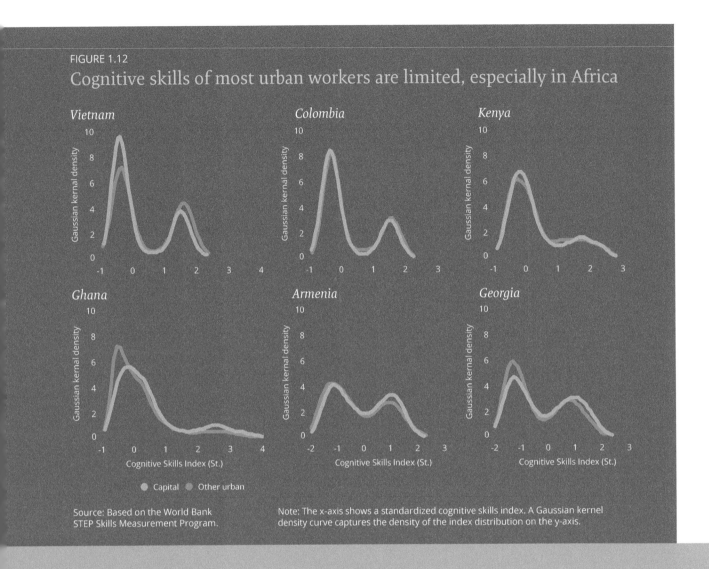

FIGURE 1.12

Cognitive skills of most urban workers are limited, especially in Africa

Source: Based on the World Bank STEP Skills Measurement Program.

Note: The x-axis shows a standardized cognitive skills index. A Gaussian kernel density curve captures the density of the index distribution on the y-axis.

Africa's cities are crowded, and they lack the structures need to make them livable. They are not more densely populated than cities elsewhere, but more of their people live in slums.

Concentrated urban populations should enjoy economic benefits from firm clustering, agglomeration, and productivity. Instead, in Africa they endure substandard living conditions, because cities are not dense with economic activity and structures and capital levels are low (low building stock values, poor shelter and infrastructure amenities, and low worker skills).

One reason Africa's city perform poorly is that Africa is poorer than other regions were at comparable stages of urbanization. As a result, housing investment lags such investment in low- and middle-income economies elsewhere, and cities are relatively unbuilt.

Also important are the relatively high concentrations of economic density within African cities. Urban workers crowd into informal settlements near the city center in order to access job opportunities not found elsewhere. The lack of economic density outside downtown districts can be seen, literally, in the low intensity of nighttime lights.

Poverty itself is not the problem, however: It locks cities into low development traps only if cities are spatially dispersed and disconnected, unable to attract investment with efficiencies from agglomeration. Even poor cities can become livable when they are developed in a more integrated manner, as chapter 2 shows.

References

Bacolod, M., B.S. Blum, and W.C. Strange. 2009. "Skills in the City." *Journal of Urban Economics* 65 (2): 136–153.

Bertaud, Alain. 2001. Metropolis: A Measure of the Spatial Organization of 7 Large Cities. Available: http://alainbertaud.com/wp-content/uploads/2013/06/AB_Metropolis_Spatial_Organization.pdf

Cattaneo, M. D., S. Galiani, P.J. Gertler, S. Martinez, and R. Titiunik. 2009. "Housing, health, and happiness." *American Economic Journal: Economic Policy* 1 (1): 75–105.

Charlot, S., and G. Duranton. 2006. "Cities and workplace communication: Some quantitative French evidence." *Urban Studies* 43 (8): 1365–1394.

Dasgupta, B., S. V. Lall, and N. Lozano-Gracia. 2014. "Urbanization and Household Investment." Policy Research Working Paper 7170, World Bank, Washington, DC.

Demographia. 2015. Demographia World Urban Areas. 11th Annual Edition ed. St. Louis: Demographia. Available at: http://www.demographia.com/db-worldua.pdf.

Devoto, F., E. Duflo, P. Dupas, W. Parienté, and V. Pons. 2012. "Happiness on Tap: Piped Water Adoption in Urban Morocco." *American Economic Journal: Economic Policy* 4 (4): 68–99.

Fujita, M., and J. Thisse. 2002. *The Economics of Agglomeration. Cambridge University Press*, Cambridge.

Galiani, S., P. Gertler, and E. Schargrodsky. 2005. "Water for Life: The Impact of the Privatization of Water Services on Child Mortality." *Journal of Political Economy* 113 (1): 83–120.

Gamper-Rabindran, S., S. Khan, and C. Timmins. 2010. "The Impact of Piped Water Provision on Infant Mortality in Brazil: A Quantile Panel Data Approach." *Journal of Development Economics* 92 (2): 188–200.

Gollin, Douglas, Martina Kirchberger, and David Lagakos. 2016. "Living Standards across Space: Evidence from Sub-Saharan Africa." March 31. Available at: https://collaboration.worldbank.org/docs/DOC-20505.

Gulyani, Sumila, Debabrata Talukdar, and Darby Jack. 2010. "Poverty, Living Conditions, and Infrastructure Access: A Comparison of Slums in Dakar, Johannesburg, and Nairobi." Policy Research Working Paper 5388, World Bank, Washington, DC.

Henderson, Vernon, and Dzhamilya Nigmatulina. 2016. "The Fabric of African Cities: How to Think about Density and Land Use. Draft, April 20. London School of Economics.

Iacovone, L., V. Ramachandran, and M. Schmidt. 2014. "Stunted Growth: Why Don't African Firms Create More Jobs?" Working Paper 353, Center for Global Development, Washington, DC.

Ishizawa, O., and R. Gunasekera. 2016. "Economic Values of Buildings in Four African Cities." Background paper for this report.

J-PAL. 2012. "J-PAL Urban Services Review Paper." Cambridge, MA: Abdul Latif Jameel Poverty Action Lab.

Jones, Patricia, Julia Bird, J.M. Kironde, Lussuga, and Anne Laski. 2016. Dar es Salaam: City Narrative. Available: https://collaboration.worldbank.org/docs/DOC-20828.

Kariuki, Mukami, and Jordan Schwartz. "Small-Scale Private Service Providers of Water Supply and Electricity: A Review of Incidence, Structure, Pricing and Operating Characteristics." Policy Research Working Paper 3727, World Bank, Washington, DC. 2015.

Kolenikov, Stanislav, and Gustavo Angeles. 2009. "Socio-economic status measurement with discrete proxy variables: Is principal component analysis a reliable answer?" *Review of Income and Wealth* 55 (1): 128–165.

Linn, Justin. 1979. "Policies for efficient and equitable growth of cities in developing countries." Staff Working Paper 342, World Bank, Washington, DC.

Lozano-Gracia, Nancy, and Cheryl Young. 2014. "Housing Consumption and Urbanization." Policy Research Working Paper 7112, World Bank, Washington, DC.

Mtoni, Yohana, and Kristine Walraevens. 2010. "Saltwater intrusion in the quaternary aquifer of the Dar es Salaam region, Tanzania." *Geologica Belgica*, 15(1-2), 16-25.

Nakamura, Shohei. 2016. "Spatial Analysis of Greater Maputo: Housing, Infrastructure, and Poverty." Background paper for *Greater Maputo Urban Poverty and Inclusive Growth*. World Bank, Washington, DC.

Sclar, E. D., P. Garau, and G. Carolini. 2005. "The 21st Century Health Challenge of Slums and Cities." *Lancet* 365 (9462): 901–03.

Spalding-Fecher, R. 2005. "Health Benefits of Electrification in Developing Countries: A Quantitative Assessment in South Africa." *Energy for Sustainable Development* 9 (1): 53–62.

Thomson, H., M. Petticrew, and D. Morrison. 2001. "Health Effects of Housing Improvement: Systematic Review of Intervention Studies." *British Medical Journal* 323 (7306): 187–90.

Trojanis, Z., and N. Lozano-Gracia. 2016. "Policy Note: Intermediate Cities in Peru." World Bank, Washington, DC.

UNDESA (United Nations Department of Economic and Social Affairs). 2014. *Electricity and Education: The Benefits, Barriers, and Recommendations for Achieving the Electrification of Primary and Secondary Schools*. New York: UNDESA.

United Nations Department of Economic and Social Affairs, Population Division. 2014. World Urbanization Prospects: The 2014 Revision, CD-ROM Edition.

United Nations. 2015. *Millenium Development Goals Indicators. Indicator 7.10 Proportion of Urban Population Living in Slums*. http://mdgs.un.org/unsd/mdg/seriesdetail.aspx?srid=710.

World Bank. 2005. "Affordability of Public Transport in Developing Countries. Transport Paper No. 3, Washington, DC: World Bank.

———. 2013. Planning, Connecting, and Financing Cities Now: Priorities for City Leaders. Washington, DC: World Bank.

———. 2015a. *Ethiopia Urbanization Review: Urban Institutions for a Middle-Income Ethiopia*. Washington, DC: World Bank.

———. 2015b. *From Oil to Cities. Nigeria's Next Transformation. Nigeria Urbanization Review*. Washington, DC: World Bank.

———. 2015c. *Measuring Living Standards within Cities. Households Surveys: Dar es Salaam and Durban*. Washington, DC: World Bank.

———. 2015d. *Rising through Cities in Ghana: Ghana Urbanization Review Overview Report* Washington, DC: World Bank.

———. 2016. *Côte d'Ivoire Urbanization Review. Diversified Urbanization*. Washington, DC: World Bank.

Wu, T., L. Borghans, and A. Dupuy. 2010. "Energy Infrastructure and Left Behind Villages in Indonesia: Effects of Electric Energy on Children's Educational Outcomes." Maastricht University, the Netherlands.

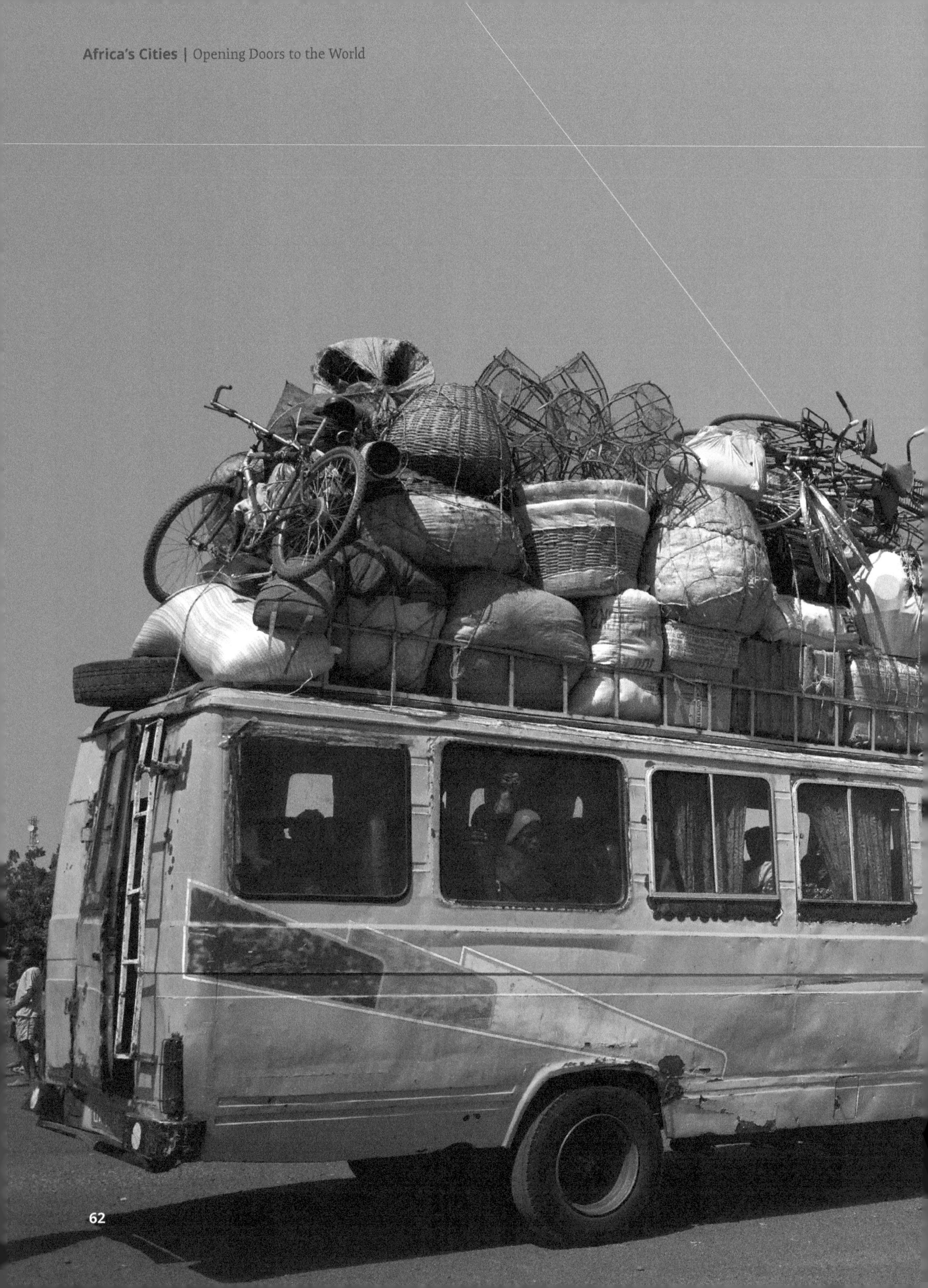

Chapter 2
Disconnected —
people and jobs

Even as Africa's cities are crowded with inhabitants — but not dense with capital — they are physically fragmented and dispersed. They develop as collections of small, scattered neighborhoods. Without adequate roads or transportation systems, commuting is slow and costly, so workers lack access to jobs in the larger urban area. Many people and firms are disconnected — from one another and from economic opportunity.

The lack of connections among neighborhoods means that — compared with developed and developing cities in other regions — African cities show both lower exposure and higher fragmentation in the intensity of how land is used near the city center.

- Low exposure means that people are disconnected from one another. At a set distance (usually 10 kilometers), they cannot interact with as many people as in a city with higher exposure.

- High fragmentation means that within a specified area, population varies widely, with scattered peaks rather than the clustered ones that can enhance scale economies. Fragmentation increases infrastructure costs and lengthens travel times between homes, jobs, and businesses.

There are several aspects to African cities' low exposure and high fragmentation. The first is the paucity of new building cover and volume near city centers. Although many African cities have tall buildings, there are patches of either undeveloped land or land developed with low building volume. The result is a lack of concentration of capital near the center, or infill on unbuilt parcels. Development tends to push the boundaries of the city outward (a type of development known as expansion).

African cities also suffer from a large number of "leapfrog patches" — small parcels of newly built land that do not border on or overlap existing development. Their isolation from existing development undermines city governments' efforts to provide the networked services that benefit from scale economies — and that undergird urban productivity.

The prevalence of expansion, particularly leapfrog, development is just one pattern that makes urban commuting challenging in African cities. Another is deficient transportation infrastructure. Traffic congestion cripples the economy in cities such as Nairobi, where the average journey-to-work time is one of the longest among 15 cities studied (IBM 2011).

Economically, the ideal city can be viewed as an efficient labor market, matching employers and job seekers through connections (Bertaud 2014). With matching, cities benefit because, by increasing the size of their labor force and its diversity, employers and job seekers are more likely to find an appropriate match that makes the best of workers' skills and aspirations. The typical African city fails in this matchmaker role. Its land use is fragmented and its transport infrastructure insufficient — so its residents lack access to jobs. The separation of formal housing areas from commercial and industrial areas, which makes commuting slow and costly, is made worse by emphasis on expansion development. The lack of connections within the city stymies agglomeration economies, keeping costs high and closing the doors of African cities to regional and global trade and investment. In short, because African cities are fragmented (disconnected) and their infrastructure inadequate, people are disconnected from people, and people are disconnected from jobs.

Disconnected land

Collections of small and fragmented neighborhoods

Nearly all African cities look like collections of small neighborhoods. Outside the high-density city core of a stylized African city, infrastructure is poor, specialization is low, and land has mixed uses — often unregulated and informal. New satellite towns develop in peri-urban areas, where land is cheaper. But because these new towns have few economic opportunities; lack social amenities (schools, markets); and are not well connected to the urban core, they do not become viable, supporting centers. Instead, they emerge as secondary, disconnected neighborhoods. Large and mushrooming informal settlements emerge along the few axes of connectivity, usually major arterial roads or rivers and canals. On the outskirts, the city's rural areas see construction in pockets of private investments (Huang 2016).

With cities physically dispersed, Africans in urban areas are disconnected from one another. Urban expansion has increasingly occurred as leapfrog patches that do not border or intersect with existing urban built-up areas, leading to high transportation costs and lower access to markets and other people in the city. Within the urban core, population densities vary widely across locations, reducing the chances for large sections of the population to interact with other groups in the city.

Cities exist because they reduce economic distance by concentrating, in a limited area, workforce, employers, capital, costly infrastructure, ideas, and buyers and sellers. Connected people and firms enjoy labor market pooling, savings in the transport of inputs, and technological and information spillovers (Cervero 2001). Disconnectedness reduces the opportunity to benefit from agglomeration, costing opportunities to learn from others and match needs.

Disconnectedness can stem from a combination of few people to interact with, long physical distances between people, and long travelling times to reach other people. The three factors depend on the dispersion of people and capital. The scale of interactions depends on the density of people in the city, distance depends on how close buildings are to one another, and time depends on infrastructure availability (figure 2.1). African cities lag in all three areas.

FIGURE 2.1
Three aspects of being connected

Scale
Potential for interaction

Distance
Contiguity of built-up area

Time
Infrastructure to support interactions

Spatial fragmentation

On measures such as population density gradients or the share of open space surrounding built-up areas inside urban areas, African cities do not appear to be more spatially fragmented than cities in other regions (see chapter 1). The data, however, are unreliable: There is no comprehensive, up-to-date dataset on built-up fragmentation in cities. The latest data, for 2000 (Angel and others 2011), show that most African cities were on average similar to other cities of the world. The average openness index—the average share of open space in the walking distance circle around each built-up pixel in the city — is 39 percent for African cities, similar to the average in land-rich developed countries, Europe and Japan, and Southeast Asia (figure 2.2).

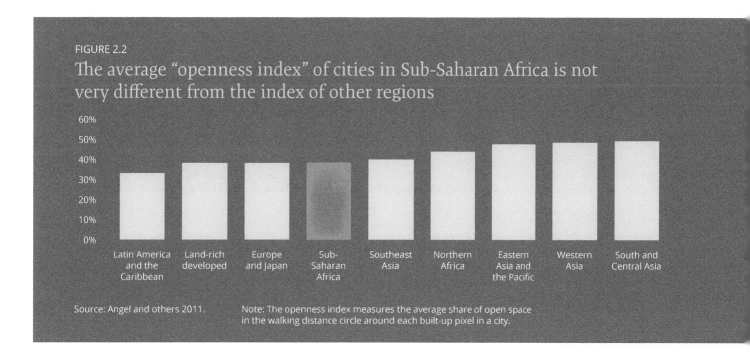

FIGURE 2.2
The average "openness index" of cities in Sub-Saharan Africa is not very different from the index of other regions

Source: Angel and others 2011.

Note: The openness index measures the average share of open space in the walking distance circle around each built-up pixel in a city.

The average city footprint ratio — the ratio of the city footprint to the built-up area in the city — is 1.8 in African cities — similar to Latin America, North Africa, and Europe and Japan. Sub-Saharan Africa's cities thus do not appear to be more fragmented because they have more urbanized open space than cities elsewhere.

African cities may be more fragmented than the global norm close to the city center. City centers have higher economic dynamism and are thus important spots for exchanging goods, services, and ideas. They also usually have the most valuable land in the city. When

land is underutilized in the center, the city loses the opportunity to use some of its most productive land.

Not all land in the vicinity of the center needs to be built up; land can also be left empty for green spaces. In Paris, for example, 14 percent of the city center is unbuilt; in Singapore, about 20 percent of the land in the center is intentionally left undeveloped. In contrast, in cities like Antananarivo, Madagascar; Brazzaville, the Republic of the Congo; and Harare, Zimbabwe, noncontiguous built-up areas are scattered throughout the center, with more than 30 percent of land within 5 kilometers of the city center left unbuilt (figure 2.3).

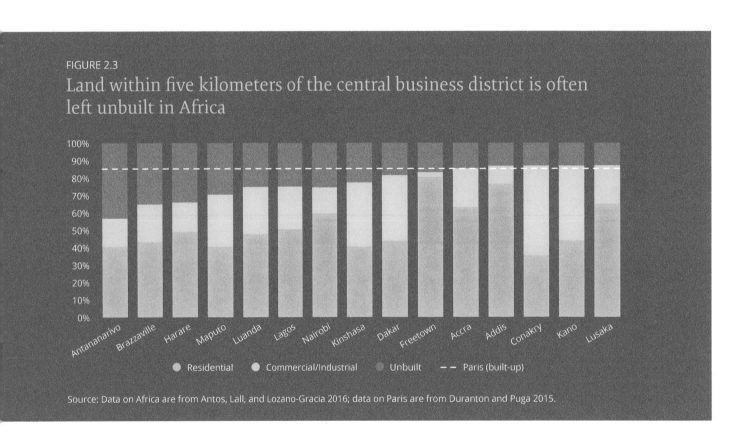

FIGURE 2.3
Land within five kilometers of the central business district is often left unbuilt in Africa

Source: Data on Africa are from Antos, Lall, and Lozano-Gracia 2016; data on Paris are from Duranton and Puga 2015.

African cities are also characterized by lower exposure and higher fragmentation in the intensity of land occupation around the city center during the day. Controlling for differences in city population and country GDP per capita, African cities are about 33 percent less exposed than Asian cities and somewhat less exposed than Latin American cities, as measured by the de la Rocha and Puga index described in box 2.1.[12] They are also about 25 percent more fragmented near the city center than either Latin American or Asian cities (Henderson and Nigmatulina 2016).[13]

Lower exposure and higher fragmentation create scattered density peaks instead of clustered densities that could enhance scale economies. Henderson and Nigmatulina (2016) use Landscan (see box 2.1) to measure these and other aspects of the urban form in 265 cities in 70 countries in Africa, Asia, and Latin America. They find, for example, that Nairobi is more fragmented in the city center than Pune, India, with lower clustering of high-ambient densities (as evident from the smaller number of blue peaks in figure 2.4). Kampala, Uganda is more fragmented than Surat, India.

FIGURE 2.4

African cities are more fragmented in the center than comparably sized cities in India

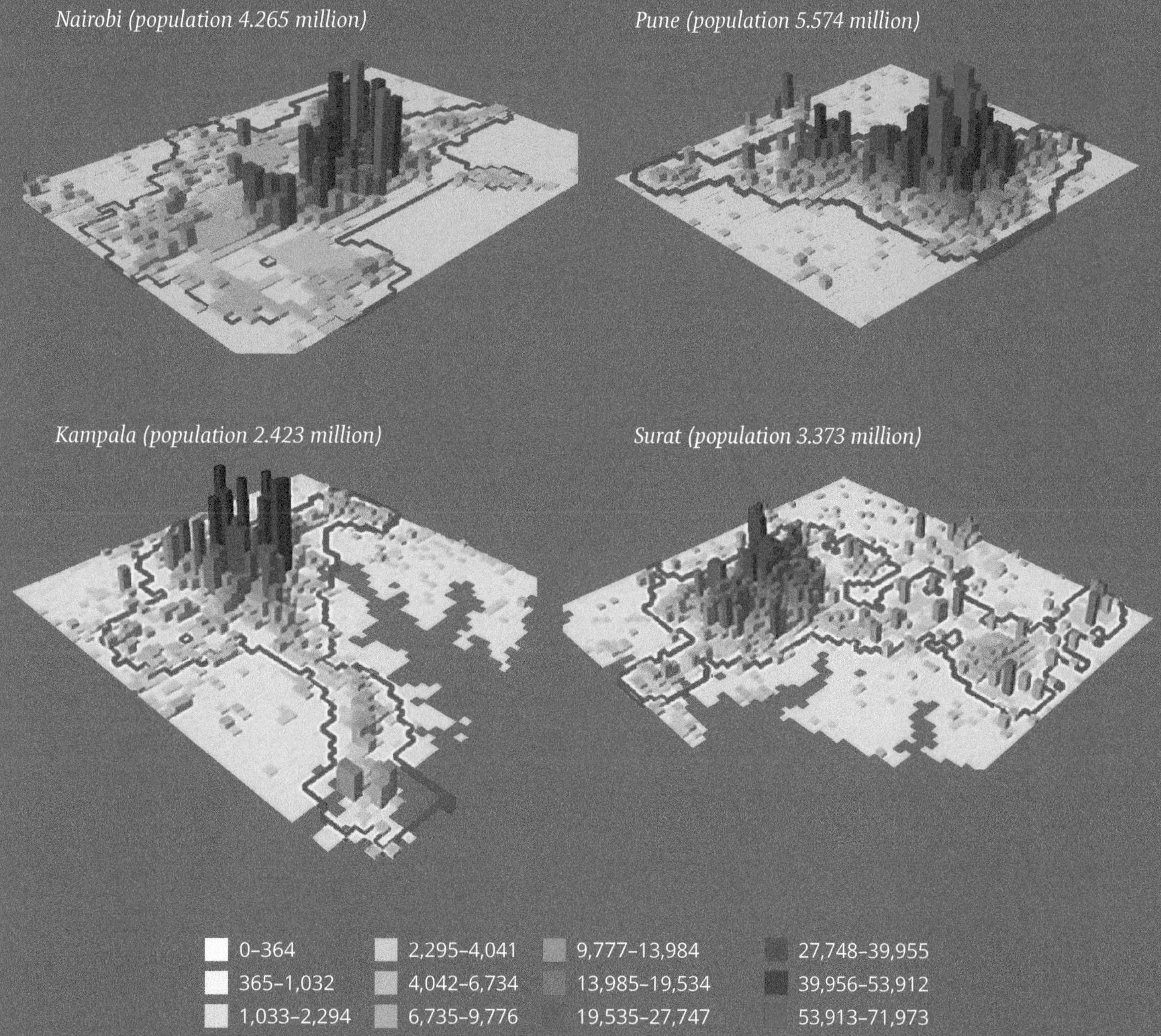

Nairobi (population 4.265 million)

Pune (population 5.574 million)

Kampala (population 2.423 million)

Surat (population 3.373 million)

■	0–364	■	2,295–4,041	■	9,777–13,984	■	27,748–39,955
■	365–1,032	■	4,042–6,734	■	13,985–19,534	■	39,956–53,912
■	1,033–2,294	■	6,735–9,776		19,535–27,747		53,913–71,973

Source: Henderson and Nigmatulina 2016.

BOX 2.1
Measuring fragmentation in urban form

- **Exposure**: The de la Roca and Puga (2016) index of population exposure measures potential interactions at the city level. It measures the exposure ("interaction") of an average person to other people working and living in a city within a certain radius. The Landscan data focus on the ambient population: where people live and work in a city over a 24-hour time period. The index is calculated by taking the sum of the ambient population within 5 or 10 kilometers from each 1 square kilometer cell within the city. The citywide measure is the sum of the exposure measures for every cell in the city, weighted by its share of the population. Using Landscan data from 2012, Henderson and Nigmatulina (2016) calculated this index for 263 cities in Africa, Asia, and Latin America.

- **Fragmentation**: The coefficient of variation of density of the ambient population near the city center is the standard deviation of all cells near the center normalized by the mean density of these cells. The index reported uses the 8 percent of urban area cells closest to the city center. Using Landscan data from 2012, Henderson and Nigmatulina (2016) calculated this coefficient.

- **Fragmented built-up area**: The fragmentation of built-up area is measured by the number and area of leapfrog patches, controlling for initial city built cover and population, population growth, and other factors. The analysis draws on Baruah (2015).

Why are some cities more fragmented than others? When population grows rapidly, cities struggle to provide infrastructure to new settlements. When land management and urban planning are weak and decentralized, new households tend to settle on the outskirts (where land is cheaper), in a scattered, fragmented manner. The intertwined effects of population size, rates of growth, affordability and availability of land, and land management and urban planning lead to different levels of fragmentation.

The persistence of institutions from colonial times may explain the development patterns of many African cities today. Former British colonial cities appear more fragmented than former French colonies; their development has been patchier, more scattered and strung out, with more open space (Baruah, Henderson, and Peng 2016).

Baruah and Henderson (2016) regress fragmentation on a dummy variable for anglophone cities and control for time-invariant geographic features, population growth, and time-varying country and city characteristics. Their results consistently show that anglophone cities are more fragmented than other cities in Africa. All other things equal, compared to French cities, they have a sprawl index 25 percent

higher, about 50 percent more leapfrog patches, and about 40 percent more area dedicated to leapfrog development.

The findings suggest that the different development paths followed by anglophone and francophone cities are linked with the colonial legacy. Three hypotheses on why this might be need to be studied:

- Legal systems and governance structures have persisted and are more integrated in former French colonies than elsewhere, enabling governments to implement urban plans and enforce land use regulations. The French tended to reject customary land management, establishing a state monopoly on land markets and management systems. In contrast, the British established a dual mandate with a dual local government structure: Different laws governed the colonists' plantations (or townships) and land held under indigenous or customary titles (Baruah, Henderson, and Peng 2016). If francophone cities remained more centralized, their procedures for allocating land use (for example) might be more standard across the city. In contrast, decentralization in anglophone cities may have allowed local governments to assign land under various local rules.

- In addition to being more centralized, legal systems in francophone countries were more prescriptive. Procedures to assign land as well as zoning were well defined, possibly resulting in standard procedures for permitting new construction and stricter zoning regulations. Land use in anglophone cities may have been more haphazard, driven by the interests of local governments.

- The training of francophone urban planners — through scholarships and education in French polytechnic schools — may have induced greater conformity and led to compact, centralized plans.

People not connected to people: High fragmentation, low exposure, little potential for interaction

Urban Africans have little connectivity in their neighborhoods, as shown by the low exposure and high fragmentation in the intensity of land occupation. They also have less potential for interaction, as the dense population near the city center quickly diminishes with distance. People living outside the center have very few neighbors to interact with: The Puga index at 10 kilometers is much lower in African cities than in Asian cities of similar size (see box 2.1). African cities in the sample are mostly small and medium-size, with fewer than 3 million inhabitants. Johannesburg's exposure is about one-fourth that of similar-size cities in Latin America and Asia (figure 2.5, left-hand panel).

African cities are more fragmented in the intensity of land use near the city center. Development in the city center is often fragmented, with low exposure punctured by random towers (Huang 2016). The coefficient of variation of densities within the 8 percent of pixels closest to the city center captures this pattern. Small and medium-size cities, such as Addis Ababa, Ethiopia; Antananarivo, Madagascar; and Bujumbura, Burundi are more fragmented than comparable cities in Asia and Latin America (figure 2.5, right-hand panel).

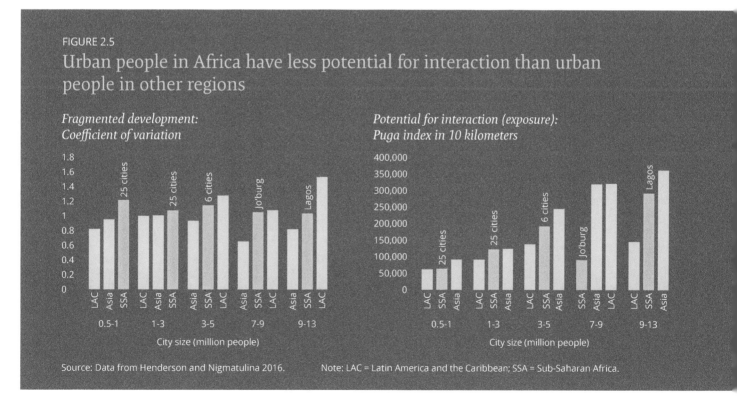

FIGURE 2.5

Urban people in Africa have less potential for interaction than urban people in other regions

Fragmented development: Coefficient of variation

Potential for interaction (exposure): Puga index in 10 kilometers

Source: Data from Henderson and Nigmatulina 2016.   Note: LAC = Latin America and the Caribbean; SSA = Sub-Saharan Africa.

A physically fragmented city, with much empty space between built-up areas, raises the costs of providing services such as road networks, sewerage systems, and schools (Squires 2002). It increases air pollution, creates losses of natural land, and fragments the ecosystem (Johnson 2001). Conversely, the clustering associated with nonfragmented development makes cities potentially more productive and welfare enhancing.

Harari (2014) analyzes 400 Indian cities. She finds that compact (nonfragmented) cities are associated with higher population density, higher welfare, and higher concentration of productive establishments. A one standard deviation deterioration in city form is associated with 0.9 standard deviation decline in population density and a welfare loss equivalent to a 5 percent decrease in income.

Leapfrog development increased in many African cities between 2000 and 2010, sowing the seeds for fragmentation. Regardless of their size, these patches increase the costs of providing network infrastructure. Among 21 African cities studied, only in Windhoek, Namibia did the share of total new fragments fall between the 1990s and 2000s. The number of leapfrog patches per square kilometer of footprint fell in only four cities: Windhoek; Addis Ababa; Lusaka, Zambia; and Ouagadougou, Burkina Faso. Cities such as Maputo, Mozambique; Nyala, Sudan; and Nairobi are becoming increasingly fragmented. In Maputo, for instance, 51 percent of the patches created between 2000 and 2010 were leapfrogged. In 2010, there were 95 new patches per square kilometer of land in the city (figure 2.6).

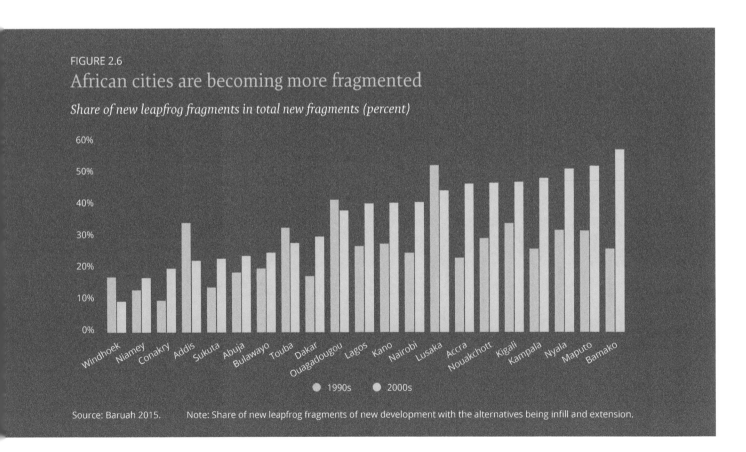

FIGURE 2.6
African cities are becoming more fragmented

Share of new leapfrog fragments in total new fragments (percent)

Source: Baruah 2015.   Note: Share of new leapfrog fragments of new development with the alternatives being infill and extension.

People not connected to jobs

Lack of transportation infrastructure

African cities are allocating little land to roads. In a sample of 30 cities around the world, the 8 African cities rank in the bottom 12 spots for road density, including Kigali (19th), Addis Ababa (24th), and Nairobi (27th). African cities devote less than 16 percent of their land to roads (figure 2.7); cities in developed countries usually allocate more than 20 percent. Lower infrastructure provision, coupled with low affordability of motorized transportation (see chapter 3), makes it difficult to access locations across the city. Low affordability increases the number of people who must walk; low road provision increases congestion and pollution.

Roads tend to be concentrated in the city center, providing little accessibility for people on the periphery. Cities with well-developed transportation infrastructure, like Paris, devote a larger share of land to roads throughout the city, providing the connectivity required for compact development. These cities still follow a monocentric model, but their population densities and the share of roads decline more gradually.

Kigali, Rwanda and Nairobi dedicate a large share of land in the city center to roads, but the share of built-up area falls steeply as the share of roads almost disappears, as it does in all four cities in map 2.1: the share of land for built-up areas (in orange) goes hand in hand with the share of roads (in dark blue).

African cities are usually serviced by radial arterial roads emanating from the center, sometimes with concentric ring roads. From a spatial planning perspective, a radial-ring structure is less efficient than a grid structure, which allows for scalability and easy orientation and provides alternative routes and thus enhanced travel efficiency. Increasingly, African cities are adopting the grid structure, especially for expansion areas or new satellite development, as in, for example, Bahir Dar, Ethiopia and Ouagadougou, both of which have adopted a scalable grid modular unit at the neighborhood level, with a clear hierarchy for roads, amenities, and services.

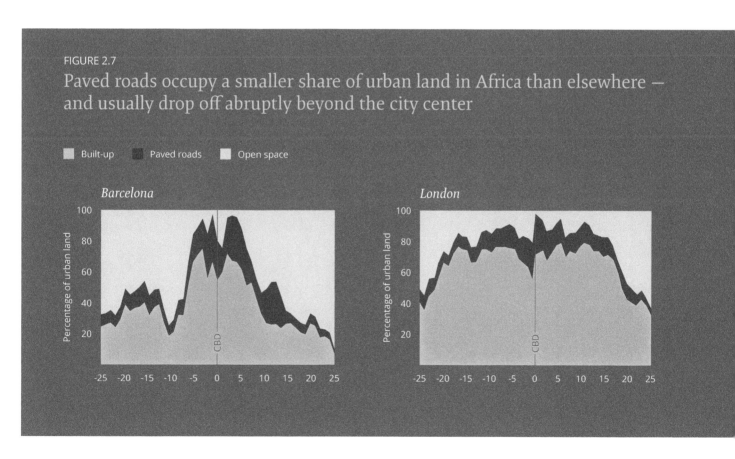

FIGURE 2.7

Paved roads occupy a smaller share of urban land in Africa than elsewhere — and usually drop off abruptly beyond the city center

■ Built-up   ■ Paved roads   ■ Open space

FIGURE 2.7 *(cont.)*

Paved roads occupy a smaller share of urban land in Africa than elsewhere — and usually drop off abruptly beyond the city center

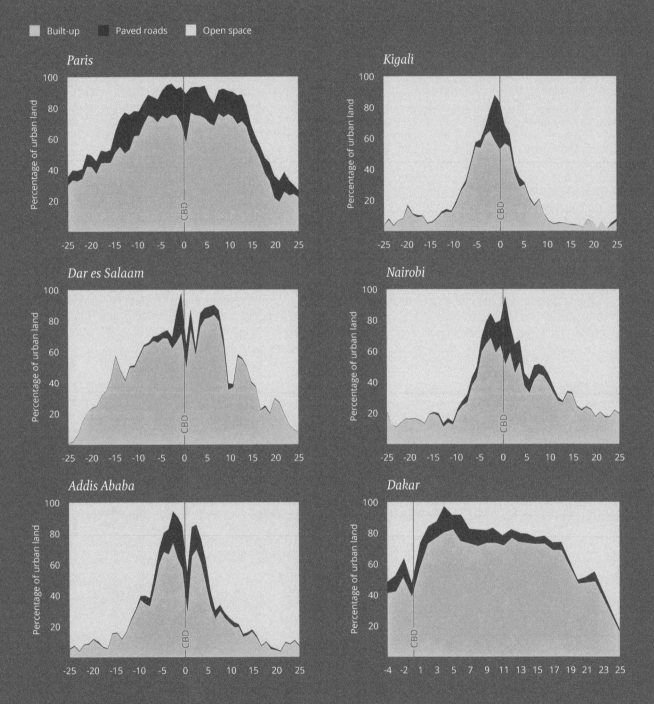

Source: Data from Antos, Lall, and Lozano-Gracia 2016 and Felkner, Lall, and Lee 2016.

Note: CBD = Central Business District. The data for African cities come from very high-resolution (< 1m) imagery using a semiautomated supervised classification approach (leveraging both textural and spectral data). The images are circa 2012 for Nairobi and Kigali, circa 2013 for Dar es Salam, circa 2014 for Dakar, and circa 2011 for Addis Ababa. The European data come from the Urban Atlas, published by the European Environment Agency (EEA) (http://www.eea.europa.eu/data-and-maps/data/urban-atlas). The layers in this atlas were created in 2010, based on 2005–07 imagery. The central business district was identified using the location of the oldest building as a proxy (or a government building if necessary).

Investments in infrastructure shape how land is used.
Roads and transit systems affect commuting costs
and times differently across the city, incentivizing
densification in some corridors and allowing
households to locate farther from the city center.
In the four cities in map 2.1, investments in road
infrastructure increased population density by 17–37
percent within a 1 square kilometer of the road
(Felkner, Lall, and Lee 2016).

MAP 2.1

Change in land used by paved roads across four African cities

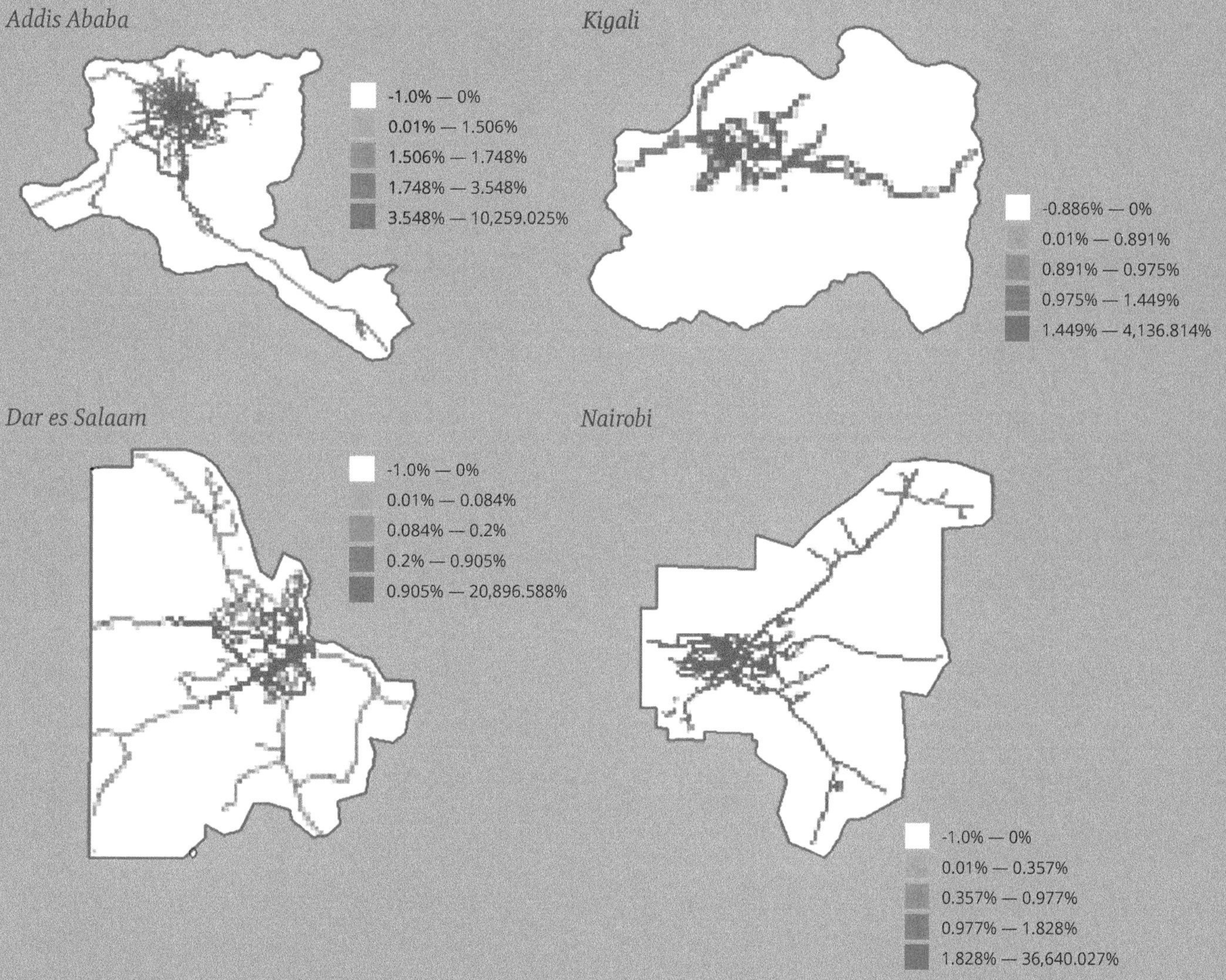

Addis Ababa

- -1.0% — 0%
- 0.01% — 1.506%
- 1.506% — 1.748%
- 1.748% — 3.548%
- 3.548% — 10,259.025%

Kigali

- -0.886% — 0%
- 0.01% — 0.891%
- 0.891% — 0.975%
- 0.975% — 1.449%
- 1.449% — 4,136.814%

Dar es Salaam

- -1.0% — 0%
- 0.01% — 0.084%
- 0.084% — 0.2%
- 0.2% — 0.905%
- 0.905% — 20,896.588%

Nairobi

- -1.0% — 0%
- 0.01% — 0.357%
- 0.357% — 0.977%
- 0.977% — 1.828%
- 1.828% — 36,640.027%

Source: Felkner, Lall, and Lee 2016.

Lack of money for transportation

Sub-Saharan Africa is urbanizing rapidly, but it is doing so at low per capita incomes, limiting the funds available for transportation. In 2013, it was roughly 37 percent urbanized, and income per capita was a little over $1,000 in 2005 dollars. Latin America and the Caribbean reached 40 percent urbanization in 1950, with a per capita income of $1,860. The Middle East and North Africa reached the threshold in 1968, when per capita incomes was $1,800; East Asia and Pacific reached it in 1994, when per capita income was $3,620 (WDI 2015).

With lower incomes, urban residents in Sub-Saharan Africa's cities spend a large share of their budgets on food, leaving little for transportation, housing, or other basic items. Food accounts for 60 percent of total expenditures for the bottom 20 percent of Sub-Saharan Africa's urban households and 35 percent even for the wealthiest quintile (figure 2.8). Transportation expenditures are very low, at 3–8 percent of total spending (Lozano-Gracia and Young 2014). The small monetary share reflects the fact that most commuting involves walking, trips for which people in Asia and Latin American cities would use cars, scooters, or public transit.

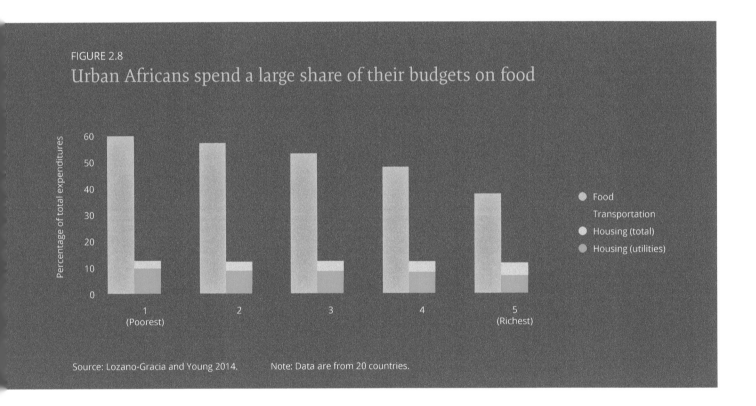

FIGURE 2.8

Urban Africans spend a large share of their budgets on food

Source: Lozano-Gracia and Young 2014.   Note: Data are from 20 countries.

High out-of-pocket commuting costs disproportionately affect the disadvantaged (poor, young, unskilled) by creating a spatial mismatch. Physical segregation of unskilled workers from job opportunities leads to high commuting and job search costs, which partially explain higher unemployment rates and lower average wages. In Addis Ababa, for example, a randomized experiment to provide young residents in peripheral neighborhoods with a nonfungible transit subsidy that could be used to search for employment in the city center increased employment (26 percent versus a mean of 19 percent) and led to better-quality jobs (more formal, less likely

to be part time, and usually better paying) within four months (Franklin 2015). Within the control group, the employed were more likely to have part-time, informal, and local jobs requiring less commuting — a pattern repeated in Kigali (figure 2.9).

Travel budgets in Europe and the United States display a remarkable regularity (about 10–15 percent of personal expenditures) (box 2.2). Monetary travel budgets in Japan are lower and closer to African averages (about 7 percent), because many Japanese use public transit rather than cars (Schafer and Victor 2000).

FIGURE 2.9

In Kigali, workers in the informal sector have shorter commutes

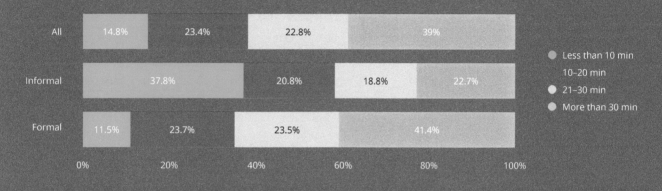

All: 14.8% | 23.4% | 22.8% | 39%
Informal: 37.8% | 20.8% | 18.8% | 22.7%
Formal: 11.5% | 23.7% | 23.5% | 41.4%

- Less than 10 min
- 10–20 min
- 21–30 min
- More than 30 min

0%   20%   40%   60%   80%   100%

Source: NISR and MPSL 2013.

BOX 2.2

Is there a constant travel time budget? The Zahavi conjecture

Zahavi (1973, 1974; later with Talvitie) observed that daily urban travel times in the United States and Europe were similar, despite wide differences in transportation infrastructure; geography; and the incomes, cultural norms, and habits of residents of different cities. Zahavi found that these average travel times are nearly constant for individual cities over time and similar over space for different cities, at about one hour a day. He concluded that travel times are therefore spatially transposable, leading to the idea of a predictable travel time budget. He also observed the regularity of a "travel monetary budget."

This observation led to the formulation of an assumption, known as the Zahavi conjecture, that postulates that decreases in travel time caused by increases in transportation speeds (switching from slower to faster transportation modes) are entirely reinvested in more trips and longer travelled distances. If the conjecture is accurate, it means that there is a natural travel time budget

that, combined with average travel speeds in an urban area, constrains the distances that can be travelled and hence the space of accessibility. It is this space of accessibility that urban dwellers seek to maximize given transportation constraints. This reasoning appears to be compatible and may even explain urban areas' growth through sprawl and increased travelled distances.

Looking at a large variety of settlements (cities and countries), Schafer and Victor (2000) find some empirical evidence to support these regularities, in particular for the travel time budget, which they estimate at about 1.1 hours a day (box figure 2.2.1). The travel monetary budget displays slightly less regularity; it depends on the motorization rate but tends to converge beyond a certain rate. Schafer (2000) shows that travel monetary budgets were virtually constant, oscillating between 10 and 15 percent, for a panel of six developed countries from 1970 to 2004. *(continued overleaf)*.

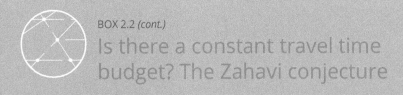

BOX 2.2 *(cont.)*

Is there a constant travel time budget? The Zahavi conjecture

BOX FIGURE 2.2.1

Average per capita daily travel times in selected cities

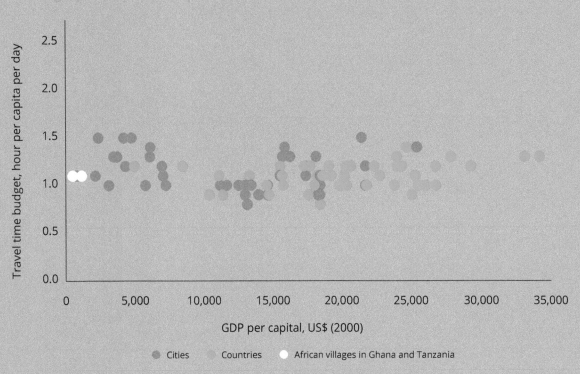

Source: Schafer and Victor 2000; Schäfer and others 2009.

Zahavi himself did not believe that there was a fundamental law that would lead to constant travel times over time, irrespective of local conditions. When developing the unified mechanism of travel model (Zahavi 1981), he linked travel time budgets to the motorization rate (equivalent to an average speed in the urban area). He did find that there is a speed beyond which travel time budgets converge and become nearly insensitive to future speed increases. His modeling found that threshold to be about 10 kilometers an hour, which would correspond to a speed at which a large share of travelers no longer walk for all trips. Before that threshold is reached, travel time budgets can exceed one hour and decrease strongly with any increase in travel speeds. This subtlety of Zahavi's modeling, which is rarely appreciated, may explain some findings for African cities in which travel time budgets appear higher than elsewhere.

The cost of collective motorized urban transportation, which dominated in Africa by informal minibuses, is high relative to household budgets in Sub-Saharan Africa's major cities, rendering it largely unaffordable on a daily basis, especially for the poorest (Kumar and Barrett 2008). In 8 out of 11 cities studied, the average household could not afford one round-trip a day using the minibus network. Figure 2.10 shows actual average budget shares on transport and then what these shares would be for first the average households and then a poor household if they made two trips a day using the minibus network.

These potential budget shares show wide variation. In Dakar, a round-trip commute costs only 3.1 percent of the average household's total expenditures. For most of the other cities, it costs 5.1–27.5 percent. For the bottom quintile, the situation is even worse. Excluding Dakar, the poorest households in these cities would need to spend an average of about 19 percent of their budget to afford a round-trip motorized commute. For the poorest quintile, the figure is 53 percent in Dar es Salaam and more than 100 percent in Lagos.

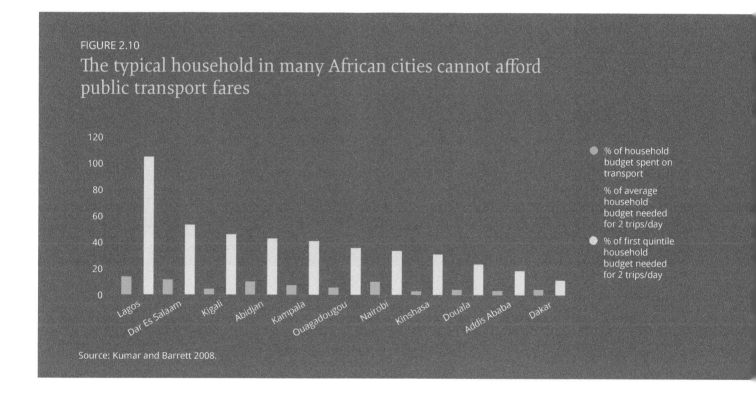

FIGURE 2.10

The typical household in many African cities cannot afford public transport fares

Legend:
- % of household budget spent on transport
- % of average household budget needed for 2 trips/day
- % of first quintile household budget needed for 2 trips/day

Cities (x-axis): Lagos, Dar Es Salaam, Kigali, Abidjan, Kampala, Ouagadougou, Nairobi, Kinshasa, Douala, Addis Ababa, Dakar

Source: Kumar and Barrett 2008.

The World Bank (2015b) conducted comprehensive travel demand surveys in Nigeria in Abuja (2013), Kano (2012), and Lagos (2009, 2012). They revealed that low-income households in these cities spend 49, 40, and 33 percent, respectively, of their household budgets on public transport; the average household spent 31, 32, and 24 percent, respectively; and middle- and upper-income households spent 18, 19, and 10 percent, respectively. These high costs relative to household budgets lead to travel patterns dominated by walking, greatly limiting access to economic opportunities.

The prevalence of minibuses rather than larger vehicles increases the monetary costs of transportation, contributing to its unaffordability for a large segment of the population in African cities; starting from the central business district and traveling outward, travel per passenger-kilometer can be provided at lower cost by bus than minibus and by minibus than car (figure 2.11).

The cost per passenger kilometer increases with distance from the central business district because density declines (Eskeland and Lall 2015). The increase is steeper (more convex) for buses than for minibuses because they have more seats to fill. They have to spend more than minibuses to be sufficiently frequent and close to demand. Cars have the flattest curve, because they carry only a few passengers.

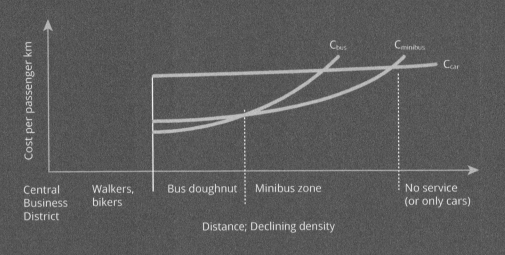

FIGURE 2.11

Scale economies in vehicle size should lead to the provision of collective transportation through large vehicles toward the city center and smaller ones as distance to the city center increases

Source: Eskeland and Lall 2015. Note: The dotted lines indicate a change in the most cost effective means of transport. The 'bus doughnut' corresponds to the dense urban area served competitively by buses.

Larger vehicles are more efficient if they can be filled; where population density falls, they may not be efficient. The size of the vehicle that can operate cost effectively declines with the distance from the center. Travel costs therefore increase more than proportionally with distance from the city center (Eskeland and Lall 2015). If the prices of transportation reflect the costs, larger buses leveraging scale economies could significantly reduce transportation costs for users in African cities.

The percentage of trips made by foot is very high in major African cities, largely because of the high cost of bus trips. The figure is 30–45 percent in Nairobi, Lagos, and Addis Ababa and nearly 70 percent in Dar es Salaam (figure 2.12).

Generously assuming that pedestrians can travel at an average of 4 kilometers an hour in a straight line, a large share of city residents can access opportunities only within a 50 square kilometer area of where they live by walking for an hour — a problem in metropolises that often cover more than 1,000 square

kilometers. Such a catchment area would cover only about 7 percent of Nairobi's core city, for example.

In Dar es Salaam, households travel only small distances to get to work: Household heads' average commuting distance is less than 6 kilometers, and other adults travel no more than 4 kilometers on average (World Bank 2015c). These figures indicate that Dar es Salaam, although a city of more than 5 million people, functions as a set of villages with extremely local labor markets.

In Durban, South Africa, labor markets do not appear to be as fragmented, with most people traveling 30–40 minutes from home to work; commuting modes are also more diverse than in Dar es Salaam. A third of Durban's population uses minibuses as the main mode of transportation, and almost 30 percent use private vehicles. A still considerable 21 percent walk to work.

Another striking feature of African cities is that collective transportation is primarily informal. *Matatus* in Nairobi and Kampala, *cars rapides* (or *ndiaga ndiaye*)

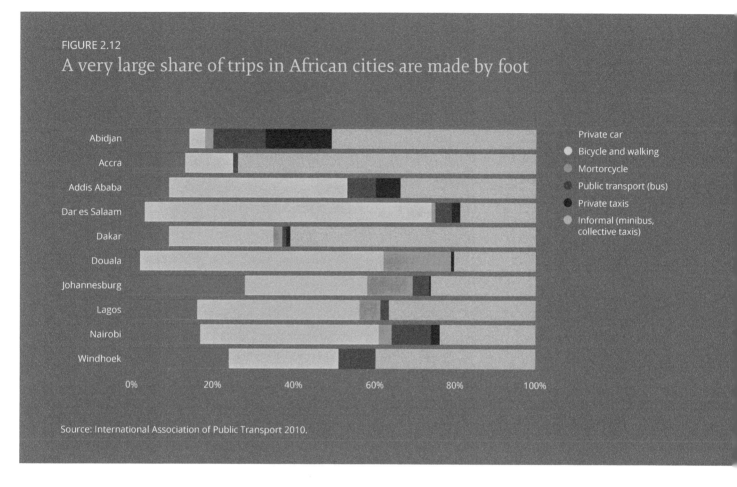

FIGURE 2.12

A very large share of trips in African cities are made by foot

Source: International Association of Public Transport 2010.

in Dakar, *dala dalas* in Dar es Salaam, *tro* in Accra, and *gbaka* in Abidjan are all informal (and often colorful) minibuses. Collectively, they are the main form of motorized collective transportation in most African cities. The service they provide is highly valued, as demonstrated by their large share of trips. However, because public or collective transportation is informal, the networks are mostly reactive: They accompany the growth of the city rather than structure it. In contrast, in many developed country cities (Paris, London, Barcelona), transportation helps determine the structure of the city (Brooks and Lutz 2013).

Inaccessible employment

For cities to act as integrated labor markets and match jobs seekers and employers, they need to make employment accessible. African cities are failing to do so. Activities are scattered instead of clustered, because capital is misallocated. Fragmentation prevents labor market pooling — leaving workers with access to few jobs, keeping productivity low, and locking cities into the nontradable sector. Such a climate does not reward workers for investing in their

human capital or facilitate the accumulation of the soft skills they need to succeed.

Mobility is essentially a derived demand, meaning that it is desired not for itself but because it can provide access to other goods and services. Cities' matchmaking function is to provide employers with candidates who seek their needs and for job seekers to find employment opportunities that suit their talents and aspirations; it is an important reason why cities are more productive than the rest of an economy (World Bank 2015a). Employment accessibility can be commonly defined as the number or share of jobs that can be reached within a given time.

Avner and Lall (2016) study access to formal jobs in Nairobi. They find that accessibility is much higher for car users than for users of *matatus* (privately owned minibuses). Indeed, map 2.2 suggests that Nairobi is a city built for car owners, who can reach about 90 percent of jobs within an hour, But car use accounts for only 13 percent of trips for all purposes; 28 percent of trips are made with *matatus* and 41 percent are

MAP 2.2

Most job opportunities in Nairobi are inaccessible to people without cars

Shares of job opportunities accessible within an hour by car

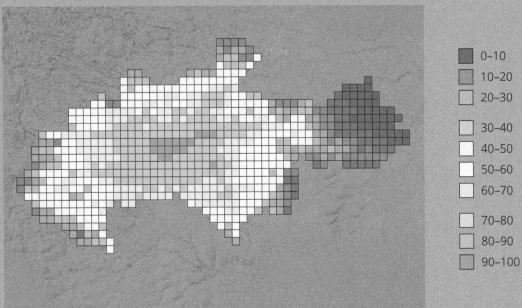

0–10
10–20
20–30

30–40
40–50
50–60
60–70

70–80
80–90
90–100

Shares of job opportunities accessible within an hour by matatu (minibus)

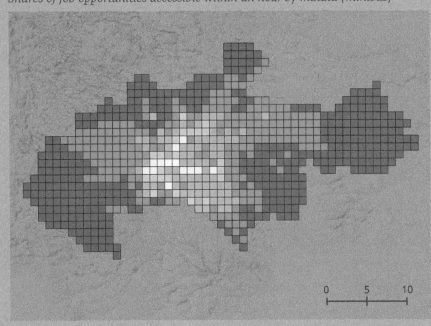

0   5   10

Source: Avner and Lall 2016.

made on foot (JICA 2013, 2014). A central resident can access only 20 percent of all jobs within an hour using the *matatu* network.

In contrast, in 2013, a resident of London could reach 2.5 million jobs (54 percent of all jobs in Greater London) within 45 minutes of the city center using the public transit network (TfL 2014). From any location in the urban area, the average number of jobs accessible within 45 minutes using transit in Greater London in 2013 was a little under a million (21.6 percent of all jobs). By comparison, in Nairobi, matatu users' had access to only 5.8 percent of all jobs within 45 minutes.

These figures do not account for the distribution of residents throughout the urban areas. As people tend to settle in denser patterns in zones that benefit from greater employment accessibility, residents' location affects the outcome (table 2.1).[10]

Table 2.1 Accessibility to formal jobs in Nairobi

Maximum travel time (minutes)	Cars		Matatus + walking	Walking only
	Uncongested	Congested	Congested	
30	57%	31%	4%	3%
45	85%	58%	10%	7%
60	96%	77%	20%	11%

Source: Avner and Lall 2016.

Heavy congestion, high rates of walking, informal collective transportation, and the spatial distribution of jobs and residents lead to low employment accessibility in Nairobi and the misallocation of labor. Matatu users on average can access only 4 percent of jobs within 30 minutes, 10 percent within 45 minutes, and 20 percent within 60 minutes. These figures are very low: In metropolitan Buenos Aires, equivalent accessibility figures using public transportation are 7 percent, 18 percent, and 34 percent for the same time thresholds (Peralta Quiros 2015). In Ugandan cities, 70 percent of work trips are on foot (Uganda Bureau of Statistics 2010), with the average share of jobs reachable within one hour standing at just 19 percent (Bernard 2016).[11]

The early deployment of collective transportation systems preserves an option value (Henry 1974) by limiting urban-form irreversibility. Early deployment also reduces the need for transportation infrastructure. Rode and others (2014) show that although the upfront costs of collective transportation infrastructure are on the same order of magnitude as — or even higher than — the costs of high-capacity highways, collective transportation has the edge when cost estimates take carrying capacity into account (table 2.2). Compact cities (associated with collective transportation) also mitigate the impacts of higher oil prices.

Table 2.2 Estimated capital costs of building various types of transportation infrastructure

Type of infrastructure	Capacity (pers/h/d)	Capital costs (dollars per kilometer)	Capital costs/ capacity (dollars)
Dual-lane highway	2,000	10–20 million	5,000–10,000
Urban street (car use only)	800	2–5 million	2,500–7,000
Bike path (2m)	3,500	100,000	30
Pedestrian walkway/ pavement (2m)	4,500	100,000	20
Commuter rail	20,000–40,000	40–80 million	2,000
Metro rail	20,000–70,000	40–350 million	2,000–5,000
Light rail	10,000–30,000	10–25 million	800–1,000
Bus rapid transit	5,000–40,000	1–10 million	200–250
Bus lane	10,000	1–5 million	300–500

Source: Rode and others 2014, based on Rode and Gipp 2011, Litman 2009, Wright 2002, and Brilon 1994.

High transportation costs, crippling congestion, and slow commuting speeds have prevented African cities from acting as matchmakers and fostering agglomeration economies through firm clustering. Such mixed land-use patterns — with jobs and people dispersed throughout urban areas — penalize large-scale transit systems, which need high ridership to function efficiently.

African cities are locked into low-level equilibria that are unkind to their residents and unproductive for firms. Coordination mechanisms are needed to harness the forces of urbanization through kinder, more efficient development trajectories (chapter 6).

These coordination mechanisms can take many forms. All, however, include synchronized action on land use and transportation infrastructure. Whatever shape a city assumes — and various urban forms are consistent with more productive and inclusive cities — leaders must think very carefully about the long-term consequences of their decisions. Given the high inertia and path dependencies of urban areas, these decision makers are building their cities for decades and possibly centuries to come.

References

Alonso, W. 1964. *Location and Land Use*. Cambridge, MA: Harvard University Press.

Angel, Shlomo, Jason Parent, Daniel L. Civco, and Alejandro M. Blei. 2011. "Making Room for a Planet of Cities." Policy Focus Report, Lincoln Institute of Land Policy, Cambridge, MA.

Antos, Sarah E., Nancy Lozano-Gracia, and Somik V. Lall. 2016. "The Morphology of African Cities." Draft, World Bank, Washington, DC.

Arthur, W. B. 1986. *Industry Location Patterns and the Importance of History*. Center for Economic Policy Research, Stanford University, Stanford, CA.

Avner, Paolo, and Somik V. Lall. 2016. "Matchmaking in Nairobi: The Role of Land Use." Policy Research Working Paper 7904, World Bank, Washington, DC.

Baruah, Neeraj. 2015. "Splintered and Segmented? Fragmentation of African Cities' Footprints." Paper presented at the Spatial Development of African Cities Workshop, World Bank, Washington DC, December 16–17.

Baruah, Neeraj, and Vernon Henderson, with Cong Peng. 2016. "Fragmentation of African Footprints. Colonial Legacies in Shaping African Cities." Paper presented at the Annual Bank Conference on Africa 2016: Managing the Challenges and Opportunities of Urbanization in Africa, Oxford University, June 14.

Baum-Snow, N. 2007. "Did Highways Cause Suburbanization?" *Quarterly Journal of Economics* 122 (2): 775–805.

Baum-Snow, N., L. Brandt, J. V. Henderson, M. A. Turner, and Q. Zhang. 2016. "Roads, Railroads and Decentralization of Chinese Cities." LSE Working Paper, London School of Economic, London.

Bernard, Louise. 2016. "Job Access in Kampala." University of Oxford.

Bertaud, Alain. 2014. "Cities as Labor Markets." Working Paper 2, Marron Institute on Cities and the Urban Environment, New York University.

Brooks, Leah, and Byron Lutz. 2013. "Vestiges of Transit: Urban Persistence at a Micro Scale." Trachtenberg School of Public Policy and Public Administration, George Washington University, Washington, DC.

Cervero, Robert. 2001. "Efficient Urbanisation: Economic Performance and the Shape of the Metropolis." Urban Studies 38 (10): 1651–71.

de la Roca and Puga. 2016. "Learning by Working in Big Cities." *Review of Economic Studies*.

Duranton, Gilles, and Diego Puga. 2004. "Micro-Foundations of Urban Agglomeration Economies." In *Handbook of Regional and Urban Economics*, vol. 4, 2063–117. Amsterdam: Elsevier.

———. 2015. "Urban Land Use." In *Handbook of Regional and Urban Economics*, vol. 5, 467–60. Amsterdam: Elsevier.

Ellison, G., and E. L. Glaeser. 1997. Geographic Concentration in U.S. Manufacturing Industries: A Dartboard Approach. *Journal of Political Economy* 105 (5): 889–927.

Eskeland, Gunnar S., and Somik V. Lall. 2015. "A Crowded City: Agglomeration and Mobility in Urban Development." Draft, August 20, World Bank, Washington, DC.

Felkner, John S., Somik V. Lall, and Hyun Lee. 2016. "Synchronizing Public and Private Investment in Cities: Evidence from Addis Ababa, Dar es Salaam, Kigali and Nairobi." April 22, World Bank, Washington, DC.

Franklin, Simon. 2015. "Location, Search Costs and Youth Unemployment: The Impact of a Randomized Transport Subsidy in Urban Ethiopia." CSAE Working Paper WPS/2015-11, Oxford..

Fujita, Masahisa, and Ogawa, Hideaki, 1982. "Multiple Equilibria and Structural Transition of Non-Monocentric Urban Configurations." *Regional Science and Urban Economics* 12 (2): 161–96.

Gobillon, Laurent, Harris Selod, and Yves Zenou. 2007. "The Mechanisms of Spatial Mismatch." *Urban Studies* 44 (12): 2401–28.

Harari, M. 2014. "Cities in Bad Shape: Urban Geometry in India." Economics Department, MIT, Cambridge, MA.

Henderson, Vernon and Nigmatulina, Dzhamilya. 2016. "The Fabric of African Cities: How to Think about Density and Land Use." Draft, April 20, London School of Economics.

Henry, Claude. 1974. "Investment Decisions under Uncertainty: The 'Irreversibility Effect.'" *American Economic Review* 64 (6): 1006–12.

Huang, Chyi-Yun. 2016. "Enabling Structure: Role of Public Sector and Institutions." Background paper for this report.

Iacovone, L., V. Ramachandran, and M. Schmidt. 2014. "Stunted Growth: Why Don't African Firms Create More Jobs?" Working Paper 353, Center for Global Development, Washington, DC.

International Association of Public Transport (UITP). 2010. *Major Trends and Case Studies*. Brussels, Belgium: International Association of Public Transport.

IBM. 2011. "IBM Global Commuter Pain Survey: Traffic Congestion Down, Pain Way Up." Available at: http://www-03.ibm.com/press/us/en/pressrelease/35359.wss.

JICA (Japan International Cooperation Agency). 2013. *JICA Nairobi Personal Travel Survey*. Tokyo.

———. 2014. *The Project on Integrated Urban Development Master Plan for the City of Nairobi in the Republic of Kenya*. Draft. Tokyo.

MCLAU (Ministère de la Construction, du Logement, de l'Assainissement et de l'Urbanisme), SDUGA, and JICA (Japan International Cooperation Agency). 2014. Le Projet de Développement du Schema Directeur d'Urbanisme du Grand Abidjan (SDUGA). Rapport Interimaire, Volume I, Resume. Oriental Consultants Co. Ltd., Japan Development Institute, JICA, and Asia Air Survey Co. Ltd.

Johnson, M. 2001. "Environmental Impacts of Urban Sprawl: A Survey of the Literature and Proposed Research Agenda." *Environment and Planning* A 33: 717–35.

Krugman, P. R. 1991. *Geography and Trade*. Cambridge, MA: MIT Press.

Kumar, Ajay, and Fanny Barrett. 2008. "Stuck in Traffic: Urban Transport in Africa." Africa Infrastructure Country Diagnostic Background Paper. World Bank, Washington, DC.

Lall, S. V. 2009. "Shrinking Distance: Identifying Priorities for Territorial Integration." Draft, World Bank, Washington, DC. http://ec.europa.eu/dgs/policy_advisers/docs/15_paper_lall.pdf.

Lall, S. V, E. Schroeder, and E. Schmidt. 2009. "Identifying Spatial Efficiency-Equity Tradeoffs in Territorial Development Policies: Evidence from Uganda." Policy Research Working Paper 4966, World Bank, Washington, DC.

Lecocq, Franck, and Zmarak Shalizi. 2014. "The Economics of Targeted Mitigation in Infrastructure." *Climate Policy* 14 (2): 187–208.

Levinson, David. 2013. *Access across America*. CTS 13-20, Center for Transportation Studies, University of Minnesota, Minneapolis.

Lozano-Gracia, Nancy, and Cheryl Young. 2014. "Housing Consumption and Urbanization." Policy Research Working Paper 7112, World Bank, Washington, DC.

Lucas, Robert E., and Esteban Rossi-Hansberg. 2002. "On the Internal Structure of Cities." *Econometrica* 70 (4): 1445–76.

Marshall, Alfred. 1920. *Principles of Economics*. London: Macmillan.

Muth, R. F. 1969. *Cities and Housing: The Spatial Pattern of Urban Residential Land Use*. Chicago: University of Chicago Press.

Mills, E. S. 1972. *Studies in the Structure of the Urban Economy*. Baltimore, MD: Johns Hopkins Press.

NISR (National Institute of Statistics), and MPSL (Minister for Public Service and Labour). 2013. *Rwanda National Manpower Survey 2011–2012*. National Institute of Statistics of Rwanda, Kigali.

Owen, Andrew, and David Levinson. 2014. Access across America: Transit. CTS 14-11, Center for Transportation Studies, University of Minnesota, Minneapolis.

Peralta Quiros, Tatiana. 2015. "Mobility for All: Getting the Right Urban Indicator." Note 25, Connections Series, World Bank, Washington, DC. http://www.worldbank.org/en/topic/transport/brief/connections-note-25.

Rode, Philipp, Graham Floater, Nikolas Thomopoulos, James Docherty, Peter Schwinger, Anjali Mahendra, and Wanli Fang. 2014. "Accessibility in Cities: Transport and Urban Form." New Climate Economy Cities, Paper 03. LSE Cities, London School of Economics and Political Science, London, UK.

Rosenthal, Stuart S., and William C. Strange. 2004. "Chapter 49: Evidence on the Nature and Sources of Agglomeration Economies." In *Handbook of Regional and Urban Economics* 4: 2119–71. Amsterdam: Elsevier.

Schäfer, Andreas. 2000. "Regularities in Travel Demand: An International Perspective." *Journal of Transportation and Statistics* 3 (3): 1–31.

Schäfer A., J. B. Heywood, H. D. Jacoby, and I. A. Waitz. 2009. Transportation in a Climate-Constrained World. Cambridge, MA: MIT Press.

Schäfer, Andreas, and David G. Victor. 2000. "The Future Mobility of the World Population." *Transportation Research Part A: Policy and Practice* 34 (3): 171–205.

Squires, G. 2002. *Urban Sprawl: Causes, Consequences, & Policy Responses*. Urban Institute, Washington, DC.

Syverson, C. 2004. "Market Structure and Productivity: A Concrete Example." *Journal of Political Economy* 112 (6): 1181–222.

TfL (Transport for London). 2014. Travel in London. Report 7, Transport for London.

Uganda Bureau of Statistics. 2010. *Uganda National Household Survey 2009–2010*. Kampala.

WDI (World Development Indicators). 2015. Washington, DC. http://data.worldbank.org/data-catalog/world-development-indicators.World Bank. 2009. *World Development Report 2009: Reshaping Economic Geography*. Washington, DC: World Bank.

World Bank. 2009. *World Development Report 2009: Reshaping Economic Geography*. Washington, DC: World Bank.

———. 2015a. *Competitive Cities for Jobs and Growth*. Washington, DC: World Bank.

———. 2015b. From *Oil to Cities. Nigeria's Next Transformation. Nigeria Urbanization Review*. Washington, DC: World Bank.

——— 2015c. *Measuring Living Standards within Cities. Households Surveys: Dar es Salaam and Durban*. Washington, DC: World Bank.

———. 2015d. *Rising through Cities in Ghana: Ghana Urbanization Review Overview Report* Washington, DC: World Bank.

Zahavi, Yacov. 1973. "The TT-relationship: A unified approach to transportation planning." Traffic engineering and control, 205–212.

———. 1974. "Travel Time Budgets and Mobility in Urban Areas." Report prepared for the U.S Department of Transportation, Washington, D.C. and Ministry of Transport, Federal Republic of Germany, Bonn.

———. 1981. *The UMOT Project*. Washington, DC: US Government Printing Office.

Zahavi, Yacov, and Antti Talvitie. 1980. *Regularities in Travel Time and Money Expenditures*. Transportation Research Record 750: 13–19.

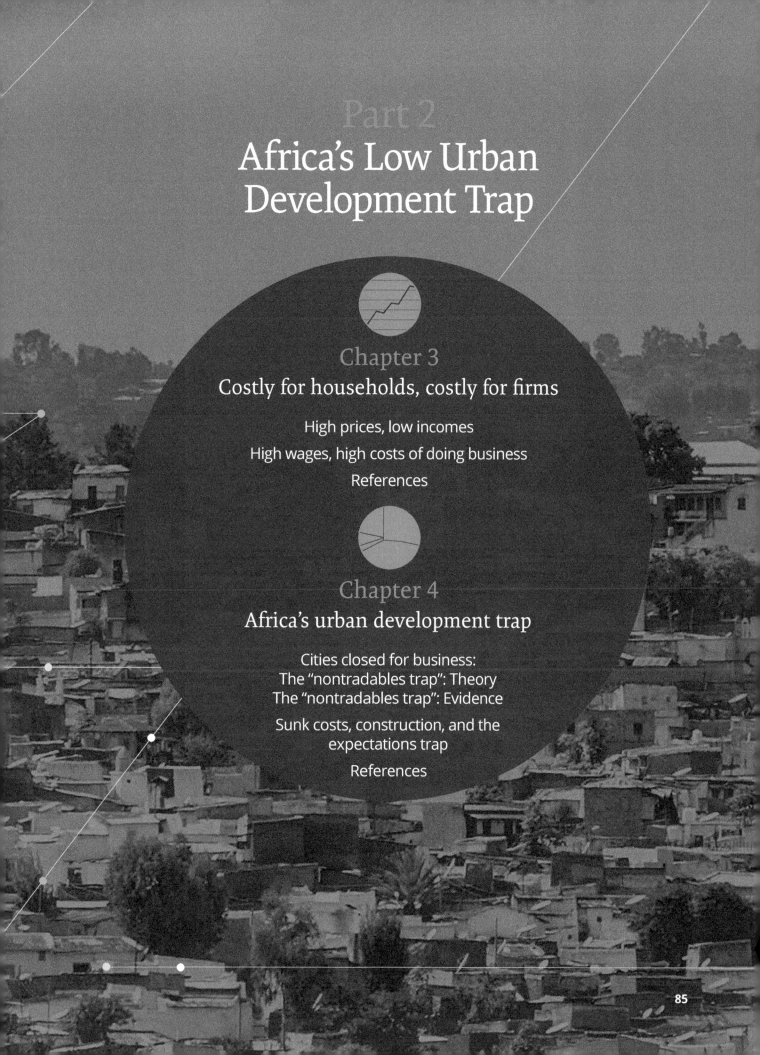

Part 2
Africa's Low Urban Development Trap

Chapter 3
Costly for households, costly for firms

High prices, low incomes

High wages, high costs of doing business

References

Chapter 4
Africa's urban development trap

Cities closed for business:
The "nontradables trap": Theory
The "nontradables trap": Evidence

Sunk costs, construction, and the
expectations trap

References

African firms face multiple obstacles to becoming competitive on global markets. Among the usual suspects are corruption; low access to finance; limited domestic goods markets; and unreliable infrastructure for water, transport, and electricity (Malikane 2015 reviews the main findings).

A less obvious constraint is the fragmented spatial form of the typical African city. This type of urban form burdens firms with high costs. By hindering agglomeration economies and necessitating high wages, fragmented cities lock African firms into producing nontradables — a low urban development trap.

When urban forms are fragmented, workers and households face higher living costs — and firms face constraints and indirect costs as a result. For example, commuting by vehicle is unaffordable for most workers, who thus have difficulty finding jobs that match their skills. High food and building costs directly challenge families who are trying to remain healthy and secure decent housing. But when firms pay a high nominal wage to cover workers' high living costs (or compensate them for living in poor conditions), that higher wage — driven by high urban costs instead of high labor productivity — makes the firms less competitive. They can survive selling nontradable goods in local markets, but are not able to compete in tradable goods production or break into international markets.

Fragmented cities thus have higher business costs. They are less attractive sites for investment in infrastructure and in commercial, industrial, and residential structures. And they are less able to realize scale economies. As a result, African firms find it harder to break into global markets. But this is not the end of the story. This difficulty retards income growth in African cities and lowers expectations about future income growth. As a consequence, residential investment decisions get delayed, resulting in a lower quality housing stock. This contributes further to the fragmented and high cost urban form of African cities, creating a low level development trap in which many African cities appear to be trapped.

The next two chapters present evidence and analysis in support of this view of African cities. Research for this report confirms that Africa's urban living costs are relatively high and that this contributes to high labor costs. Wages are about 15 percent higher in African cities than in non-African ones (at official exchange rates, conditional on national per capita GDP), while overall labor costs are estimated at up to 50 percent higher. Chapter 3 documents these facts about cost and wages. Chapter 4 shows how these features, together with those described in chapters 1 and 2 can combine to create an urban development trap, in which African cities become locked into poor urban form and unable to break in to production of internationally tradable goods and services.

Reference

Malikane, Christopher. 2015. "The Theory of the Firm in the African Context." In The Oxford Handbook of Africa and Economics: Volume 1: Context and Concepts. Edited by Célestin Monga and Justin Yifu Lin. Oxford, United Kingdom: Oxford University Press.

Chapter 3

African households face higher costs relative to their per capita GDP than households in other regions. According to a new study of price level indices at the urban level, based on data collected by the International Comparison Program, urban households in 39 Sub-Saharan African countries pay 20–31 percent more overall than urban households in other countries at similar income levels (Nakamura and others 2016). A similar comparison of urban prices — based on data from 125 cities, including nine in Sub-Saharan Africa (the Economist Intelligence Unit's Worldwide Cost of Living Survey) — finds African cities to be about 31 percent more costly for households than cities in low- and middle-income countries elsewhere (Nakamura and others 2016).

Housing and transport are especially costly in urban Africa. Relative to their income levels, urban residents pay 55 percent more for housing in Africa than they do in other regions.

Urban transport, which includes prices of vehicles and transport services, is about 42 percent more expensive in African cities than in cities elsewhere. Urban workers in Sub-Saharan Africa incur high commuting costs — or they simply cannot afford to commute by vehicle, leaving them no option but to walk (or possibly bike). The informal, often colorful minibus systems that dominate collective motorized transport in most African cities are far from cost-efficient: the buses' small size and low load factors (passenger capacity) prevent them from realizing scale economies. For the poorest urban residents especially, the cost of vehicle transport in some cities is prohibitive. The need to walk to work limits these residents' access to jobs. The price premium for food is also large (about 35 percent).

In deciding where to live, households choose the best home they can afford, with the amenities they value most, and make tradeoffs in allocating their budgets over time. Some choose to live in the center of a city, where rents are higher, sacrificing size for access to amenities. When public amenities are limited, basic services lacking, and connective infrastructure deficient, households may underconsume housing and make suboptimal decisions on housing quality in order to access these services. For example, when transport systems are unavailable, households may choose to live in close-in slums so that they can access jobs, schools, or health care. Recent work suggests that low investments in formal housing may be pushing households into searching for informal solutions.

The high costs and lack of amenities faced by households also matter for firms. Workers need to be compensated for the high costs of living that they face, which translates into higher wage costs for firms. Wages are generally at least 15 percent higher than wages in comparable countries.

High prices, low incomes

Price levels are generally higher in high-income countries, and they are higher in urban areas than rural ones (Nakamura and others 2016). Goods and services in lower-income African countries are generally less expensive than in higher-income countries. For example, the price level of food and nonalcoholic beverages in Ethiopia is almost half that in the United States. Within countries, urban areas generally have higher prices than rural, partly because the costs of commuting, land, rent, and some goods are also high.

These relationships hold quite widely, but the data reveal that African cities have particularly high prices relative to their level of development. Figure 3.1 plots a measure of the cost of living in cities in various countries relative to their GDP per capita (adjusted for purchasing power parity). It confirms that richer countries generally have higher price levels, but it also shows that African countries face price levels that are higher than expected given their low income levels (Nakamura and others 2016).

The figure is based on data from the 2011 round of the International Comparison Program. It covers 62 countries (including 39 in Sub-Saharan Africa), with price level index data collected mainly in urban areas. Where the price information is not entirely urban based, adjustment was made using within-country data for urban–rural differentials.[20] Price level indices are calculated by dividing the purchasing power parities by the nominal exchange rate for each country.

Econometric analysis of these data show that, controlling for income levels, price levels for household expenditures (excluding housing rent) are on average 31 percent higher in Sub-Saharan African countries than in other countries. A group of relatively expensive countries includes Angola, Mozambique, Malawi, Niger, Chad, and the Central African Republic. By contrast, The Gambia, Mauritania, Madagascar, and Tanzania have relatively low price levels. Map 3.1 (overleaf) illustrates the spatial pattern in Sub-Saharan Africa by showing the residuals from the regression.

FIGURE 3.1

African cities face high prices for their income levels

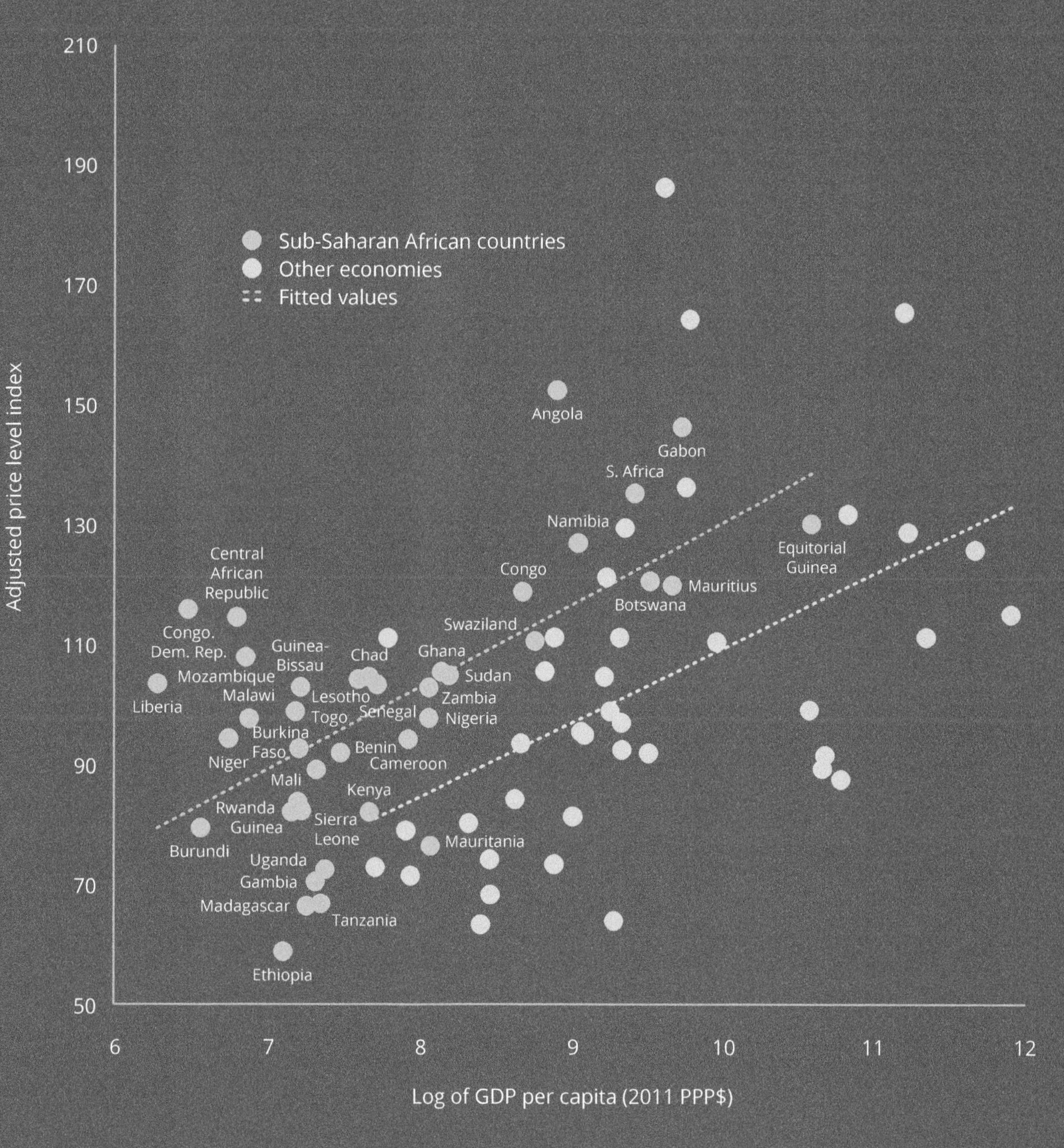

Sub-Saharan African countries
Other economies
Fitted values

Adjusted price level index

Angola
Gabon
S. Africa
Namibia
Congo
Equitorial Guinea
Mauritius
Botswana
Central African Republic
Swaziland
Congo. Dem. Rep.
Guinea-Bissau
Chad
Ghana
Mozambique
Sudan
Malawi
Lesotho
Zambia
Liberia
Togo
Senegal
Nigeria
Burkina Faso
Benin
Niger
Cameroon
Mali
Kenya
Rwanda
Guinea
Sierra Leone
Mauritania
Burundi
Uganda
Gambia
Madagascar
Tanzania
Ethiopia

Log of GDP per capita (2011 PPP$)

Source: Nakamura and others (2016), based on 2011 International Comparison Program data.

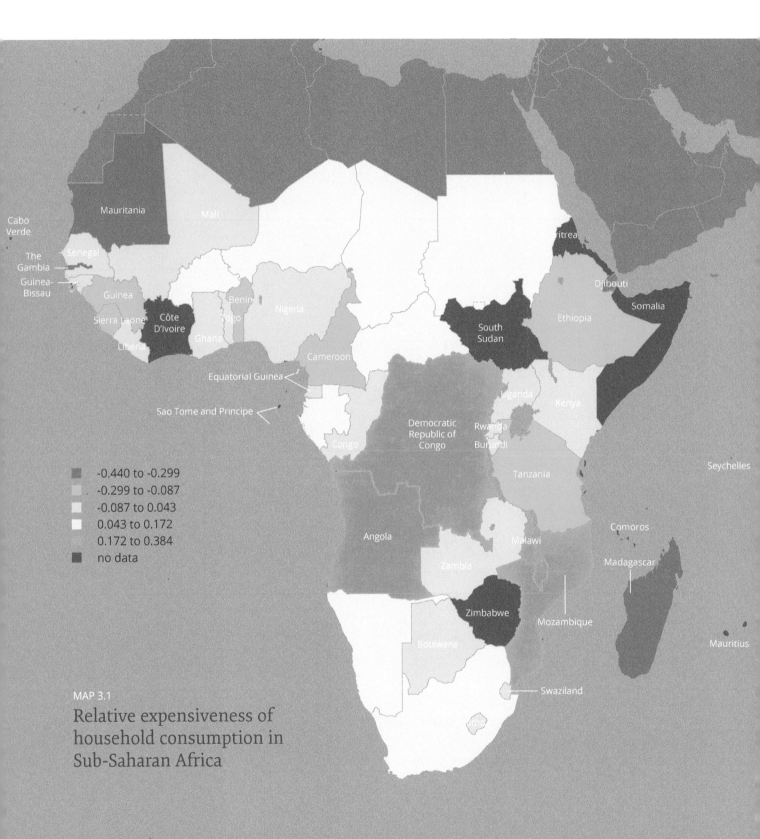

Similar findings are obtained using data collected by the Economist Intelligence Unit. These data are compiled for quite different purposes — the cost of living of expatriates traveling from developed countries for business. Its price survey therefore collects data on items typically consumed by expatriates. Using these data, Nakamura and others (2016) find a highly significant positive Africa effect, indicating that (controlling for income levels), African cities are about 30 percent more expensive than comparable cities elsewhere.

What goods and services are most important in driving this price premium? The Africa price premium varies depending on the groups of goods and services. It is particularly large on essentially urban commodities, such as housing (55 percent), followed by communication (46 percent), and urban transport (42 percent). But food and nonalcoholic beverages are also relatively expensive in African cities (35 percent premium); particularly expensive among food items are fresh or chilled vegetables, eggs and egg-based products, and fresh milk (figure 3.2).

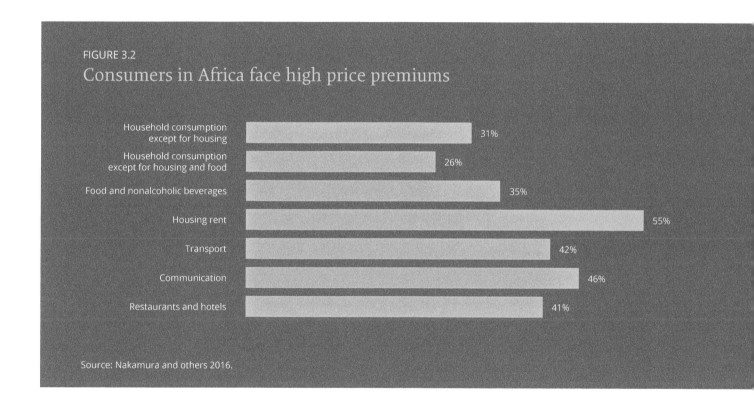

FIGURE 3.2

Consumers in Africa face high price premiums

Household consumption except for housing	31%
Household consumption except for housing and food	26%
Food and nonalcoholic beverages	35%
Housing rent	55%
Transport	42%
Communication	46%
Restaurants and hotels	41%

Source: Nakamura and others 2016.

Given the expenditure patterns of urban households in Africa, higher prices of food deepen livability challenges for households and impose a severe constraint on the choices they have on where to live or work. The budgets of the poor are spent mainly on food, reducing their opportunities to spend on health, education, and housing. According to household surveys collected in several African countries between 2003 and 2010, spending on food accounts for 39–59 percent of monthly expenditures by urban households (figure 3.3). The poorest households (households in the bottom expenditure quintile) spend an even larger share on food, ranging from 44 percent in Uganda to 68 percent in Zambia. Rising incomes allow for consumption of nonfood items, such as housing, recreation, and so forth (Dasgupta and others 2014).

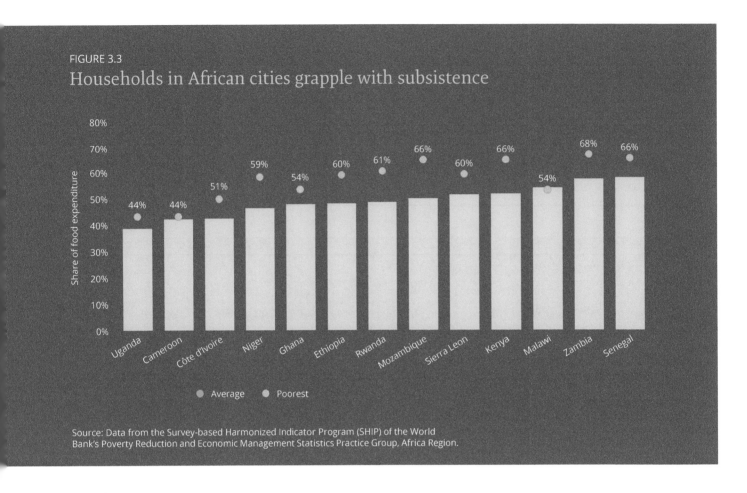

FIGURE 3.3

Households in African cities grapple with subsistence

Source: Data from the Survey-based Harmonized Indicator Program (SHIP) of the World Bank's Poverty Reduction and Economic Management Statistics Practice Group, Africa Region.

Two other observation about the cost of urban living in Africa are important. The first is that building formally is expensive. Registering property in Sub-Saharan Africa is generally more time consuming and costly (relative to property value) than in other regions of the world (figure 3.4); dealing with construction permits is fairly quick but still costly (relative to income per capita) (figure 3.5). On average in Sub-Saharan Africa, it takes 59 days and 9 percent of property value to register property — more than twice as long and three times as much as in Europe and Central Asia (26.5 days and 2.8 percent of property value) and high-income OECD countries (24 days and 4.4 percent

of property value). Obtaining construction permits in Sub-Saharan Africa takes on average 171 days and costs 737 percent of income per capita. This average time is comparable to other regions; it is lower than in South Asia, Latin America and the Caribbean, and Europe and Central Asia. However, the average cost is second only to South Asia and, at 84 percent of per capita income, nearly nine times as expensive relative to incomes as in the high-income OECD countries (World Bank 2015). The high costs of obtaining property registration and construction permits in Sub-Saharan cities contributes to further growth of informal settlements.

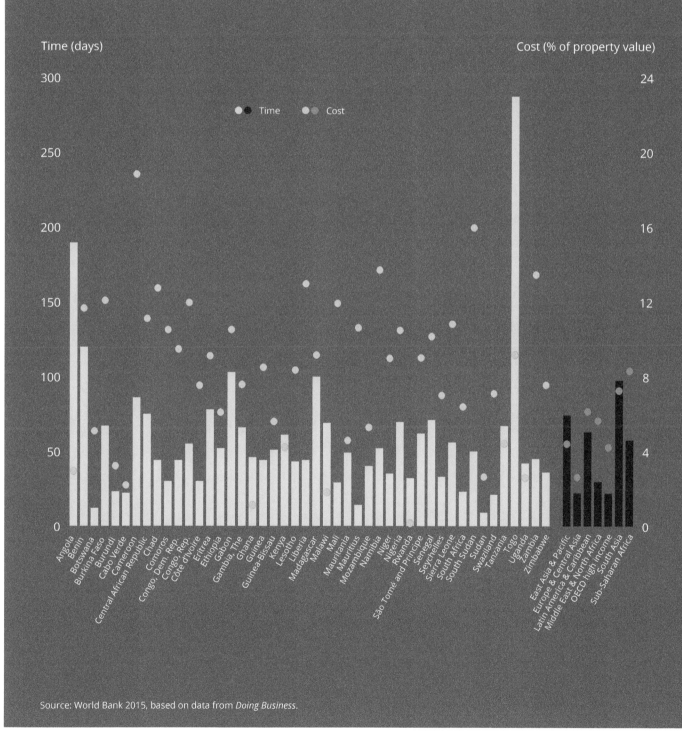

FIGURE 3.4

Average time and cost to register property in Sub-Saharan countries and international benchmarks

Time (days)

Cost (% of property value)

Source: World Bank 2015, based on data from *Doing Business*.

FIGURE 3.5

Average time and cost to deal with construction permits in Sub-Saharan countries and international benchmarks

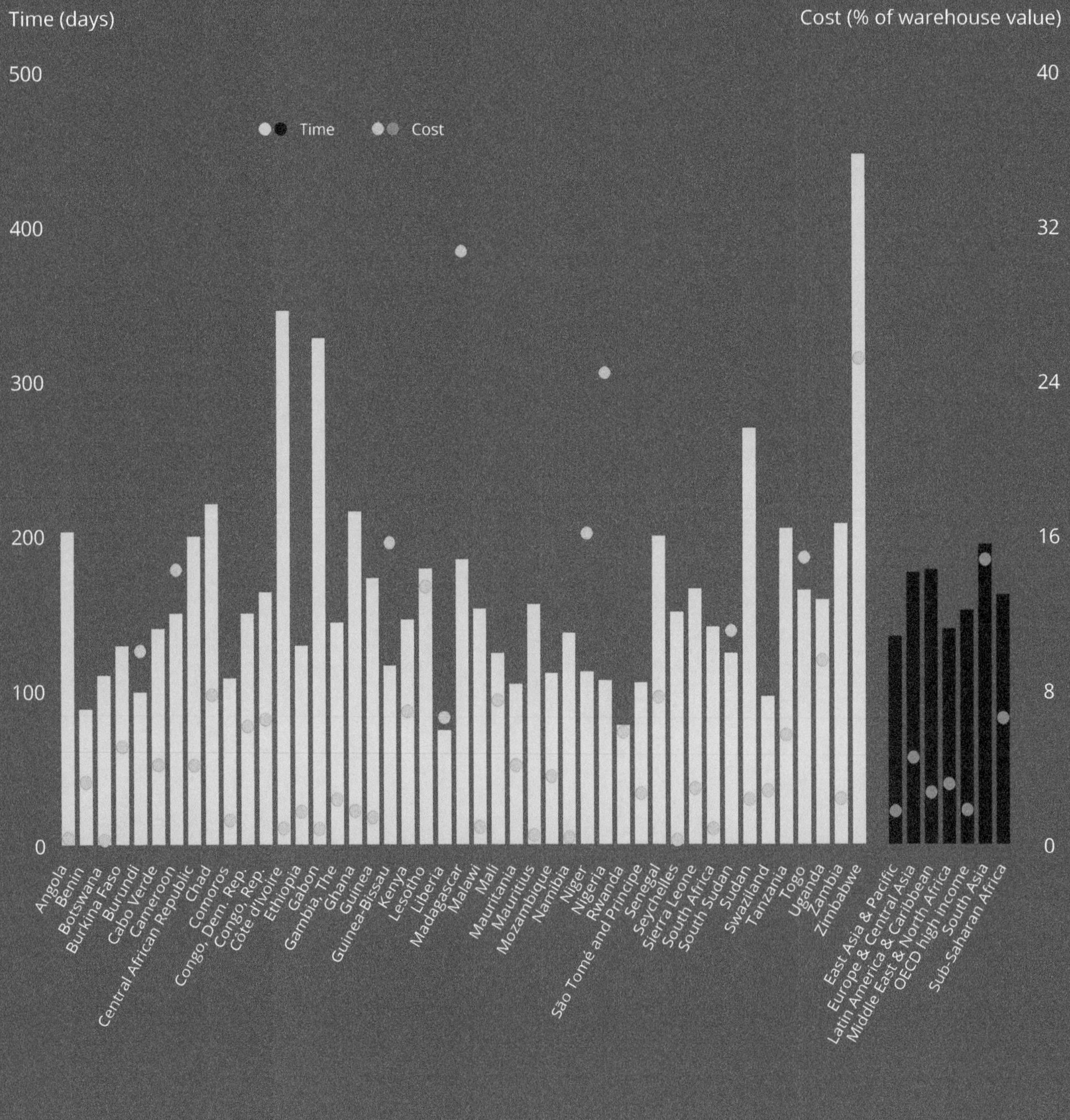

Source: World Bank 2015, based on data from Doing Business.

The second observation is that there appears to be a positive association between urban costs and the extent to which a city fails to provide density or is fragmented. Estimates of the cost of proving urban infrastructure indicate that doubling urban density reduces the per capita cost of a package of infrastructure improvements by about 25 percent (Foster and Briceno-Garmendia 2010). The decrease is particularly large for infrastructure associated with high capital cost per capita, as shown in figure 3.6.

Figure 3.7 also shows that a fragmented urban form is associated with higher costs. Using the Puga measure of urban fragmentation (discussed in chapter 2),

higher "exposure" for the largest city in a country is associated with a lower urban price index. When the urban form is fragmented, economies of scale in service delivery are sacrificed, opportunities for agglomeration economies are lost, and transportation is more expensive, because people are dispersed and more kilometers of road network are needed. Ordinary least squares regressions show that a 1 percent increase in the Puga index is associated with urban costs that are lower by 12 percent, controlling for income levels and city population. Alongside high urban costs, lack of urban amenities and high congestion reduces household wellbeing in Africa's cities.

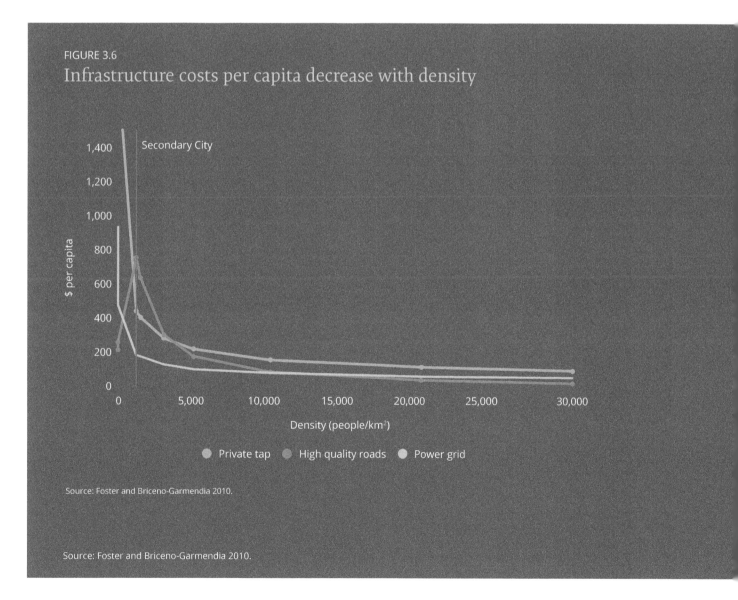

FIGURE 3.6
Infrastructure costs per capita decrease with density

Source: Foster and Briceno-Garmendia 2010.

Source: Foster and Briceno-Garmendia 2010.

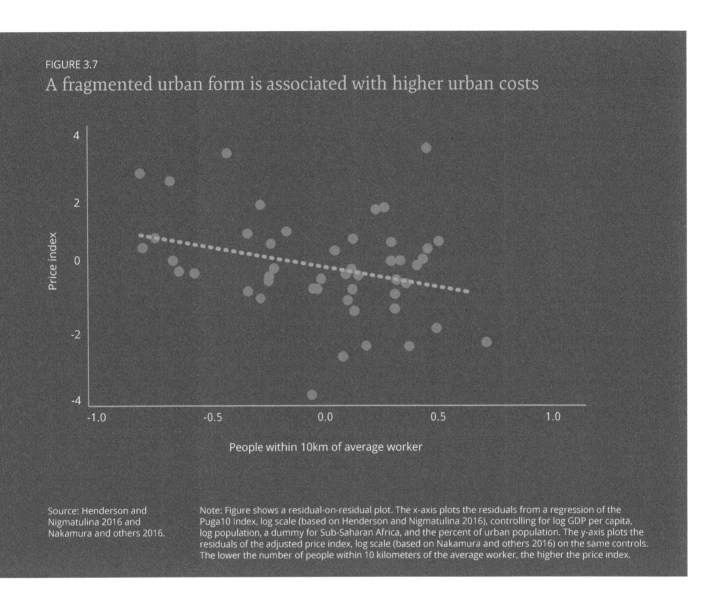

FIGURE 3.7

A fragmented urban form is associated with higher urban costs

People within 10km of average worker (x-axis), *Price index* (y-axis)

Source: Henderson and Nigmatulina 2016 and Nakamura and others 2016.

Note: Figure shows a residual-on-residual plot. The x-axis plots the residuals from a regression of the Puga10 Index, log scale (based on Henderson and Nigmatulina 2016), controlling for log GDP per capita, log population, a dummy for Sub-Saharan Africa, and the percent of urban population. The y-axis plots the residuals of the adjusted price index, log scale (based on Nakamura and others 2016) on the same controls. The lower the number of people within 10 kilometers of the average worker, the higher the price index.

High wages, high costs of doing business

Chapters 1 and 2 point to many aspects of African cities that impose costs on firms. An important additional factor is that firms need to pay high nominal wages to compensate workers for their high cost of living as well as for their poor living conditions. African firms pay significantly higher nominal wages than firms in other regions at comparable levels of real income.

Data from World Bank Enterprise Surveys indicate that urban wages in manufacturing are higher in African cities than in other cities at comparable levels of economic development. Manufacturing firms in African cities pay a wage premium of about 15

percent (in nominal terms) over equivalent firms in other developing country cities (figure 3.8). Slightly larger estimates can be found when comparing industrial labor costs across countries with the same data: African firms paid 50 percent more in labor costs than equivalent firms elsewhere (Gelb, Meyer, and Ramachandran 2013). Higher wages may be one reason why Africa's manufacturing sector is so small and has been declining (as a share of global output) since the 1980s (UNIDO 2009). Today, the average firm in Africa hires about 20 percent fewer employees than equivalent firms elsewhere (Iacovone, Ramachandran, and Schmidt 2014).

FIGURE 3.8

Nominal manufacturing wages in African cities are higher than in other developing country cities

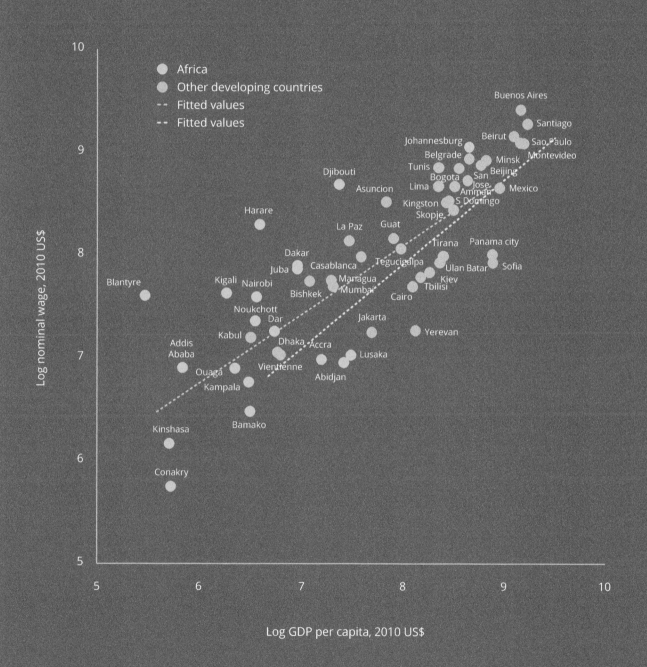

Source: Data from World Bank Enterprise Surveys.

FIGURE 3.9

Sales revenue per worker in African and other developing-country cities

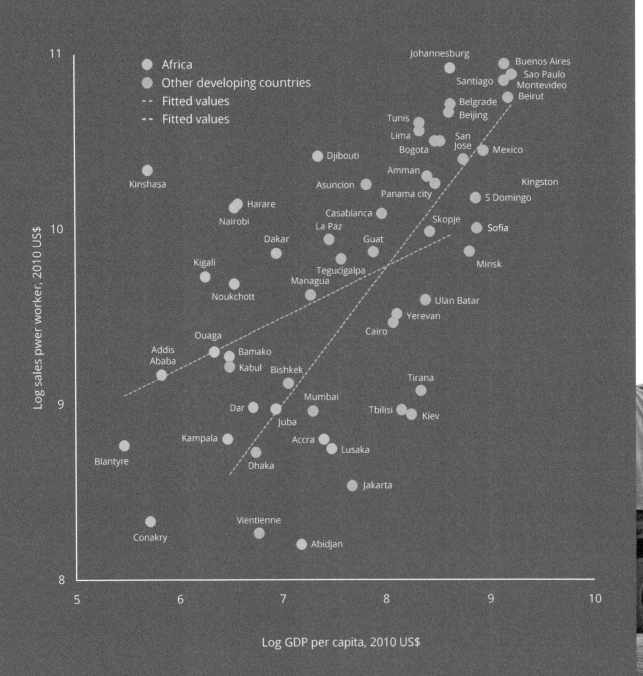

Source: Data from World Bank Enterprise Surveys.

African firms could afford to pay high wages only if revenue per worker is high. This turns out to be the case, by about 25 percent (figure 3.9). It is therefore important to ask: "Do these higher revenues reflect higher productivity (output per worker) or do they simply reflect higher prices?"

The implications of high costs is that urban wages in manufacturing are higher in African cities than in other cities at comparable levels of economic development. When a city's urban wage is higher than the international wage (for tradables), it makes it harder for the city to break into global markets. In contrast, in the nontradable sector, higher nominal wages may exist in the absence of productivity gains, because, absent competition, firms can pass labor costs on to local consumers (Venables 2016). As labor costs continue to rise in China and other Asian countries, international firms will be searching for new cities in which to invest and set up industrial plants.

References

Dasgupta, P. 2014. "Measuring the Wealth of Nations." *Annual Review of Resource Economics* 6 (1): 17–31.

Gelb, A., C. Meyer, and V. Ramachandran. 2013. "Does Poor Mean Cheap? A Comparative Look at Africa's Industrial Labor Costs." Working Paper 325, Centre for Global Development, Washington, DC.

Foster, V., and C. Briceno-Garmendia. 2010. *Africa's Infrastructure: A Time for Transformation.* Washington, DC: World Bank.

Henderson, Vernon, and Dzhamilya Nigmatulina. 2016. "The Fabric of African Cities: How to Think about Density and Land Use." Draft, April 20, London School of Economics.

Iacovone, L., V. Ramachandran, and M. Schmidt. 2014. "Stunted Growth: Why Don't African Firms Create More Jobs?" Working Paper 353, Center for Global Development, Washington, DC.

Nakamura, S., R. Harati, S. Lall, Y. Dikhanov, N. Hamadeh, W. V. Oliver, M. O. Rissanen, and M. Yamanaka. 2016. "Is Living in African Cities Expensive?" Policy Research Working Paper 7641, World Bank, Washington, DC.

UNIDO (United Nations Industrial Development Organization). 2009. Breaking In and Moving Up: New Industrial Challenges for the Bottom Billion and the Middle-Income Countries. Industrial Development Report 2009. Vienna: UNIDO.

Venables, A. J. 2016. "Breaking into Tradables: Urban Form and Urban Function in a Developing City." University of Oxford, United Kingdom

World Bank. 2015. *Stocktaking of the Housing Sector in Sub-Saharan Africa: Challenges and Opportunities.* Washington, DC: World Bank.

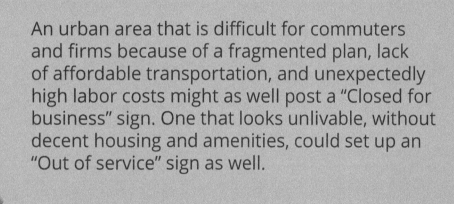

Chapter 4

An urban area that is difficult for commuters and firms because of a fragmented plan, lack of affordable transportation, and unexpectedly high labor costs might as well post a "Closed for business" sign. One that looks unlivable, without decent housing and amenities, could set up an "Out of service" sign as well.

A city that is a candidate for posting these signs has already entered a low development trap. Potential investors and trading partners quickly see the evidence of the physical and economic dysfunction that constrains public service provision, inhibits labor market pooling and matching, and prevents firms from reaping scale and agglomeration benefits. They stay away, fearing lack of return on their investment. This dynamic will keep Africa's urban economies undercapitalized, making their development even more challenging than it otherwise would be.

City and country governments should recognize the problem for what it is: not simply one of underinvestment leading to low infrastructure, but one of the interdependency of many investment decisions. Business investment decisions depend on the presence of other businesses that are their customers and their suppliers and on workplaces being reachable from residential areas. Investment in housing will occur if there is increasing demand, driven by rising incomes of workers, and if revenues from a growing city are available to finance infrastructure. These decisions are interrelated — and in all of them expectations are crucial. Investors' low expectations become self-fulfilling, as failure to implement one project reduces the return to others, locking cities in a low development trap.

This chapter looks at the form and function of African cities to spotlight key inefficiencies and their immediate effects — the signs that warn business away, limiting Africa's appeal to the business world and consigning its cities to producing mostly nontradables in the informal sector.

Cities closed for business

Chapters 1–3 laid out key features of developing country cities and documented the low levels of capital, lack of connectivity, and high costs facing households and firms in African cities. There are strong interlinkages between all these elements. Urban form (the built fabric or physical environment) shapes urban costs, such as commuting expenses and rents. Costs determine the urban function (the mix of activities undertaken in the city), in turn shaping productivity, labor demand, wages, and rents. There are feedback loops, as expectations about the city's performance — employment, productivity, wages, rents — determine investment decisions and hence urban form. These interactions can lead to virtuous cycles of rapid urban development — or to a development trap exhibiting the features described in chapters 1–3.

This chapter pulls the key elements together. It first looks at the ways in which business investment decisions in different sectors depend on the way the city functions, in particular its urban form. It then turns to residential investment decisions, in particular the ways in which they depend on expectations about future city growth.

Much of the chapter is analytical, pulling together findings from previous research and setting the stage for the chapters on housing and land tenure (chapter 5) and infrastructure (chapter 6). The analytic framework demonstrates how the different elements of the city fit together and highlights the fact that there can be several equilibrium outcomes. Expectations can be self-fulfilling, leading a city to one outcome or the other. In one outcome, a city produces only nontradable goods, with low land values, little investment in buildings, and consequent failure to achieve the scale and density required for modern tradable production. The other outcome has the city producing tradable goods and services alongside nontradables. Land values are higher, as are expectations of rents, incentivizing developers to invest more in building a taller and denser city. In both cases, expectations become self-fulfilling: If developers anticipate increased tradable production, their expectations of wages and land prices will be higher, leading them to invest more in taller buildings. "Taller" cities have greater economic density than "flatter" cities, increasing the likelihood of agglomeration economies and the future growth potential of the city and decreasing urban costs.

The "nontradables trap": Theory

Africa's failure to industrialize, and to create the jobs that come with industrialization, are a major cause of concern. Many factors lie behind this failure. The focus here is on the role that poorly functioning cities play, drawing on the framework developed by Venables (2016), which reflects the interactions that shape the performance of a developing country city.

The key ingredients are supply and demand for labor in the city. The supply curve gives the wage that the city has to offer to attract population from neighboring areas (figure 4.1). It slopes upward because cities impose "urban costs" — the additional costs workers face when living in the city because of high rent, commuting costs, and the price of many goods (as shown in chapter 3). These costs increase with city size. Urban costs — and hence the height and slope of the supply curve — also increase with urban inefficiencies in delivering housing, transportation, and public services. Labor supply will be forthcoming only if wages rise to offset the costs of living in a city.

The demand curve is drawn with two distinct sections, one representing labor demand in the nontradable sector, the other in the tradable sector. Nontradables are goods and services that are sold within the city and its hinterland (perhaps extending to national or even regional sales). They include beer and cement, construction, and many services, including retailing, as well informal sector activities. Demand for these goods and services comes from income generated within the city and its hinterland and from income transferred from outside sources, such as resource

rents, tax revenues, and foreign aid. The curve is downward sloping because of diminishing returns; the more workers employed produce nontradables, the greater will be the supply of the goods they produce and hence the lower the price of the goods. Given local demand, the more workers are crammed into this sector, the lower will be their earnings.

In contrast, the price of tradable goods is set on the world market. A city's export activities do not run into a constraint set by the size of the local or regional market. The price of imports (and import-competing products) is set largely by the possibility of supply from the rest of the world. The demand for labor curve is therefore relatively flat. It is drawn in figure 4.1 as upward sloping because these sectors are likely to experience agglomeration economies, creating increasing returns to scale.

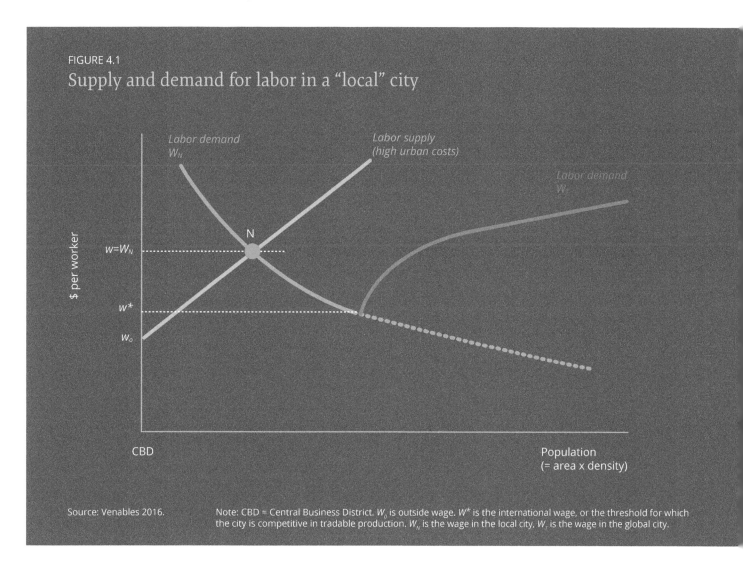

FIGURE 4.1

Supply and demand for labor in a "local" city

Source: Venables 2016.   Note: CBD = Central Business District. W_0 is outside wage. W^* is the international wage, or the threshold for which the city is competitive in tradable production. W_n is the wage in the local city, W_r is the wage in the global city.

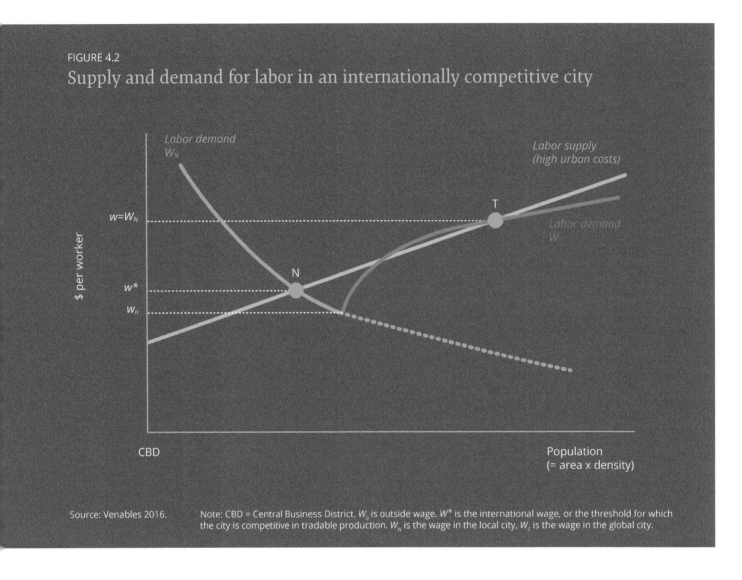

FIGURE 4.2

Supply and demand for labor in an internationally competitive city

Source: Venables 2016.

Note: CBD = Central Business District. W_0 is outside wage. W^* is the international wage, or the threshold for which the city is competitive in tradable production. W_N is the wage in the local city, W_T is the wage in the global city.

What is the outcome of the interplay between supply and demand? If urban costs are high or increase sharply, then the situation is as in figure 4.2. Labor supply equals labor at point N. Four observations can be made. First, nominal wages are high. Second, real wages remain low (they are set by the supply of labor from outside the city; high nominal wages merely compensate for high urban costs). Third, nominal wages are too high to attract any tradable sector production, so the city produces only nontradables. Fourth, unlike tradable sector firms, firms in the nontradable sector are able to afford to pay these high wages by passing them on to consumers, contributing further to the high cost of living in the city.

Figure 4.2 illustrates an outcome in which urban costs increase less rapidly with city size, so the labor supply curve is flatter. In this case, labor supply equals labor

demand at point T, where both the nontradable and tradable sectors are active. The larger the city, the flatter the labor supply curve, although nominal wages may be high. Firms in the tradable sector can afford to pay these wages because employment in these sectors is high; agglomeration economies increase productivity.

The argument so far shows how urban form — urban costs and hence the shape of the labor supply curve — determine the size of the city and its production structure. Why is production of only nontradables considered a "trap"? In figure 4.2, there are three points at which labor supply equals labor demand. The middle one is unstable and can be ignored, but points N and T are both sustainable outcomes. At N the city produces only nontradables; at T both sectors are active.

Both outcomes are sustainable because agglomeration economies make it hard to start producing in new sectors. At point N the wage is too high to trigger tradable production, because productivity in the tradable sector is low — because there is no tradable production, there are no agglomeration economies.

This situation stems from coordination failure, a standard problem in developing new clusters of economic activity (see, among others, Henderson and Venables 2009). It arises when a group of firms (or individuals) has the resources to achieve a desirable outcome but fail to do so because they cannot (or do not) coordinate their decision making. The chicken and egg problem is that no firm wants to be the first to set up but many would become established if they could coordinate their entry.

To solve the problems, cities need either a forward-looking group of firms to harmonize their plans and make a move together or a large-scale land developer or city government with strong expectations that will establish its credibility by making irreversible investments in the new location (Henderson and Venables 2009). Absent coordination, agglomeration economies will not be realized, leaving all firms stuck in the suboptimal equilibrium. Cities will develop at a smaller scale, with fragmented neighborhoods, as they have in Africa.

Three messages emerge from this analysis. First, it is possible for real incomes to be low but nominal prices and wages high. In this scenario, the city produces only nontradables, with high prices passed on to the local market; the city is too high cost for tradable sectors to be able to operate.

Second, even if urban costs are lower, it may be hard to break out of the nontradables trap. Coordination failure means that the city is stuck at point N in figure 4.2, and it is not profitable for any firm to start up tradable production.

Third, there is a dichotomy of urban types. Some cities — including many in Asia — produce tradable goods at scale, bringing high productivity and high real incomes. Others — such as most in Africa — have not yet broken into this sector. They remain stuck at point N.

The "nontradables trap": Evidence

Chapter 3 established that the high-cost/high-wage configuration is a feature of African cities. There is also plenty of evidence that African cities — and countries — have not broken in to supplying internationally tradable manufactured goods or services. The contrast between Asia and Africa is illustrated in figure 4.3, which shows the shares of firms in tradable and nontradable sectors in selected cities. It shows that the share of tradables in Asian cities is about 70 percent, 20 percentage points higher than in African cities (about 50 percent).

Africa's failure to industrialize is a cause for concern because much of the growth in developing countries since the 1980s has been linked to the expansion of industrial production and higher-technology exports (Nallari and others 2012). Rapidly growing countries, like China, have switched from exporting mainly resource and agro-based products to increasingly participating in global production chains, in particular high-tech products like optical devices, transportation equipment, and domestic appliances as well as related assembly services. As countries are increasingly specializing in tasks rather than products, trade statistics are now moving from "naive" export valuation to domestic value added measures. The switch is particularly important in countries like China, whose share of processing exports is above 50 percent. In high-tech sectors, the share of foreign value added reaches 80 percent, resulting in an overestimated trade value for these products (Koopman and others 2008).

The big winners in China were "exports of electronic and telecommunications products and office equipment, the shares of which grew from 5.4 percent in 1985 to more than one-third in 2006" (Nallari and others 2012). Many other countries in East and Southeast Asia experienced similar transitions in their export mix during the first decade of this century (table 4.1). By contrast, the majority of African exports remain resource- and agro-based.

FIGURE 4.3

The tradables sector is much larger in Asia than in Africa

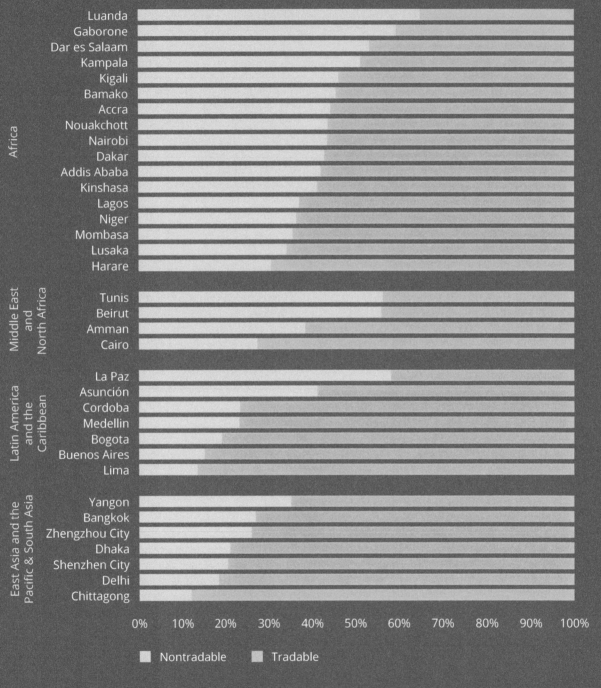

◼ Nontradable   ◼ Tradable

Source: Data from World Bank Enterprise surveys conducted since 2010.

Note: The data is from the latest WBE surveys post-2010 (with more than 15,000 firms in capital cities, or cities of at least one million inhabitants, and with at least 50 firms sampled). Only firms with five or more employees are interviewed. The sectoral specialization analyses used the UN International Standard Industrial Classification of All Economic Activities (3.1 revision). Manufacturing, wholesale and commission trade, and business services (such as travel agencies, transport, financial intermediation) are all tradable activities. By contrast, construction, local services, retail trade, health and social work, and other local activities are classified as nontradable.

Table 4.1 Top 10 commodity exports from Asia and Africa, 2000–10

Commodity	Trade value (billions of dollars)
Asia (East Asia, South Asia, and Oceania)	
Electrical, electronic equipment	7,409.6
Nuclear reactors, boilers, machinery, etc.	5,044.7
Vehicles other than railway, tramway	2,175.4
Mineral fuels, oils, distillation products, etc.	1,926.4
Optical, photo, technical, medical apparatus, etc.	1,085.4
Plastics	903.9
Articles of apparel, accessories, knit or crochet	798.2
Articles of apparel, accessories, not knit or crochet	774.1
Iron and steel	744.0
Pearls, precious stones, metals, coins, etc.	722.5
Africa	
Mineral fuels, oils, distillation products, etc.	1,224.4
Pearls, precious stones, metals, coins, etc.	169.7
Iron and steel	74.3
Ores, slag, and ash	64.0
Articles of apparel, accessories, not knit or crochet	62.2
Vehicles other than railway, tramway	59.3
Electrical, electronic equipment	57.4
Nuclear reactors, boilers, machinery, etc.	54.3
Cocoa and cocoa preparations	43.5
Inorganic chemicals, precious metal compound, isotopes	35.5

Source: Data from UN Comtrade Database.

Globally, urbanization is strongly correlated with the expansion of manufacturing (figure 4.4). For most countries, manufacturing as a share of GDP rises with urban shares until about 60 percent of the population lives in cities and manufacturing accounts for about 15 percent of GDP.

Sub-Saharan Africa has not developed in this way: its pattern of growth has been described as "urbanization without industrialization" (Fay and Opal 2000; Jedwab 2013; Gollin, Jedwab, and Vollrath 2016). This theory argues that Africa's urbanization growth has been driven by natural resource exports, a third explanation for relatively high demand for nontradable services produced in cities (box 4.1).

FIGURE 4.4

Urbanization and manufacturing share of GDP in Africa and outside Africa

Outside Africa

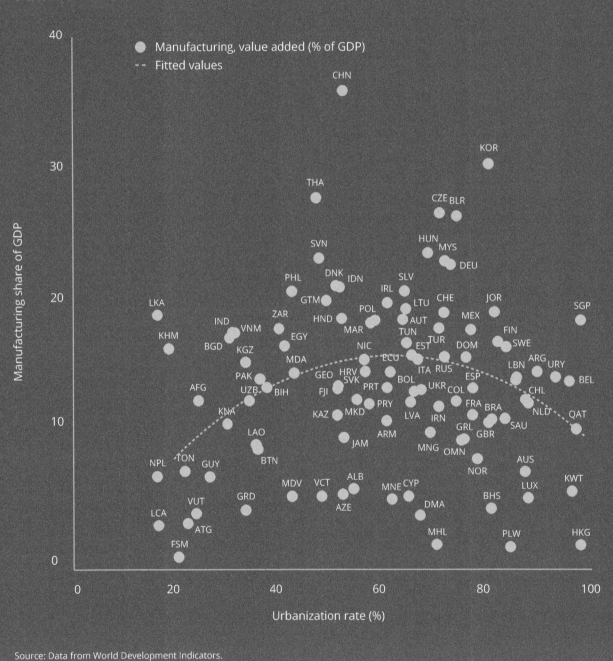

Source: Data from World Development Indicators.

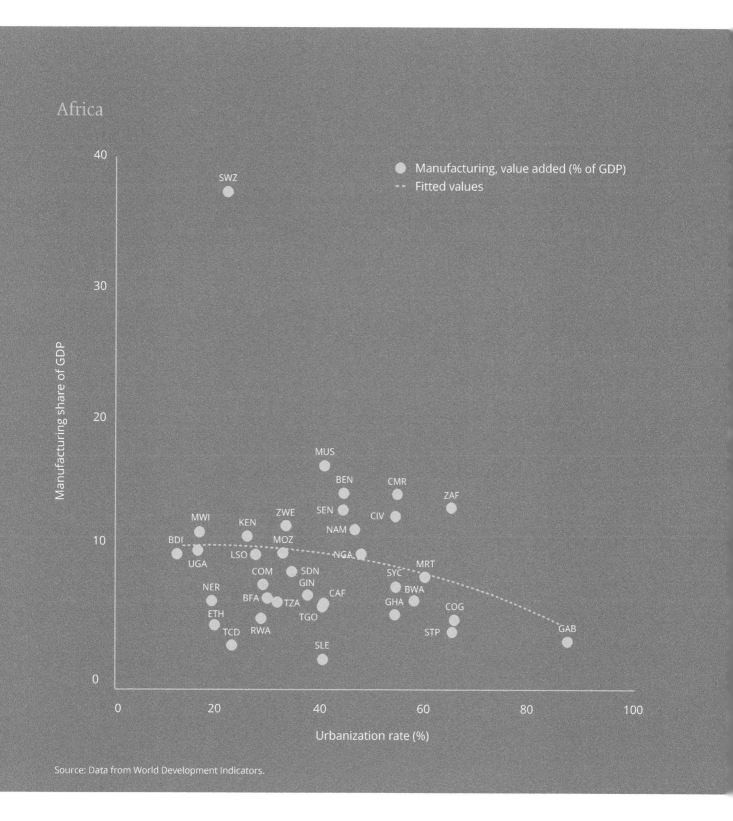

Africa

Source: Data from World Development Indicators.

BOX 4.1

Do natural resource exports explain why African cities specialize in nontradables?

Countries can follow one of two paths to achieve higher urbanization rates as they structurally transform. The first path moves workers out of agriculture and into manufacturing (box figure 4.1.1). This type of structural change — the path taken by most countries in Europe, Latin America, and Asia — creates "production cities," which produce tradable goods for domestic and international markets.

The second urbanization path reflects the experience of African countries with large natural resource endowments. Positive productivity shocks to the resource sector shift workers into the sector and out of the food and tradable sectors. Surplus income generated from natural resource productivity shocks causes a disproportionate rise in the demand for urban goods and services (relative to food). This added demand is met largely through imports (except for urban services, which are produced locally). Urbanization is driven by consumption, not production, creating "consumption cities" (Gollin, Jedwab, and Vollrath 2016).

BOX FIGURE 4.1.1

Urbanization and industrialization take different paths in resource exporters and nonresource exporter

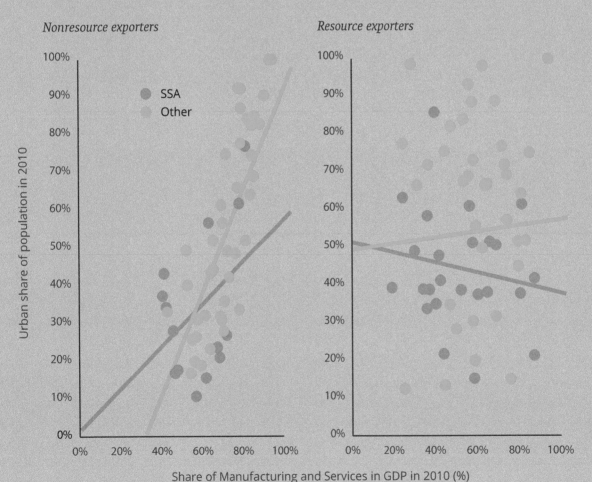

Nonresource exporters

● SSA
● Other

Resource exporters

Urban share of population in 2010

Share of Manufacturing and Services in GDP in 2010 (%)

Source: Gollin, Jedwab, and Vollrath 2016.

If this analysis is correct, urbanization in Sub-Saharan Africa may not generate the same productivity effects as urbanization in other developing regions — in part because of rapid growth in the natural resource sector, which increases urban employment mostly in the nontradable sector. The different growth paths taken by countries that do and do not rely on natural resource exports appear in box figure 4.1.1.

Disproportionate demand for nontradables can offset efforts to reduce urban costs — one of the factors that keeps cities locked into local markets.

In box figure 4.1.2, heavier demand for nontradable goods and services shifts the labor demand curve to the right. Starting from a city with two equilibria, an increase in demand for nontradables leads to the single equilibrium that specializes in nontradables.

BOX FIGURE 4.1.2

Large natural resource rents lead to an equilibrium dominated by nontradables (urban "Dutch disease")

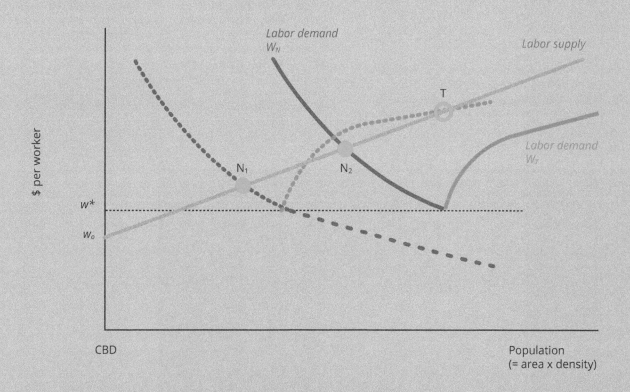

Source: Venables 2016.

Note: N is a city producing nontradable goods for the domestic market. T is a city producing tradable goods for both local and international markets. CBD is central business district. W0 is outside wage. W* is the international wage, or the threshold for which the city is competitive in tradable production.

Sunk costs, construction, and the expectations trap

Urban form depends on private investment decisions, including decisions made in the residential sector. For formal sector housing, these decisions involve sinking costs in constructing long-lived structures. Such decisions depend critically on expectations about the future prospects of the city. If the city is expected to be "artisanal," based on low-value production of nontradables, then land rents will be expected to remain relatively low and it will not be worth investing in formal structures. The lack of incentive to invest perpetuates the disconnectedness and high urban costs that are one of the obstacles to investment. Expectations are therefore self-fulfilling. In contrast, more optimistic expectations increase investment in formal sector structures, including residential structures, bringing down urban costs and making the city more attractive as a place for local investment (flattening the labor supply curve).

The costs involved in building durable formal sector structures include several components. Construction costs are high, particularly in building tall. There may also be high conversion costs in going from informal to formal. They include the costs of road layout and the provision of water, sewerage, and other infrastructure. They also include legal and institutional costs. Building durable structures is unlikely to take place until ownership of land is made clear, a process

than can be a lengthy and expensive (see chapter 5). Imperfect land markets make it difficult and expensive to assemble parcels of land of size sufficient to justify infrastructure investments and other large-scale expenditures.

The future returns from building a structure are extremely uncertain in many developing cities. Lack of clarity in land rights and political risk create uncertainty about future rental incomes. Low expectations about the future growth of the city mean low expectations about the growth of rents. Even if developers expect the city to grow, they might not know where in the city that growth is likely to occur. An investor may be confident that growth will occur somewhere in the city, but if it could be in any one of many possible locations, the ensuing uncertainty means that no one will invest. These issues reflect coordination failure.

There are mechanisms for overcoming such failures. Sunk investments—made by the government or a group of investors—are one. They provide a strong signal to other potential investors and can have long-run effects. It has been argued that "investments sunk historically, even small ones that have now depreciated completely, might serve as a mechanism to coordinate contemporary investment" (Bleakley

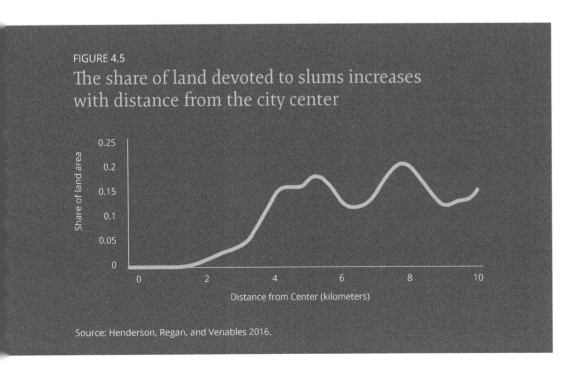

FIGURE 4.5

The share of land devoted to slums increases with distance from the city center

Source: Henderson, Regan, and Venables 2016.

2012). This argument explains why places that have seen large sunk investments in the past (like towns along rail lines) continue to attract investment today (Jebwab and Moradi 2016; Jedwab, Kerby, and Moradi 2015).

Given these high sunk costs and low or uncertain expected returns, it is not surprising that investment in formal structures has been low. A further consequence is the patchwork of building types observed in many African cities, with informal settlements still present in central areas, adjacent to modern development.

Henderson, Regan, and Venables (2016) argue that informal settlement is likely to be part of an "efficient" urban structure in a growing low-income city but that the coexistence of formal and informal sector settlement near the center is inefficient. Their detailed study of Nairobi indicates that although there are no remaining slum areas within 2 kilometers of the city center, beyond that 10–20 percent of land is occupied by slums (figure 4.5). Slums are less tall than formal areas but have a higher proportion of land area covered by buildings (so less space is used for road and other amenities). The building volume per unit land is similar in slum and formal areas. However, the land rent differential between uses is large, indicating inefficient use of land. They estimate that the capital value forgone by not developing Kibera, Nairobi's largest slum, is on the order of $1 billion.

An inefficient level of housing investment has implications that go beyond the housing sector. The supply curve of urban labor discussed earlier depends on, among other things, the stock of housing available to workers. Inefficiency and undersupply shift this curve to the left, raising costs and restricting the supply of workers. This shift is one of the factors that makes it more likely the city will be stuck in the nontradables trap. The coordination failure is therefore much wider than just between firms or between property developers. It intersects both sets of activities. There is an expectations trap, as developers will not construct housing unless they expect the city to grow (and other market failures in the housing market to be ironed out), and undersupply of housing is one of the factors undermining the profitability of tradable sector production, which in turn retards the growth of the city.

Countries in Sub-Saharan Africa are urbanizing rapidly. Some 472 million people live in urban areas across Africa, and this number is expected to double in the next 25 years (United Nations 2014). By 2030, Sub-Saharan African cities need to create 160 million additional jobs.

Africa's pattern of urbanization, however, is different from that underway in other developing regions, where increased urbanization has been accompanied by a rise in manufacturing activities. As two-thirds of Africa's urbanization still needs to happen, now is the moment to make African cities more productive.

Theory and evidence combine to paint a challenging picture of the current state of African cities. The urban landscape of African cities has generated economic inefficiencies that have increased urban costs. Low expectations have resulted in lack of investment in residential, commercial, and industrial buildings and in infrastructure. Such shortfalls in structures makes cities costly and forestall economic agglomeration.

References

Bleakley, H., and J. Lin. 2012. "Portage and Path Dependence." *Quarterly Journal of Economics* 127 (2): 587–644.

Fay, M., and C. Opal. 2000. "Urbanization without Growth: A Not-So-Uncommon Phenomenon." Policy Research Working Paper 2412, World Bank, Washington, DC.

Gollin, D., R. Jedwab, and D. Vollrath. 2016. "Urbanization with and without Industrialization." *Journal of Economic Growth* 21 (1): 35–70.

Henderson, J. V., T. Regan, and A. J. Venables. 2016. "Building the City: Sunk Capital, Sequencing, and Institutional Frictions." CEPR Discussion Papers 11211, Center for Economic and Policy Research, Washington, DC.

Henderson, J. V., and A. J. Venables. 2009. "The Dynamics of City Formation." *Review of Economic Dynamics* 12 (2): 233–254.

Jedwab, R. 2013. *Urbanization without Structural Transformation: Evidence from Consumption Cities in Africa.*

Jedwab, R., E. Kerby, and A. Moradi 2015. "History, Path Dependence and Development: Evidence from Colonial Railroads, Settlers and Cities in Kenya." *Economic Journal.* Accepted Author Manuscript.

Jedwab, R., and A. Moradi. 2016. "The Permanent Effects of Transportation Revolutions in Poor Countries: Evidence from Africa." *Review of Economics and Statistics* 98 (2): 268–284.

Koopman, R., Z. Wang, and S.-J. Wei. 2008. *How Much of China's Exports is Really Made in China?* U.S. International Trade Commission. Office of Economics Working Paper, Washington, DC.

Linden, G., K. Kraemer, and J. Dedrick 2007. "Who Captures Value in a Global Innovation System? The Case of Apple's iPod." Personal Computing Industry Center, Irvine, CA.

Nallari, R., B. Griffith, and S. Yusuf. 2012. *Geography of Growth: Spatial Economics and Competitiveness.* Washington, DC: World Bank.

United Nations. 2014. *World Urban Prospects, the 2014 Revision.* New York: United Nations.

Venables, A. J. 2016. "Breaking into Tradables: Urban Form and Urban Function in a Developing City." University of Oxford, United Kingdom.

Part 3

Springing Africa from Its Low Urban Development Trap

Chapter 5

Clarifying property rights and strengthening urban planning

Chapter 6

Scaling up and coordinating investments in physical structures and infrastructure

To create an internationally competitive tradable sector, African cities must cease to be crowded, disconnected, and costly, and instead become livable, connected, and productive. How?

The answer lies in swift action by mayors and ministers to enhance the functioning of land markets (the factor market most urgently in need of reform) and to strengthen urban planning, regulation, and enforcement — followed by actions to coordinate and scale up investment in cities' physical structures and infrastructure. In short, city leaders must make decisive and concerted efforts to:

1. **Reform urban land markets and regulations.** Leaders can act immediately to improve the institutional and capacitive structures that govern land markets and land use — structures that depend on human capital, and that will ultimately determine a city's ability to mobilize investment capital. Leaders should do this by:

    *   Simplifying and clarifying transfers of property rights among land market participants (freeing these procedures from today's unclear, overlapping property-rights regimes).

    *   Supporting the effective management of urban development through foresighted planning, realistic regulation, and predictable enforcement.

2. **Coordinate and increase early infrastructure investments.** After taking firm and decisive steps to improve institutional structures, authorities can build on those efforts to adapt physical structures and infrastructure — including housing, transport infrastructure (including roads), and basic services — to a future of urban productivity. Leaders should do this by:

    *   Making infrastructure investments early, and coordinating them with land market intentions and with the plans and regulations that guide physical structures (ensuring that infrastructure investments will be integrated with the growth of neighborhoods and structures in predictable ways).

    *   Intensifying these early, coordinated infrastructure investments to take full advantage of scale economies in housing, transport, and services (avoiding inefficient and fragmented investments that diverge from market demand).

Both efforts should aim at structural improvements in the allocation of a city's land, capital, and structures. Their aim should be to achieve urban development at scale and for scale, while fostering economic specialization. Chapters 5 and 6 provide findings from emerging empirical studies on the key policy areas outlined above.

Chapter 5

Over the next 20 years, the growth of Africa's urban populations will propel new demand for infrastructure, housing and other physical structures, and amenities. To meet this new demand, city leaders and planners will need adaptable strategies. Plans and regulations should allow the best use of land — but they must also permit uses, and users, to change over time, as demand evolves further.

Three key considerations are as follows:

> *How to handle land and property rights*
> *How to manage land valuation and prices*
> *How to strengthen land use and urban planning*

Africa's cities are not developing in a well-planned fashion. Instead, they grow informally and develop informally. Public planning is ineffective; private development is hobbled or repelled by opaque or inappropriate regulations. Informal dwellings house not only poor but also middle-income households, essentially because of constraints on formal land markets. These land market constraints also do much to explain the typical African city's spatial fragmentation and the relatively low capital investment near its core.

The crowded streets of African cities attest to a lack of formative, integrated urban plans. Traffic congestion stems from limited road infrastructure, limited parking, and the lack of formal addresses. And the informality and small scale of public and collective transport in African cities indicate that these networks are mostly reactive — they emerge in response to the city's growth. They do not structure growth, as did the introduction of rail infrastructure or streetcars in well-developed cities like Paris and London (Brooks and Lutz 2013).

Households in African cities find it difficult to locate outside the central business district because the lack of paved roads makes commuting from the periphery impractical (Felkner, Lall, and Lee 2016). Increased investments in roads could increase productivity, even while affecting commuting costs and times differently across the city — but only if such investments are well thought through in advance. Similarly, African cities have an urgent need for well-planned and forward-thinking transportation systems. All transportation development plans are not equal.[17]

The lack of physical and technological structures — housing, services, and transportation — in Africa's cities points to the need for planning capacity. Without proper local planning guidance, it is impossible to coordinate and implement infrastructure, public amenities, and other investments. No planning, or poor planning, is one of the fundamental reasons why African cities are too crowded, too disconnected, and too costly to attract regional and global investors and trading partners.

Reforming land markets is a necessity in any policy effort to transform city growth patterns — to get African urbanization right. Success will bring large payoffs in economic efficiency. If land market reform enables Africa's cities to tap the potential of rising land values, the ability to finance infrastructure and other public goods will follow.[18]

Why African cities fail to attract investment: An urban planner's perspective

Beyond the poor connective infrastructure discussed in chapter 2, three features of African cities directly explain their low appeal to investors, which undermines their prospects for economic development. The first feature is capital misallocation. The second is institutional constraints. The third is ineffectual property rights.

Capital misallocation

Central to the problem of "cities out of service" is capital allocation in urban structures, which is shaped by sunk capital, sequencing, and institutional frictions. Because urban investments in structures are durable and long-lived, investment decisions are based on expectations about future land rents, as driven by future incomes, populations, and policy.

Henderson, Regan, and Venables (2016) develop a core analytic model to examine these issues. It shows the importance of expectations in shaping urban investment decisions: Low expectations of the city's future development distort investment levels below their efficient levels. Investment is deterred by market failures, including inappropriate regulation and land titling or capital market imperfections. The consequences of such imperfections are long-lasting.

Institutional constraints

Restrictive regulations are strangling development in African cities, discouraging investment and limiting formal housing options for the poor. For example, Dar es Salaam (box 5.1) requires lots to be at least 400 square meters. Anyone who wants to buy a stand-alone house in the formal sector near the center must be able to afford a lot this size. The only ownership alternative is informal — and one-fourth of Dar es Salaam's homeowners have no documentary proof of ownership (World Bank 2015d).

Another kind of regulatory burden can be imposed by the system of land ownership itself. A majority of land in Kampala, Uganda operates under a complex land tenure regime that recognizes independent rights over land and structures, giving rise to legal disputes and blocking development (Muinde 2013).

BOX 5.1

Inappropriate building regulations hamper affordability

Land use regulations, zoning, and building regulations are some of the most valuable tools for governments to guide development and promote livability. Yet certain interventions in urban land markets can negatively affect affordability and access to serviced land if they are not benchmarked against what the local population can afford to pay. Evidence from around the world indicates that inappropriate minimum standards actually increase informal development, even on formally titled land.

Many cities in India have imposed strict limits for building heights. In Bangalore, the policy resulted in horizontal low-density expansion of built-up area and increased housing costs by 3–6 percent of median household income. In Mumbai, which is constrained by the surrounding topography, the impact was even more pronounced. Building heights were limited to less

than one-tenth those allowed in other Asian cities. The restriction increased housing prices by an estimated 15–20 percent of income, according to Buckley and Kalarickal (2006).

In Dar es Salaam, inappropriate size regulations make the majority of buildings de facto illegal, regardless of formal land title or the quality of the structure. Developments that are out of compliance (building areas below 375 square meters) are condemned to be unplanned and excluded from water and sanitation services, making it extremely costly and difficult to redevelop the land later legally. A more effective approach would be to rationalize standards for development based on performance (for example, structural integrity) and affordability by the local population.

BOX FIGURE 5.1.1

Distribution of buildings in Dar es Salaam by distance from center

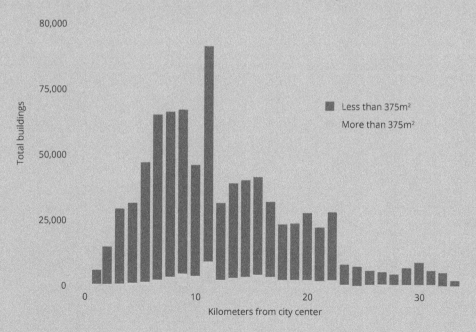

Source: World Bank Staff calculations

119

In Nigeria, high costs and burdensome regulations have stymied the formal development of urban land. Titling expenses alone can reach as high as 30 percent of construction costs in Lagos and Port Harcourt, where total transaction costs range from 12 to 36 percent of a property's value (World Bank 2015c). Zoning can also push people out of the formal sector and into unplanned development. In Ibadan in 2000, researchers found that 83 percent of homes violated city zoning rules (Arimah and Adeagbo 2000).

As challenging as the stranglehold of overregulation is the lack of connective infrastructure. Given faster and more affordable transportation, more African city dwellers might forgo a downtown location for a house with better amenities a few kilometers from the center. But long commutes are an obstacle for most residents (see chapter 2). Some people live on the outskirts of the city, but many others settle for more centrally located informal housing — the only affordable kind.

In Dar es Salaam, for example, people live in Tandale — the informal district — not for its services and amenities but despite its lack of them. Its central location puts people close to where most jobs and economic opportunities are. In 2010, Dar es Salaam's informal housing areas were on average much closer than formal ones to commercial and industrial areas (figure 5.1). Similar evidence is found for Kigali. Across cities, households are willing to compromise on living conditions. In Nairobi, most residents of informal settlements have jobs and comparatively high levels of education relative to those living in formal housing, yet their living conditions remain basic (Gulyani, Talukdar, and Jack 2010). This choice probably reflects the premium they place on accessibility.

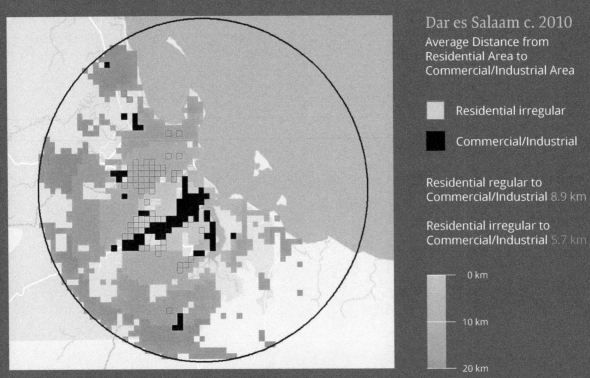

FIGURE 5.1

Average distances to commercial and industrial areas from formal and informal settlements in Dar es Salaam, Tanzania and Kigali, Rwanda

Dar es Salaam c. 2010
Average Distance from Residential Area to Commercial/Industrial Area

Residential irregular

Commercial/Industrial

Residential regular to Commercial/Industrial 8.9 km

Residential irregular to Commercial/Industrial 5.7 km

0 km

10 km

20 km

Source: Antos, Lall, and Lozano-Gracia 2016.

Ineffectual property rights

Clear rights to urban land are a precondition for the emergence of a formal land market, whether formal, customary, or informal. But many African cities struggle with overlapping and sometimes contradictory systems, severely constraining urban land redevelopment and imposing high costs. And even where formal titles or clear land rights exist, basic mapping, geographic, or ownership information is often inaccurate or land records maintained poorly, causing disputes.

Applying for formal recognition can also be a tedious process. Land administration systems (such as registries and cadaster records) are incomplete and underused for enforcing legal claims and landholders' fiscal obligations, so lenders cannot always use land as collateral. In Sub-Saharan Africa, only 10 percent of rural land is registered (Byamugisha 2013).

In West Africa, only 2–3 percent of land is held with a government-registered title (Toulmin 2005).

The lack of a proper registration system prevents urban land markets from functioning well. It creates obstacles to the raising of capital for development and investment — and to the raising of revenue by the local authority.

These dysfunctions distort the price and availability of land for efficient urban development, prompting recourse to informality in building. Henderson, Regan, and Venables (2016) distinguish between formal and informal sector construction. Formal buildings involve sunk capital costs, can be built tall, and are hard to modify once constructed. Because they are durable, investment decisions are based on expectations about future land rents, as driven by future incomes and populations. As the city grows, there will be periodic demolition and redevelopment of formal

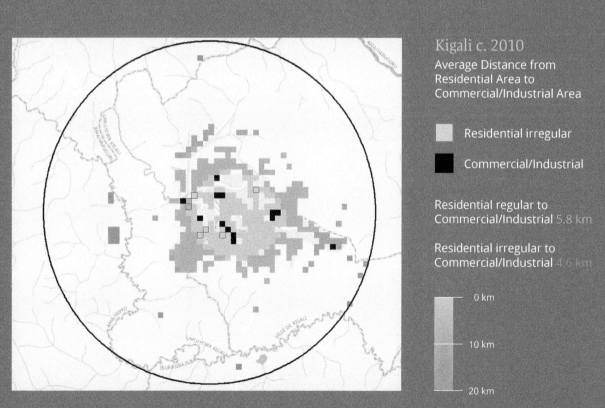

Kigali c. 2010

Average Distance from Residential Area to Commercial/Industrial Area

Residential irregular

Commercial/Industrial

Residential regular to Commercial/Industrial 5.8 km

Residential irregular to Commercial/Industrial 4.6 km

0 km

10 km

20 km

Source: Antos, Lall, and Lozano-Gracia 2016.

areas. The city may also contain informal or slum structures. Given the technology and materials used in construction, these building are not likely to be built tall; they can be rebuilt and adjusted after their initial construction. The capital used in such structures is not sunk but remains malleable.

The cost of converting informal to formal land use varies over time and even across properties in the city. The process can be hindered by institutional issues. Barriers can include poor enforcement of land rights when multiple tenure systems coexist. In slums, rules are often "split between a galaxy of private sector actors, landlords, chiefs, bureaucrats and gangs" (Marx, Stocker, and Suri 2013, quoted in Henderson, Regan, and Venables 2016). The core insight from the framework of Henderson, Reagan, and Venables is that urban form (the size and shape of the city) is sensitive to the expected returns to durable investments and to the costs of converting informal to formal sector usage.

More broadly, the lack of affordable formal housing in Africa's cities stems partly from the difficulty of adding new stock onto the old with the building methods now in use. Housing and other structures in Africa employ cheap methods that do not allow substituting capital for land (Bernard, Bird, and Venables 2016). By contrast, in much of developing East Asia — as in developed countries — building methods allow for various floor areas and building heights. In Bangkok, for example, the average height of the tallest buildings is 62 floors; in Kuala Lumpur it is 84 floors. In contrast, in Dar es Salaam it is just 15 floors.

More than 60 percent of African's urban population lives in areas with some combination of overcrowding, low-quality housing, and inadequate access to clean water and sanitation (UN Habitat 2015). The result is urban dysfunction that, across the region, keeps expectations low and deters investment.

The example of Nairobi

In Nairobi, informal building volume per unit of land is lower than formal development (map 5.1). As land prices decrease with distance to the center, the gains from conversion are larger closer to the central business district and usually exceed the cost of conversion. For example, converting informal slums to formal structure would increase building volumes by up to 148 percent at 2 kilometers from the center and by 53 percent at 4 kilometers from the center (Henderson, Reagan, and Venables 2016). Most slum structures are built with unimproved materials (57 percent of slum dwellings are built with sheet metal and 15 percent of mud and wood) that are cheaper but not suitable for taller buildings. Ninety percent of formal residences are built with stone, brick, or cement block. There has been redevelopment up to about 2 kilometers from the center in Nairobi; beyond that distance, development is much less than what the model of Henderson, Reagan, and Venables (2016) predicts.

They argue that the 1,000 acres covered by the Kibera slum (3.5 kilometers from downtown Nairobi) is too large and too complex for conversion costs to be tractable. The land is owned by the government but managed by slumlords and political elites who control the land and have no interest in redevelopment (because they do not own the land), which would take away their very profitable slum business. Rough calculations based on 1,000 acres of land at 4 kilometers from the center suggest that the gains of converting Kibera would reach $1 billion. The surplus generated by such a transformation could be used to help relocate tenants and potentially buy off the people blocking redevelopment, but transformation would require making deals with slumlords.

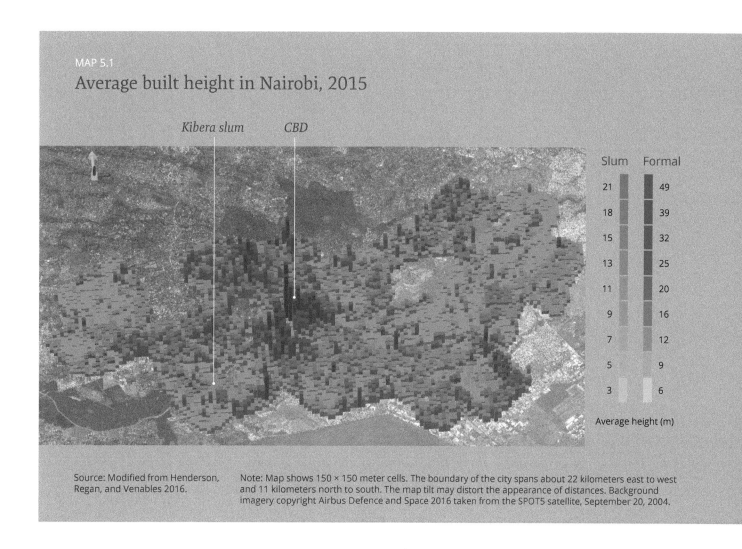

MAP 5.1

Average built height in Nairobi, 2015

Kibera slum   *CBD*

Slum	Formal
21	49
18	39
15	32
13	25
11	20
9	16
7	12
5	9
3	6

Average height (m)

Source: Modified from Henderson, Regan, and Venables 2016.

Note: Map shows 150 × 150 meter cells. The boundary of the city spans about 22 kilometers east to west and 11 kilometers north to south. The map tilt may distort the appearance of distances. Background imagery copyright Airbus Defence and Space 2016 taken from the SPOT5 satellite, September 20, 2004.

Clear land and property rights

Clear rights to urban land are a precondition for the emergence of a formal land market. Informal, illegal markets can function in almost any conditions. But informality in land markets is distinctively limiting. Informal asset transactions are viable only if the purchaser can rely on some enduring, extra-legal means of having new ownership recognized (such as sanction by the local community). In contrast, a formal market does not merely offer purchasers the protection of the state, it also generates the public good of accurate valuation through transactions that are readily observable and recorded.

African cities struggle with overlapping and sometimes contradictory property rights systems — formal, customary, and informal (map 5.2). Under the customary rules for land tenure that control much

peri-urban and urban land, property rights depend on the consent of local chiefs or family elders. Many countries (mostly in Central Africa) have a wide range of land rights systems in urban and suburban areas (traditional, customary, collective, religious, and "modern"). This diversity is problematic.

Tenure insecurity, measured as the share of the population with no formally recognized land tenure rights, increased in Africa from about 55 percent in 2009 to about 66 percent in 2012, with "strong tension" more prevalent (and rising) in larger agglomerations than in average-sized towns (figure 5.2). Overlapping property rights are common in Durban, South Africa (box 5.2) and in Ghana, Lesotho, Mozambique, and Zambia.

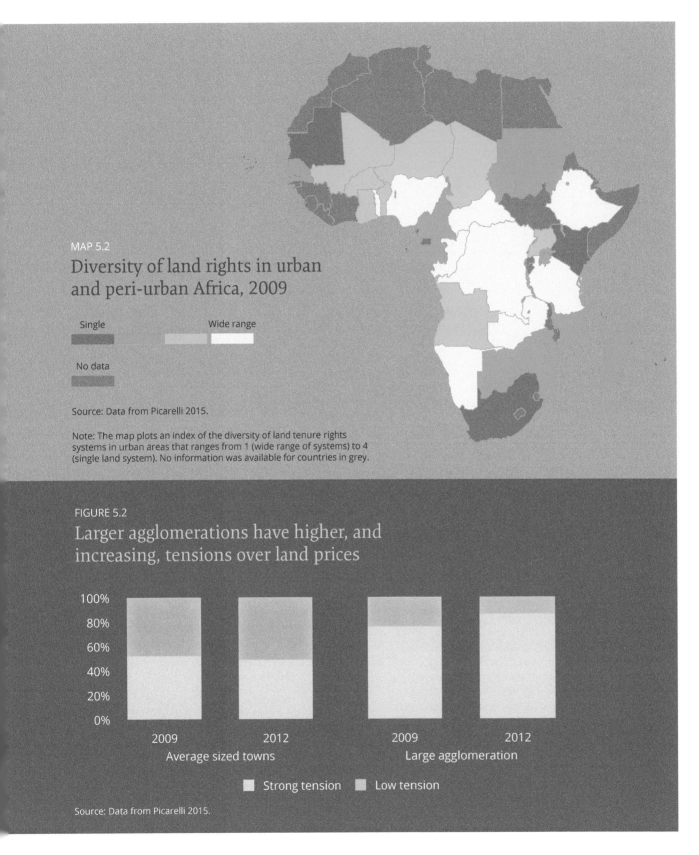

MAP 5.2

Diversity of land rights in urban and peri-urban Africa, 2009

Single   Wide range

No data

Source: Data from Picarelli 2015.

Note: The map plots an index of the diversity of land tenure rights systems in urban areas that ranges from 1 (wide range of systems) to 4 (single land system). No information was available for countries in grey.

FIGURE 5.2

Larger agglomerations have higher, and increasing, tensions over land prices

Average sized towns — 2009, 2012
Large agglomeration — 2009, 2012

Legend: Strong tension, Low tension

Source: Data from Picarelli 2015.

BOX 5.2

Customary land rights in Durban, South Africa

Customary property rights systems retain a strong influence on land tenure in Africa, particularly in peri-urban and rural areas. For example, in Durban, areas formally administered by the eThekwini Municipality occupy just 36 percent of the eThekwini Metropolitan Area (EMA). Another 27 percent of the EMA falls under non-scheme agriculture areas, administered jointly by local and provincial governments. The remaining 37 percent of the EMA is jointly administered by the municipality and the traditional authority (the Ingonyama Trust Board), with primary responsibilities falling to the latter.

The municipality and the board operate two entirely different and separate administrative regimes, and their planning and implementation systems are not aligned. The link to the formal administration occurs at the central level, where the board reports to the national Minister for Rural Development and Land Reform. At the local level, the board in effect decides how to govern and manage activities within its lands. The board is required to inform and seek advice from the municipality on land use decisions within the Trust Lands, but such coordination does not occur consistently, a marker of how hard it is to overcome entrenched divisions.

Source: Huang 2016.

Kampala, Uganda also labors under multiple systems (map 5.3), including the dual-ownership Mailo system (instituted by the British government in 1900), which helps makes Uganda's regime among the world's most complicated (Muinde 2013). Under Mailo, the tenant owns the structures on each plot while the Mailo landowner — typically the Buganda Kingdom but possibly one of a few other private landholders — owns the land. The tenant pays below-market rent, determined by the Land Board at the Ministry of Lands. Developing the land requires permission from the landowner and the structure owner.

Recent research led by Tony Venables (as part of this project) examines the broader welfare consequences of the land tenure system in Kampala. Bernard, Bird, and Venables (2016) developed a spatial computable general equilibrium model for the city. They find that land tenure and geographic constraints explain up to 38 percent of the variation in productivity and 48 percent of the variation in amenity value across Greater Kampala. The negative effect is particularly strong for customary land tenure, which if converted to leasehold would increase productivity by 3 percent in manufacturing, 4 percent in business services, and 11 percent in local services. A parish's share of Mailo land also has a detrimental effect on service sector productivity, especially local services.

Mailo tenure is prominent close to the central business district and thus particularly bad for productivity. Productivity in local services would rise 8 percent by switching entirely to leasehold from Mailo, removing the strict regulation of freehold areas that may well impede small businesses in setting up easily.

Turning to where people choose to live, customary land is less attractive than leasehold land for high-skilled workers. Mailo land is associated with high residential densities of low-skilled workers. Paired with the fact that Mailo land has a negative impact on local services, this finding suggests that this land is particularly residential and undersupplied with small shops relative to other areas in the city. In Kampala City, the high end of the skilled distribution seems to value settling on Mailo land, suggesting that people make a tradeoff between being close to the central business district and having a tenure system without incentives to invest in better housing (under which mainly low-skill, low-income people informally reside).

MAP 5.3

Land tenure systems in Greater Kampala

Freehold
Owner has full rights.

Leasehold
Leaseholder has rights for 49 years. Needs approval of the Land Board for use, transfer, and development.

Customary
Residents gain rights by long-term presence, but rights are hard to convert to free- or leasehold. Cannot be used as collateral or redeveloped.

Mailo
Dual ownership: Tenants own the structures and landowner the land. Tenants pay below-market rents (determined by the Land Board). Development needs approval from both parties, and both are compensated.

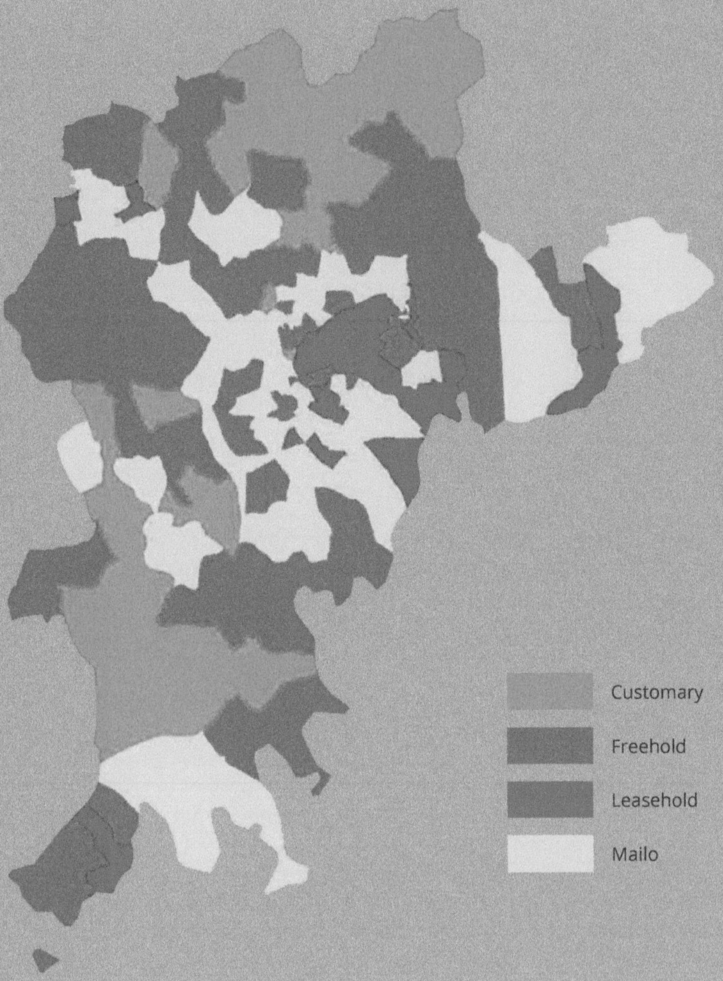

Customary

Freehold

Leasehold

Mailo

Source: Bernard, Bird, and Venables 2016.

Across Africa, when barriers to urban land access arise from an overly complex property rights regime, they impede consolidation of plots and transfer of land among users and among uses. Firms cannot readily buy downtown land to convert it from low-density residential use to higher-density apartments or build clusters of new commercial structures. Land transactions are long, costly, and complicated (World Bank 2015d). Such market constraints reduce the collateral value of structures, giving developers little incentive to invest in residential height while tempting all parties to make informal arrangements.

Unclear land rights severely constrain urban land redevelopment throughout the continent, imposing high costs. In Nairobi, the cost of misallocating 1,000 acres of land within 4 kilometers of the city center — the edge of Kibera — is huge (box 5.3). Unclear land rights also impede the collateral value of buildings constructed on the land, constraining investment in residential structures.

BOX 5.3

Welfare costs of stymied redevelopment in Nairobi

In 1912, the British government set up Kibera as a settlement for Nubians who fought in the King's African Rifles regiment of the British Army. Nubians were the only people with settlement permits for the land until independence, in 1969, when the Kenyan government revoked their claims. Other migrants, who never had permits, settled informally on the land not directly occupied by the Nubians. Today Kibera is one of the largest slums in Africa, with 600,000 inhabitants.

Failure to convert this land from informal to formal uses imposes high welfare costs. Kibera is located on some of Nairobi's most desirable land. The welfare cost of misallocating 1,000 acres within 4 kilometers of the city center — the edge of Kibera — amounts to $1 billion, or about $200 per person in Greater Nairobi (about 70 percent of Kenya's per capita GDP).

Source: Henderson, Regan, and Venables 2016.

Table 5.1 Percentage of land registered and number of days required to transfer property in selected countries and regions

Country	Percentage of land registered	Number of days to transfer property
Rwanda	70–100	25
Kenya	35	73
Uganda	18	52
Tanzania	5	68
Sub-Saharan Africa	10	65
Organisation for Economic Co-operation and Development	70	30

Source: World Bank 2014.

Low land registration (table 5.1) may result partly from cumbersome, expensive registration and transfer systems loaded with survey expenses and fees, which make registration unaffordable for many (Toulmin 2005). The principal obstacles to improved land governance in Africa include land grabs, poor documentation, inefficient land administration, a lack of transparency, and low capacity and demand for professional land surveyors (Byamugisha 2013).

The good news is that African countries are taking steps to clarify land rights and strengthening land administration (box 5.4). Botswana took the bold step of regularizing customary lands in 2008, partly because the land boards faced challenges to administering tribal land. Zambia passed a new planning bill in 2015, extending planning controls across state and customary land, and designating all local authorities as planning authorities. Namibia recognizes traditional leaders as part of the formal land system; they are designated by the country's president, with their details published in the government gazette (World Bank 2015d).

BOX 5.4
Recent actions to improve land administration and common knowledge in Africa

Improving the reach of land registries

- Since 2005, Rwanda has implemented comprehensive land tenure reform that has shown early success. Between 2005 and 2012, it pursued its nationwide program to issue land titles based on photomapping technology, at a cost of less than $10 per parcel. Madagascar, Namibia, and Tanzania have undertaken similar efforts (Byamugisha 2013).

- Tanzania surveyed all its communal lands and registered 60 percent of them, at a cost of $500 per village. Ghana and Mozambique have begun to follow Tanzania's example (Byamugisha 2013).

- Ethiopia issued certificates for 20 million parcels of land at less than $1 per parcel and mapped them onto a cadastral index map at less than $5 per parcel in 2003–05 (CAHF 2013).

Streamlining registration

- In 2009, Kenya adopted a new land policy that strives to streamline land administration processes by reducing the stamp duty, from 25 percent of the principal amount to 5 percent; providing value added tax exemptions for developments with more than 20 low cost units; and reducing the tax on mortgages, from 0.2 percent to 0.1 percent (Johnson and Matela 2011).

- The introduction of Lesotho's Land Administration Authority in 2012 improved land registration by reducing wait times and improving application turnaround. It gained general support from land-holding communities (Byamugisha 2013).

- Computerizing land records and registration systems helped cut the number of days to transfer property in Ghana (from 169 to 34) and Uganda (from 227 to 48) (Byamugisha 2013).

Improving tenure security among informally settled populations

- In 2012, Namibia passed the Flexible Land Tenure Act, which allows communities to obtain blocks of multiple plots and a "starter title" that grants perpetual occupancy and transfer rights. This act is aimed at the 30 percent of Namibian residents who live in informal settlements (CAHF 2013). Residents can also apply for full, mortgageable land titles. Upon receipt of title, the communities are responsible for upgrading the site infrastructure. The legislation is regarded as innovative in its recognition of incremental tenure and building methodology (Byamugisha 2013).

- In 2011, Senegal passed a new Land Tenure Act, under which people with temporary occupancy permits in urban areas can convert the permits into permanent title deeds at no cost. Improved tenure security further helps increase housing investment and improvement, access to housing finance, and the activity of the formal land market.

- Kenya, Lesotho, and Tanzania are using bulk surveying and land use planning approaches to regularize tenure in slums (Byamugisha 2013).

Source: World Bank 2015d.

Some countries and cities are developing hybrid regimes to make formal and customary administration more compatible. For example, in Nigerian states with largely Muslim populations, the emir's representatives subdivide and allocate land with the help of volunteer professionals from the government (an example is the city of Rigasa, in the extreme west of Kaduna [Igabi Local Government Area]). In Ethiopia, local officials play a dual role for the local authority and for households. It could be formalized and extended to land subdivision and site-infrastructure-reservation authority. A similar pattern is evident in Ghana, where local authority professionals survey the land for the chiefs, who allocate it, in a manner also seen in Malawi and Zambia (World Bank 2015b). Future urban redevelopers in Africa may learn from the successes of two approaches — land sharing and land readjustment — in Asian cities (box 5.5).

BOX 5.5

Land sharing and readjustment: Two ways to include residents in urban redevelopment plans

Land sharing was used in Bangkok in the 1970s and 1980s, when rapid economic growth drove up urban land prices. Many slums were in desirable and accessible urban areas; the government brokered seven land-sharing deals with slum dwellers, accommodating commercial development without displacing the residents. Existing development was to be densified, enabling verticalization of low-rise or low-density residential uses and the opening up of some of the land for new development (Rabe 2010).

The deals — struck in cases where land rights had long been disputed by landowners and 10,000 slum dwellers — allowed the building of high rises for existing residents, releasing other portions of the land for lucrative real estate development. In all seven cases, the slum dwellers paid for part of the construction through a loan program. Land sharing can work both for squatter households, who gain the right to remain on the site (though in new, multifamily, medium- to high-rise housing), and landowners, who recover and benefit from part of their land (Rabe 2010).

Land readjustment has been used in the Republic of Korea, Japan, and Germany to assemble and plan privately owned land on the peri-urban fringe and develop it with infrastructure and services. In the Republic of Korea, 95 percent of urban land delivery between 1962 and 1981 occurred through land readjustment. In Japan, 40 percent of the total annual supply of urban building plots from 1977 to 2000 was secured in the same manner (Povey and Lloyd-Jones 2000). In land readjustment, the government pools privately owned parcels in an area and prepares a land use plan, designating spaces for public infrastructure and services such as roads and open spaces. It then implements the plan, providing trunk infrastructure, and distributes lots to landowners, proportional to the original parcels but smaller (for example, 50–60 percent). Because the new lot is serviced, it is worth more than the landowner's original parcel. The government retains selected, strategic land parcels, which it auctions or sells at market rates to recover the cost of infrastructure and service delivery (Lozano-Gracia and others 2013). Although land readjustment is useful for urban regeneration where land ownership is divided among many private parties — and avoids the need for the government to buy land outright — it presupposes strong local institutions and a sound legislative framework.

Source: Amirtahmasebi and others 2015.

Land valuation and prices

The pricing of land on the market depends partly on policies, which must be designed with great care. Taxes, charges, and subsidies can be used to complement regulatory controls on land use, creating financial incentives and disincentives. Revenues, such as those from land-based financing, can be used to finance administrative costs and infrastructure. Implementation tools such as capital investment, budgets, and phasing plans can help with planning.

Removing data and legal obstacles

Land valuation is outdated or incomplete in many African countries. In Kenya, the valuation and rating system has not been updated since colonial times, and property rolls are outdated: Mombasa's was last updated in 1992 and Nairobi's in 1981 (World Bank 2016a). In Ghana, property valuations have not changed in the past 15–20 years (World Bank 2015b). Some cities in Ethiopia do not even have such rolls (World Bank 2015a). In Malawi, only ratable areas are listed and valued for tax purposes. However, over time, some nonratable areas have become indistinguishable from ratable areas.

As a result, Lilongwe City Council's property valuation roll is estimated to list about 45 percent of the properties in the city and Blantyre's lists about a third (World Bank 2016b).

In Malawi, the Local Government Act prescribes that the preparation and updating of valuation rolls can be done only by registered valuers (that is, valuers registered under the Land Economy Surveyors, Valuers, Estate Agents and Auctioneers Act), but there are very few in the country, pushing up costs. Property valuation methods are also inappropriate and cumbersome, relying on individual, rather than mass, valuations (World Bank 2016b). In Nigeria, the sales comparison approach is the preferred method of valuation, but most cities lack the information on transactions needed (World Bank 2015c). In Kenya, the system relies on individual valuations that can be subject to ratepayer objection before the roll is finalized, leading to very outdated property rolls in the more urban counties (World Bank 2016a). Some laws even prohibit (or severely limit) land fees and taxes (World Bank 2015d).

Even if land revenue laws were sound, cities would still have little power to leverage land for revenue, because fiscal cadaster records and capacities are weak. Moreover, cities' reliance on central government transfers means that they have few incentives to make such efforts. Given the inadequacy of revenues from intergovernmental transfers, Africa's cities should consider land and property taxes to finance urban infrastructure and public services (box 5.6).

Improving tax collection

Several cities are making improvements in their tax collection systems. In Blantyre, Malawi, minor improvements, including direct payment to a commercial bank, have led to a sharp increase in collection rates, from less than 50 percent in 2011/12 to almost 60 percent in 2013/14. The Mzuzu City Council in Malawi set a more complete reform that doubled tax collection in just one year, from MWK 120 million to more than MWK 220 million. The reform of its property tax administration system included a low-cost mass valuation method that used a Geographic Information System (GIS) and follow-up in the field by local staff. It increased the number of assessed properties from 8,000 to almost 40,000 (World Bank 2016b).

In 2004, Hargeisa, Somaliland began to create a land and property database and a method for classifying and generating property tax invoices. Data were stored in a GIS database for quick retrieval and mapping, allowing the local government to begin tax collections very quickly. The property survey,

BOX 5.6

Leveraging land values to finance urban infrastructure

To be economically dense and well connected, Africa's cities will need huge investment in infrastructure. Although revenues from the intergovernmental transfer system have been the mainstay of urban public finance, there is a need to explore how cities can leverage the value of their assets — mainly land — to finance infrastructure and provide public goods and services.

Land-based infrastructure financing has the greatest payoff where there is rapid urban growth. Rapid growth causes land prices to rise rapidly, creating an opportunity to generate significant revenue. Yet rapid growth also magnifies infrastructure investment needs, requiring substantial sources of development finance. France, Japan, and the United States used land-based financing most heavily during periods of rapid urban growth, when there were leaps in the scale of urban investment. Taxes on land can also improve the efficiency of land use, because property owners have an incentive to develop the land to its most profitable use commensurate with the market value of the property. Valuable downtown locations with higher land prices will experience densification and investment in residential and commercial structures.

Not only can such taxes incentivize dense urban development, they are also nondistortionary, because appreciation in land values is merely an economic rent for a scarce resource rather than a return on the economic activity of the owner. There is thus no behavior by the owner to be distorted.

Higher revenues from land and real estate can come from (a) improved valuation of land and properties closer to their market value, which deepens the tax base; (b) improved compliance, so that more property owners pay land and property taxes, which broadens the tax base; and (c) monetization of underused public land. However, setting in place land and real estate tax systems that support economic density is not straightforward. Strong institutions are essential to define property rights clearly; ensure standardized and objective methods of land valuation; and support and oversee the process of land management, land sales, and tax collection.

prepared over one year, cost only $48,500, or $0.82 per property (excluding equipment such as personal digital assistants, office computers, and software but including satellite imagery). The new system enabled the local government to increase tax collections from $60,000 in 2008 to $282,725 in 2011. Between 2006, when the GIS became operational, and 2013, the share of taxed properties increased from 5 percent to 45 percent; the number of properties on record also climbed, from 15,850 to 59,000, in five districts (UN-Habitat 2013).

In 2014, the Arusha City Council became the first of seven Tanzanian cities to switch from a manually administered own-source revenue system to a modern local government revenue collection information system integrated with a GIS platform. The new system allows the local government to use satellite data to identify taxpayers and includes an electronic invoicing system that notifies and tracks payments. The city identified 102,904 buildings with this new method, a huge increase from the 23,000 in past databases. In the first 15 months after the switch to the new system, the number of eligible taxpayers more than trebled, from 31,160 to 104,629. Within one year, the city council boosted annual revenues by 75 percent, from 2.6 billion shillings in 2012/13 to 4.6 billion shillings in 2013/14 (World Bank 2015e).

Uban planning institutions and land use regulation

Land and property rights affect the transfer of land between users; land prices determine the intensity of investments in structures. Both land transfers and land prices are affected by land use regulation and urban planning — the policies that determine how and where land is used.

Urban planning and land use regulations are central for enhancing urban connectivity, productivity, and livability because of externalities and coordination failures. Unregulated markets are unlikely to get urban densities and form right, because the productivity of firms and the job-generating aspects of increased density are positive externalities accruing freely to all, whereas the increased costs of construction, such as buildings, roads, and network utilities necessary for higher density to remain efficient, are not fully internalized by firms and households.

These market and coordination failures lead to less than optimal investment and ultimately to weaker productivity gains, less job creation, and lower wages. Further, well-functioning cities require that economies of scope and complementarities be leveraged in the provision of physical infrastructure (roads, drainage, street lighting, electricity, water, sewerage, and waste disposal) alongside policing and health care. Although each infrastructure sector and service can be addressed by appropriate government policies, addressing only one or two has little payoff if the others remain unresolved. With foresight and strong implementation, urban planning can help prevent these failures.

Strong urban planning institutions have a unique power of enforcement that is valuable in many aspects of urbanization. Strong public authorities are essential to enforce private property rights. Because building the city depends on private rights over land and structures, such enforcement is fundamental to successful urbanization. For land registers and mortgage collateral to perform their core functions of supporting a market in parcels of land, and providing finance for investment in structures, they need well-functioning on-the-ground enforcement.

Beyond enforcing property rights, public authorities are important for enforcing building regulations in two areas: coordination and information. Costs are often lower if design is standardized: Firms can coordinate on a common publicly set standard. Some features of a structure, such as its foundations, can be observed only during construction. It is therefore useful for standards on foundations to be publicly enforced, so that subsequent purchasers know what they are buying. Standardization and information make valuation easier, which enhances the collateral value of structures.

Across Africa today, urban plans and planning institutions appear ineffective. They are not coordinating investment in structures or managing the spatial form of cities. One source of difficulty is the inappropriate adoption of regulatory codes and planning models inherited from colonial regimes or imported from developed countries (Goodfellow 2013). Another problem is that plans do not give credible accounts of finance, market dynamics, or distributional impacts. Minimum lot sizes, for example, may be intended as pro-poor land use regulations, but in practice they limit households' investment choices (and in Brazil they have been associated with increased slum formation [Lall and others 2006]). Yet another challenge arises from capacity and resource constraints.

Strengthening capacity and resources for urban planning

City and national authorities will have to make tough political decisions based on technical evidence and assessments. They will need to increase urban planning capacity and resources, even given competing funding priorities. In 2011, a survey of 12 African countries found, on average, 0.89 planners for every 100,000 people (Africa Planning Association and UN-Habitat 2014) — a far lower the ratio than in three high-income countries (table 5.2). It reported that recruiting skilled urban planners in a reasonably short time is a challenge in Africa, although institutional processes may have been at fault, given that ministry-level staff have to be recruited centrally through the Ministry of Public Services. The lack of staff capacity constrains effective management. It is even more crippling to enforcement, often the greatest challenge even where all necessary structures and regulations are in place.

Addressing coordination constraints across levels of government

Urban planning has traditionally been largely the function of the central government. Only gradually since the mid- to late 1900s has decentralization gained momentum. These shifts are usually formalized through some form of local government act that empowers local governments to undertake their own urban planning activities.

However, such devolution of responsibilities is not entirely clear-cut or always accompanied by the necessary fiscal empowerment. At the local level, the systems and institutions to support inclusive and effective community participation may also be lacking.

Most African countries have vertical institutional fragmentation and a complex relationship among the multiple bodies, as exemplified by Tanzania and Uganda (figure 5.3). Both national and city-level agencies are often still involved in land and urban

Table 5.2 Ratio of registered planners to population in selected countries, circa 2011

	Population (million) 2011	No. of accredited planners	No. of planners per 100,000	Year of estimate
APA Countries				
Burkina Faso	16,970,000	14	0.08	2011
Ghana	24,970,000	150	0.60	2011
Nigeria	162,500,000	2,333	1.44	2011
Mali	15,840,000	50	0.32	2011
Kenya	41,610,000	194	0.47	2011
Uganda	34,510,000	90	0.26	2011
South Africa	50,800,000	1,690	3.33	2011
Malawi	15,300,000	30	0.20	2011
Mauritius	1,286,000	27	2.10	2011
Tanzania	46,200,000	158	0.34	2011
Zambia	13,400,000	60	0.45	2011
Zimbabwe	12,700,000	262	2.06	2011
Other countries				
United Kingdom	61,126,832	23,000	37.63	
United States	304,059,724	38,830	12.77	2010
Australia	18,972,350	4,452	23.47	2009/10
Pakistan	173,593,383	755	0.43	2010
India	1,210,193,422	2,800	0.23	2011

* Countries that regulate the registration of planning at a national level.

Source: Africa Planning Association Survey, Newman 2012.

management and in infrastructure and services provision, often with overlapping or unclear regulatory scope and responsibilities. Such ambiguities muddy lines of accountability and complicate planning, implementation, monitoring, and enforcement. A "silo" mentality across sectors and departments also perpetuates institutional fragmentation, working against coordination.

In Dar es Salaam, the central government retains multiple controls over local authorities. For example, it appoints senior personnel to run the urban authorities, and the Minister for Local Government approves the urban authorities' bylaws, budgets, and proposals for generating own-source revenue. (Most local government authorities are still largely dependent on central transfers.) Several central government agencies or national parastatals are crucial in areas under the jurisdiction of these authorities, in service provision (roads, water, electricity, drainage), land use regulations (especially land use planning and land allocation), and environmental management, for example (Kironde 2009).

Urban regulations

Urban regulations are key instruments to put urban plans into action, because they determine the pattern of future land use. Yet many African cities' urban regulations make it economically infeasible for households and firms to acquire planned land, forcing them to seek alternative land sources and contributing to extensive informal settlements. Typically, at least two forms of urban regulation need to be satisfied: administrative procedures (steps that individuals have to take in order to apply for and acquire planned land) and planning standards (such as minimum plot size) (Jones and others 2015).

Streamlining administrative procedures

Registering property in Africa is generally more time consuming and costly than in other regions of the world. This contributes to the growth of informal settlements. Formal property registration in Africa takes, on average 58.9 days and costs 9 percent of the property value. Both figures are more than twice the comparable figures in Europe and Central Asia (26.5 days and 2.8 percent) and OECD high-income countries (24.1 days and 4.4 percent). Time and costs vary widely in Africa (figure 5.4, overleaf): Rwanda's values, for example, are below even those in Europe and Central Asia, while registration can take almost 300 days in Togo and can cost more than 20 percent of the property value in the Republic of Congo.

In response to such rigidities, alternative systems and mechanisms to recognize ownership and facilitate market transactions have developed informally. In the Kampala informal settlements of Kamwokya, Mbuya, and Busega, for example, most land transfers are accompanied by a "letter of agreement" that acknowledges the transaction between seller and buyer or an informal "certificate of title" to prove ownership (Nkurunziza 2007). In many places, recognized leaders in the community witness the processes, to lend them credibility. Although these documents may not be legally recognized, they are considered socially legitimate and in some cases help reduce fraud and offer greater security to dwellers in informal settlements. Informal landholding may also be more gender sensitive, privileging widows' or orphans' rights over extended family claims, as in Malawi (UN-Habitat 2010).

Relaxing planning standards

Excessively stringent planning standards help keep housing out of the formal sector. In particular, large minimum lots make formal land unaffordable, so the poor often have no option but to illegally access and subdivide land into very small parcels, creating slums. A survey of regulations in five countries shows that Kenya has the lowest minimum plot size, at 112 square meters (figure 5.5). Rwanda does not specify a minimum size nationally; minimums are likely to be set by a local authority.

Cities outside Africa cities have set lower minimum plot sizes, to allow access to formal tenure to the poorest population and promote formal, planned growth. When Philadelphia was settled, for instance, the city authorities set a minimum plot size of about 30 square meters.

Continuous monitoring of on-the-ground conditions to determine the appropriateness of regulations drawn up would better inform the parameters to use.

FIGURE 5.3

Key players in urban development in Tanzania and Uganda

Tanzania

	Urban planning and development	Services provision (water and sewage)	Environmental management
Central	• Ministry of Lands, Housing and Human Settlements Development	• Ministry of Water • Energy, Water, Utilities Regulatory Authority • National Water Board	• Vice President's Office, Environment Division • National Environment Management Council • Ministry of Natural Resources & Tourism • Ministry of Health

Prime Minister's Office Regional Administration and Local Government

Regional	Dar es Salaam Regional Commissioner and Sectretariat	• Basin Water Boards • Catchment Committees • Water User Associations or Groups	Dar es Salaam Regional Commissioner and Sectretariat
City	• Dar City Council, Master Planning • Temeke DLA • Ilala DLA • Kinondoni DLA	• Dar es Salaam Water and Sewerage Corporation • Dar es Salaam Water and Sewerage Authority • Dar City Council, Urban Planning, Utility Services and Environment	• Dar City Council, Public Health • Temeke DLA, Public Health • Ilala DLA, Public Health • Kinondoni DLA, Public Health

Uganda

	Urban planning and development	Services provision (water and sewage)	Environmental management
Central	Ministry of Lands, Housing and Urban Development	National Wate & Sewerage Corporation	• Ministry of Water & Environment • National Environmental Management Authority • Wetlands Department
City	• Kampala Capital City Authority • Physical Planning Department, Public Health & Environment Department, Engineering Department, etc.		

Source: Huang 2016.

FIGURE 3.4

Average time and cost to register property in Sub-Saharan countries and international benchmarks in 2015

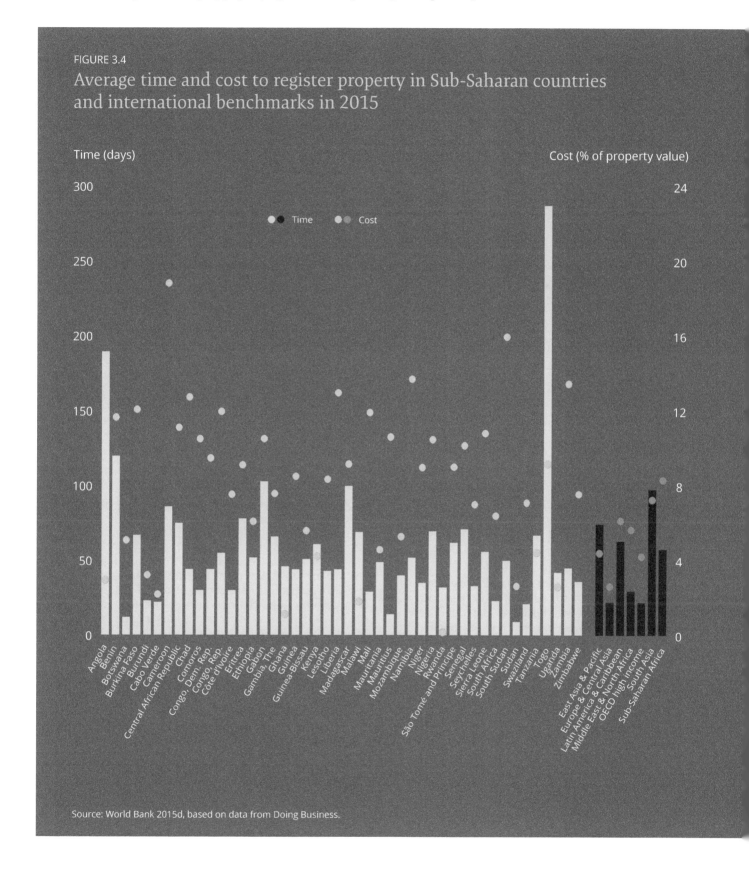

Source: World Bank 2015d, based on data from Doing Business.

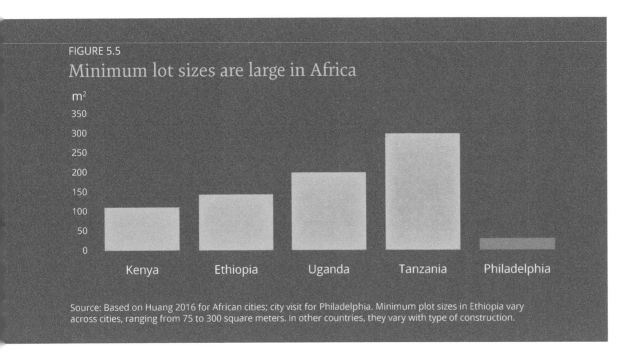

FIGURE 5.5

Minimum lot sizes are large in Africa

m²

Source: Based on Huang 2016 for African cities; city visit for Philadelphia. Minimum plot sizes in Ethiopia vary across cities, ranging from 75 to 300 square meters. In other countries, they vary with type of construction.

To build cities that work, make land markets work – nothing less will do

African cities lack the institutions needed for functional land markets, far-sighted planning, and effective regulation. As a result, their physical structures and infrastructure lag far behind the growth of the urban population. Not just housing (discussed in chapters 1–4) but other basic infrastructure and services are constantly struggling to catch up.

Africa's crowded, disconnected, and costly cities are symptoms rather than causes of urban dysfunction. They appear "closed for business" and "out of service" because of underlying distortions in the functioning of key factor and product markets. To build cities that work — cities that are livable, connected, and affordable and therefore economically dense — policy makers need to direct their attention toward the deeper structural problems that misallocate land, fragment development, and limit productivity. Above all, city and national leaders must reform land markets and urban regulations, in order to enable investment and development, reward compliance, and ensure enforcement. Titles to property must be clear and secure. Real property transactions must not be unduly costly or burdened by bureaucracy.

The key that will unlock the future for African cities is the establishment of high expectations and common knowledge through credible institutions to govern the transfer, valuation, and use of land. Such institutions are central for building economic density. Only policies that nurture them will enable Africa's cities to support dense clusters of firms; respond nimbly to changing economic circumstances; and become more kind to their residents, whose future rests in policy makers' hands.

References

Amirtahmasebi, Rana, Mariana Orloff, Sameh Wahba, and Andrew Altman. 2015. *Regenerating Urban Land. A Practitioner's Guide to Leveraging Private Investment*. World Bank, Washington, DC. Available at: http://urban-regeneration.worldbank.org/node/31.

Africa Planning Association and UN-Habitat. 2014. *The State of Planning in Africa. An Overview*. Nairobi, Kenya: UN-Habitat.

Antos, Sarah E., Nancy Lozano-Gracia, and Somik V. Lall. 2016. "The Morphology of African Cities." Draft, World Bank, Washington, DC.

Arimah, B. C., and D. Adeagbo. 2000. "Compliance with Urban Development and Planning Regulations in Ibadan, Nigeria." *Habitat International* 24 (3): 279–294.

Bernard, Louise, Julia Bird, and Anthony J. Venables. 2016. "The Urban Land Market: A Computable Equilibrium Model Applied to Kampala." Draft, July, University of Oxford.

Brooks, Leah, and Byron Lutz. 2013. "Vestiges of Transit: Urban Persistence at a Micro Scale." Trachtenberg School of Public Policy and Public Administration, George Washington University, Washington, DC.

Buckley, R. M., and J. Kalarickal. 2006. "Land Market Issues: The Mystery of Capital Revisited." *Thirty Years of World Bank Shelter Lending*. Washington DC: World Bank: 27–47.

Byamugisha, F. 2013. *Securing Africa's Land for Shared Prosperity*. Washington, DC: World Bank.

CAHF. 2013. *Housing Finance in Africa. A review of some of Africa's housing finance markets*. Parkview, South Africa: Center for Affordable Housing Finance.

Felkner, John S., Somik V. Lall, and Hyun Lee. 2016. "Synchronizing Public and Private Investment in Cities: Evidence from Addis Ababa, Dar es Salaam, Kigali and Nairobi." April 22, World Bank, Washington, DC.

Goodfellow, Tom. 2013. "Planning and Development Regulation amid Rapid Urban Growth: Explaining Divergent Trajectories in Africa." *Geoforum* 48: 83–93.

Gulyani, S., D. Talukdar and D. Jack. 2010. "Poverty, living conditions, and infrastructure access: A comparison of slums in Dakar, Johannesburg, and Nairobi." Policy Research Working Paper 5388, World Bank, Washington, DC.

Henderson, J. V., T. Regan, and A. J. Venables. 2016. "Building the City: Sunk Capital, Sequencing, and Institutional Frictions." CEPR Discussion Papers 11211, Center for Economic and Policy Research, Washington, DC.

Huang, Chyi-Yun. 2016. "Enabling Structure: Role of Public Sector and Institutions." Background paper for this report.

Johnson, S., and M. Matela. 2011. Reforming Land Administration in Lesotho: Rebuilding the Institutions. Available at: http://www.landadmin.co.uk/Documents/PN-32%20Reforming%20Land%20Administration%20in%20Lesotho.pdf.

Jones, P., J., Bird, J. Lussuga Kironde, and A. Laski. 2015. Dar es Salaam: *City Narrative*. Available at: https://collaboration.worldbank.org/docs/DOC-20828.

Kironde, J. L. 2009. Improving Land Sector Governance in Africa: The Case of Tanzania. In *Workshop on Land Governance in support of the MDGs*. World Bank, Washington DC.

Lall, S. V., H. G. Wang, and D. da Mata. 2006. *Do Urban Land Regulations Influence Slum Formation? Evidence from Brazilian Cities*. World Bank, Washington, DC.

Lavigne-Delville, P., and A. Durand-Lasserve. 2009. "Land Tenure and Development, Land Governance and Security of Tenure in Developing Countries, Summary." AFD/French Ministry for Foreign and European Affairs, Paris.

Lozano-Gracia, N., C. Young, S. V. Lall, and T. Vishwanath. 2013. "Leveraging Land to Enable Urban Transformation. Lessons from Global Experience." Policy Research Working Paper 6312, World Bank, Washington, DC.

Muinde, Damaris Kathini. 2013. "Assessing the Effects of Land Tenure on Urban Developments in Kampala." March. Available at: https://www.itc.nl/library/papers_2013/msc/upm/muinde.pdf.

Newman, K. 2012. "Benchmarking the Supply of Planning Graduates against International Practice: Its Implications for the Re-curriculation Process at the Cape Peninsula University of Technology." Paper presented at the State of Planning in Africa Conference, 17–19 September, Durban, South Africa.

Nkurunziza, E. 2007. "Informal Mechanisms for Accessing and Securing Urban Land Rights: The Case of Kampala, Uganda." *Environment and Urbanization* 19 (2): 509–526.

Picarreli, Nathalie 2015. Assessing Urban Land Tenure Rights in Sub-Saharan Africa. November 20.

Povey, M., and Lloyd Jones, T. 2000. "Mixed Use Development: Mechanisms for Sustaining the Livelihoods and Social Capital of the Urban Poor in Core Areas." Paper presented at the 17th Inter-Schools Conference on Sustainable Cities: Sustainable Development. Oxford Brookes University, Oxford, United Kingdom.

Rabe, Paul. 2010. *Land Sharing in Phnom Penh and Bangkok: Lessons from Four Decades of Innovative Slum Redevelopment Projects in Two Southeast Asian "Boom Towns*. Washington, DC: World Bank.

Toulmin, C. 2005. *Securing Land and Property Rights in Sub-Saharan Africa: The Role of Local Institutions*. Geneva: World Economic Forum.

UN-Habitat. 2008. *Mozambique Urban Sector Profile*. Nairobi, Kenya: United Nations Human Settlements Programme (UN-Habitat).

———. 2013. *Urban planning for City Leaders*. Nairobi, Kenya: United Nations Human Settlements Programme (UN-Habitat).

———. 2010. Malawi *Urban Housing Sector Profile*. Nairobi, Kenya: United Nations Human Settlements Programme (UN-Habitat).

World Bank. 2014. *Tanzania World Bank Country Economic Memorandum*. Washington, DC: World Bank.

———. 2015a. *Ethiopia Urbanization Review: Urban Institutions for a Middle-Income Ethiopia*. Washington, DC: World Bank.

———. 2015b. *Ghana Urbanization Review Overview: Rising through Cities in Ghana*. Washington, DC: World Bank.

———. 2015c. *Nigeria Urbanization Review: From Oil to Cities: Nigeria's Next Transformation*. Washington, DC: World Bank.

———. 2015d. *Stocktaking of the Housing Sector in Sub-Saharan Africa: Challenges and Opportunities*. Washington, DC: World Bank.

———. 2015e. *The Tanzanian Strategic Cities Project. Improving Local Governments' Own Source Revenues: The Arusha Experience*. Washington, DC: World Bank.

———. 2015f. *Vietnam 2035 Report*. Washington, DC: World Bank.

———. 2016a. *Kenya Urbanization Review*. Washington, DC: World Bank.

———. 2016b. *Malawi Urbanization Review: Strengthening Rural-Urban Linkages*. Washington, DC: World Bank.

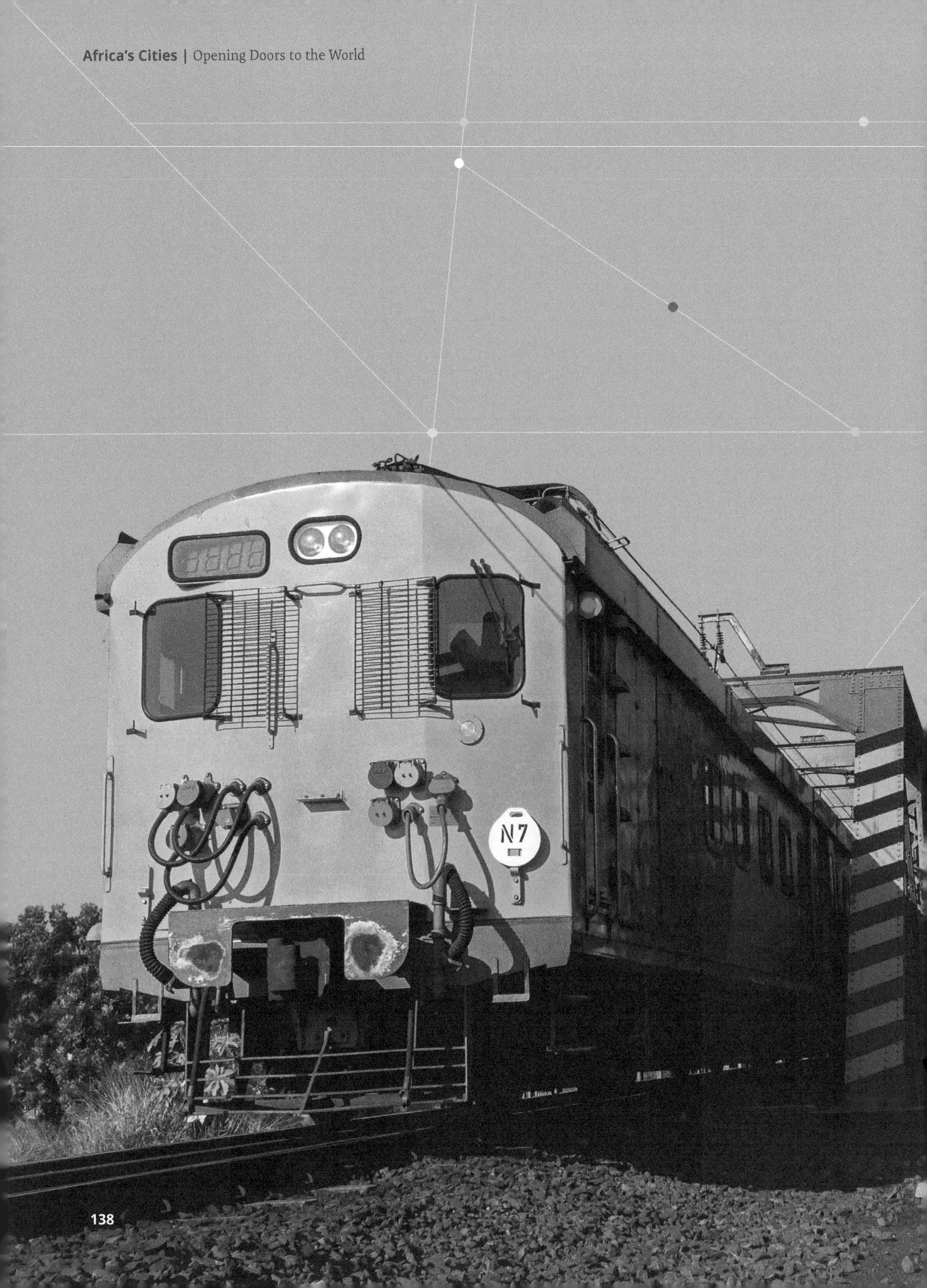
N7

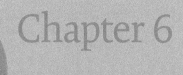

Chapter 6

At the same time as they pursue the recommendations in chapter 5, African cities have an urgent need to improve two sets of urban structures — physical and infrastructural — given that they are chronically underserviced by them. Infrastructure coverage is actually declining on some metrics, across the region.

In 2010, for example, when the urban population was 37 percent, only 34 percent of urban residents had access to piped water, down from 43 percent in 1990, when the urbanization rate was 30 percent. In 2006, the Africa Infrastructure Country Diagnostic (AICD) estimated that addressing the infrastructure backlog would require $68–$93 billion a year over the next three decades, a third of which would be for maintenance.

At the same time as they pursue the recommendations in chapter 5, African cities have an urgent need to improve two sets of urban structures — physical and infrastructural — given that they are chronically underserviced by them (Banerjee and Morella 2011). Infrastructure coverage is actually declining on some metrics, across the region (Banerjee and others 2009). In 2010, for example, when the urban population was 37 percent, only 34 percent of urban residents had access to piped water, down from 43 percent in 1990, when the urbanization rate was 30 percent (UNICEF/WHO 2012). In 2006, the Africa Infrastructure Country Diagnostic (AICD) estimated that addressing the infrastructure backlog would require $68–$93 billion a year over the next three decades, a third of which would be for maintenance (Foster and Briceño-Garmendia 2010).

Pysical structures and infrastructure pose special challenges. The first is path dependence: The costs of developing housing, infrastructure, and industrial premises depend on sequencing. Making infrastructure investments first, followed by investments in housing and then in industrial premises, reduces the cost of all three, because sewerage, drainage, electricity, clean water, and connectivity are cheaper to provide at scale than if they are added to houses and factories individually and at a later date (Collier 2016). Furthermore, urban structures share a "putty-clay" quality: Once constructed, they are difficult to modify and can stay in place for more than 150 years (Hallegatte 2009).

A second challenge is interdependence among investments in physical structures and infrastructure. For firms, the productivity of premises depends on the proximity of infrastructure, workers, and customers. For households, the utility of housing depends on

firms' investments in accessible jobs. And any social return on public infrastructure depends on the proximity of housing to premises. For example, a rapid transit system is more viable at higher densities. Policies need to leverage complementarities and manage coordination failures that lead to single-sector interventions that hinder economic density.

Effective coordination will therefore be crucial to African cities' success in managing path dependence and interdependence. A city's ability to make early and coordinated investments directly determines its later appeal to firms considering their own investments in the urban economy. Only efficient infrastructure — and service provision — will generate economic density and improve livability, job market matching, and productivity. Inefficient structures can set back urban development for decades.

Much of a structure's value is determined by complementarities with other structures in the neighborhood or city. The first structures built will dictate the options for further investments in the vicinity: Path dependence implies that investors need to anticipate what other structures will be built nearby. These expectations are self-fulfilling — investments affect expectations, which in turn affect investments (see chapter 4). The problems of path dependence and interdependence are all the more pressing because of this circularity.

This chapter provides insights from recent research on African cities that examines how early infrastructure shapes urban structures; how road investment can stimulate private investment in structures and achieve other citywide gains; how public goods can enhance livability; and what African cities will need to do to finance lumpy and huge infrastructure investments.

Investing early in infrastructure to shape urban structures

One reason for the early installation of infrastructure is that it is a coordinating device — an irreversible, and therefore credible, commitment that is highly visible and so generates common knowledge. Another reason is that, if postponed until after population settlement, it is far more expensive and difficult to install. It is more costly because all the services that need to be located underground are easier to install at scale on clear sites rather than retrofitted piecemeal beneath (or over or around) existing structures. It is harder because the inevitable disruption to private homes generates indignant political protests. For example, Freetown in Sierra Leone grew rapidly during the civil war of 1991–2002, when the government was

unable to provide new infrastructure. Now that people have settled all urban spaces, local opposition to road construction perpetuates the severe lack of roads.

A research project carried out for this study examines the longer-term benefits of "sites and services" projects that the World Bank used in the 1970s and 1980s to lay down infrastructure ahead of growth of urban settlements (Regan and others 2016). Many of these projects were undertaken with the idea of preventing slum formation or setting up durable foundations for slum upgrading into formal neighborhoods. World Bank projects covered tens of thousands of households in over 20 neighborhoods

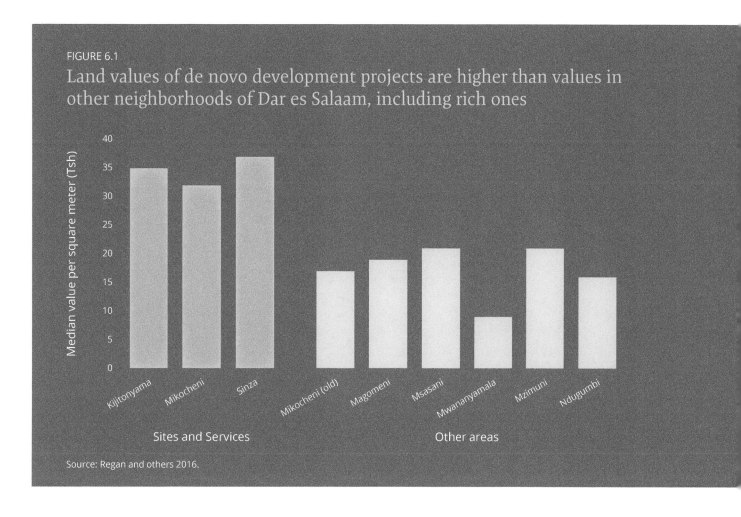

FIGURE 6.1

Land values of de novo development projects are higher than values in other neighborhoods of Dar es Salaam, including rich ones

Source: Regan and others 2016.

in cities in Brazil, El Salvador, Jamaica, Peru, Senegal, Tanzania, Thailand, and Zambia. Both types of sites and services projects — building on empty, unpopulated lands (known as de novo construction) and upgrading squatter settlements — included infrastructure investment in roads, electricity, water, and public buildings (schools, clinics, community centers, etc.). The projects were discontinued during the late 1980s because their costs were high, despite anecdotal evidence that they had beneficial long-term impacts.

Researchers evaluated the long-run outcomes of both types of projects on neighborhoods, including the costs and benefits of each program. Benefits included whether infrastructure investments increased the value of certain areas and whether and how each type of project shaped the urban landscape. In the long run, there is an expectation that the sites and services programs would increase land values, which translates into a potential tax base. Slum areas have low land value and require recurrent investments in upgrading.

In Dar es Salaam, sites with de novo development projects have higher land values than land in other parts of city, including rich neighborhoods, partly because the sites and services areas have a higher building footprint to plot area ratio (figure 6.1).

The research also shows that plots are bigger where investment was made ahead of settlement (as in Sinza, shown in the upper left of figure 6.2). These projects have higher land value per square meter than projects in upgraded areas (such as Manzese, shown in the bottom right), where roads are disorganized, plots are small and irregular, and the cost-benefit ratio of valuing for tax collections would be prohibitive. The sites and services plans drawn in the 1970s closely match the shape of today's road network, showing that investment in infrastructure is enduring, shapes urban landscapes, and leads to higher land values, which are taxable and can finance future investments.

FIGURE 6.2

Differential impacts of de novo and upgrading projects in Dar es Salaam

Source: Regan and others 2016.   Note: The upper left of the photograph shows Sinza, a de novo project. The bottom right shows Manzese, an upgrading project.

Leveraging road investment

Serious transportation problems are likely to have major implications for the overall economic performance of a city. They reduce the connectivity of firms to workers, firms to other firms, and firms to consumers — and with it both the livability and the productivity of the city. Economic theory and empirical evidence from around the world indicate that a reduction in transportation costs — which could be brought about by road investments or other improvements, such as bus rapid transit (discussed below) — can help increase connectivity between business and residential areas, improving intracity mobility and reducing commuting costs (Fujita and Ogawa 1982; Lucas and Rossi-Hansberg 2002; Glaeser and Kohlhase 2004; Srinivasan and Bhat 2005; Liu 2005; Owen and Phillips 1987).

Reductions in transportation costs and gains in mobility foster land use changes and economic growth as the city moves to a new equilibrium of urban land use patterns (Grover Goswami and Lall 2016). Gakenheimer (1999) suggests that cities in developing countries may have stronger

transportation–land use relationship than cities in more developed countries, because of weaker land use controls; the impacts on land use from road or other transportation investments are therefore likely to be more immediate. What is needed is the capacity to manage the land use shifts that are put into motion by transportation infrastructure (Cervero 2013). Ideally, such investments could be used to match land development to feasible transportation capacity, creating a more efficient balance between jobs and housing and giving workers access to a larger number of jobs (Srinivasan and Bhat 2005).

Bus rapid transit: One option among many

International evidence shows that bus rapid transit (BRT) systems can reduce commuting times. In Guangzhou (China) the introduction of the BRT in 2010 reduced travel times by 29 percent for bus riders and 20 percent for private car commuters. The change — readily apparent in figure 6.3 — has yielded total savings of 52 million hours a year, valued at RMB 158 million ($23 million) (Suzuki, Cervero, and Luchi 2010).

FIGURE 6.3

Area around the Gangding station, in Guangzhou, China, before and after construction of the bus rapid transit system

Source: Suzuki Cervero, and Luchi 2013.

In Bogota, the first BRT line reduced travel time by 15 minutes per passenger day (Hidalgo and Yepes 2004); the first and second lines reduced travel time by or 12–14 minutes per passenger day (about 19 percent) (Perdomo, Castañeda, and Mendieta 2010). BRT users in Istanbul can save 28 days' worth of commuting a year by shifting to BRT (World Bank 2015). In Johannesburg, the BRT reduce travel times 13 minutes each way (Venter and Vaz 2011, cited by EMBARQ 2013). In Lagos commuting time fell by an average of 25 minutes along a 22-kilometer corridor and wait time was reduced from 45 minutes to 10 (Peltier-Thiberge, 2015).

Other benefits of BRT are reductions in pollution and improved road safety. Bogota's BRT (TransMilenio) and new regulations on fuel quality reduce CO2 emissions by an estimated 1 million tons a year. After

implementation of the BRT, SO2 emissions declined 43 percent, NOx 18 percent, and particulate matter 12 percent (Turner and others 2012, cited in EMBARQ 2013). Car crashes and injuries fell in two of the system's main corridors (Bocarejo and others 2012, cited in EMBARQ 2013). In Lagos, the BRT project reduced CO2 emissions by 13 percent and greenhouse gas emissions by 20 percent (Peltier-Thiberge 2015).

Having boomed since the early 2000s, especially in Latin America, BRTs are starting to grow in African cities. Four were recently implemented, in Lagos (2008), Johannesburg (2009), Cape Town (2011), and Dar es Salaam (2016). Together the four systems have 104 kilometers of exclusive bus lanes. South Africa's urban BRTs have underperformed (figure 6.4). BRT projects indeed have great potential — but they must be carefully planned and implemented (box 6.1).

BOX 6.1

Bus rapid transit: Successful if handled with care

Less often noticed have been the pitfalls and shortcomings of these and other BRT projects. A World Bank review reveals key determinants of success along with certain challenges:

- Bureaucracy was circumvented. In all 11 cities studied, planning and implementation teams were formed outside existing public structures, to avoid bureaucratic obstructions.

- Political leadership was on board. Projects went forward rapidly in cities where the mayor or other political leaders had a clear vision for BRT (Bogota, Curitiba, Jakarta, and Ecuador's Guayaquil). Projects were stalled, sometimes for years, in cities where no such political commitment was present.

- Lead times were reduced to match political timetables, but the quick schedule produced gaps in planning. Steps toward project completion were hastened so that elected officials could claim credit before the end of their terms in office. As a result, crucial institutional, legal, and financial issues were sometimes neglected — though BRT planners gave thought to busway designs (median or curbside), platform types (high or low), fuel technologies (diesel or compressed natural gas), and fare collection mechanisms (on board or prepaid).

- Fares were defined by political authorities, sometimes without a complete calculation of costs and revenues.

- The public was not adequately educated about route changes. Communication failures occurred in Bogota; Santiago, Chile; Mexico City; and León, Mexico during expansion, leading to chaotic conditions and, in some cases, public protests.

- Existing transport operators protested when their interests were sidelined. For example, they were not involved in the BRT process through direct negotiations, or the bidding process failed to satisfy them.

- Fare collection systems were not integrated with public transit systems everywhere. Such disconnections occurred in Beijing, Bogota, and Mexico City. Even BRT corridors were not always integrated with one another. Examples include Jakarta and Quito.

- Bus scheduling sometimes led to overuse at peak hours and underuse at off-peak hours. Peak-hour crowding and off-peak inactivity are perhaps the most visible weaknesses in BRT operation. One or both can be seen in Beijing, Bogota, Curitiba, Guayaquil, Jakarta, León, Mexico City, and Quito.

Source: Hidalgo, Custodio, and Grafieaux 2007; ITDP 2007.

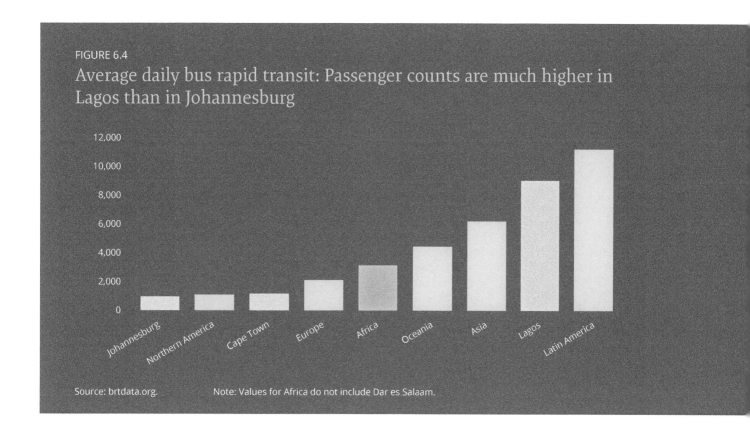

FIGURE 6.4

Average daily bus rapid transit: Passenger counts are much higher in Lagos than in Johannesburg

Source: brtdata.org.   Note: Values for Africa do not include Dar es Salaam.

Different densities require different solutions. Mass transit needs high population densities, which make it more likely that the system will be used with sufficient frequency and that high capital investments will be justified. The appropriate transportation systems for a city varies with population and job densities throughout the city. Improving logistics and designing routes and bus stops might be enough to improve connectivity in places with low densities; higher density can require a BRT, a light-rail train, or a subway. A study of the United States by Guerra and Cervero (2011) finds that to be in the top quartile of cost-effective investments, a BRT system with a cost of about $50 million per mile would need about 18 jobs and residents per acre within a half mile of the stations, a light-rail train would need 50 jobs and residents per acre, and a heavy-rail system would need about 60 per acre.

Integrated urban planning, regulation, and transportation investments

As African cities grow larger, policy makers need to carefully plan the modes of transportation that will best enhance urban mobility. Chinese cities have seen massive sprawl and huge dependence on cars (box 6.2). They have grown through a mammouth transformation of rural land into urban land and development of large-scale infrastructure. In contrast, Japan has limited the amount of rural land conversion and linked its spatial hierarchy of subcenters by the most developed subway network in the world. The result has been a vibrant urban economy and social integration.

Integrating urban planning and regulation with transport investments can help enhance ordered and efficient transport development, as it has in Curitiba, Brazil (figure 6.5b). Curitiba's 1965 master plan first envisioned the city structure. Today the city has created articulated densities along its BRT corridors, with buildings strategically built along BRT corridors. As a result, the city has lower greenhouse gas emission levels, less traffic congestion, and more livable urban spaces than similar cities in Brazil. Public transportation is also more widely used. For instance, although São Paulo has at least 10 times Curutiba's population, in 2000 the number of annual public transit trips per capita was higher in Curitiba (355 versus 330 in São Paulo) (Suzuki, Cervero, and Luchi 2013).

Alternate paths for improving urban mobility: Lessons from China and Japan

China's cautionary tale: Avoid getting locked into the "large-scale" mindset

In the early stages of urbanization, the massive and accelerated conversion of rural land into urban land brought in large amounts of capital, further fuelling the process. The resulting economic growth has led to large-scale industrialization and social transformation. China now suffers from severe urban sprawl based on giant infrastructure and isolated buildings, a marked contrast to the much finer grain of Chinese historical spatial forms. This new stage of development of Chinese cities has severed the traditional links between family generations and between neighborhoods. Spatial zoning and large-scale separation of activities has greatly increased mobility, imposed strict separations between economic classes, and increased the amount of time spent at work as opposed to leisure activities. The diversity of Chinese cities, with their different climates and cultures on a semi-continent, has been reduced to a uniform category of modern city, which consumes massive amounts of energy and will be locked into car dependency in the future. This urbanization model is not only environmentally unsustainable, it also jeopardizes the future of China's transition toward a more mature society that is less dependent on low-cost labor and more dependent on innovation-based economic growth.

China has built its intra- and interurban networks with a very large grain compared with other countries. The result has been a decline in the number of possible links and paths between urban elements in China compared with cities and city systems in Europe and the United States. This lack of medium- and small-scale street networks has a strong impact on the management of traffic flow. The system is inefficient; among the resulting problems is congestion at the level of thoroughfares and subway lines.

As a result, the deployment of a variety of transportation choices (walking, biking, buses with short distances between stops, tramways, dense subways, regional trains) is ruled out. People cannot efficiently time their commuting schedules daily. Everyone has only two choices: the large-scale mass transit system or the urban highway. The lack of short-range local choices and diversity creates strong

global inefficiency, because it obliges sizing the whole system for peaks that could be better dissipated by a variety of modal choices in a large "space of paths," fitting the distances to travel at a finer grain and creating a better-structured city organized around a variety of scales. Peaks cannot be dissipated into capillary networks, because the system lacks capillarity. To avoid congestion, the large scales are overdimensioned and segregated from the smaller scales, which prevents the emergence of intermediary and small scales connected to the large scale. This reinforces large scales against intermediary and small scales and eventually locks cities into "large-scale dependence."

Japan's successful organization, based on fine grain and local connectivity

Japan increased its rate of urbanization from 25 percent in 1950 to 65 percent in 1980, while rising, in 30 years of sustained growth from poverty after the destructiveness of World War II, to become the world's third-largest economy, after the United States and China. Japan developed the largest city in the world, Tokyo, with 38 million inhabitants, in a highly efficient way, through myriad micro-processes, creating a highly complex, well-integrated, and well-connected spatial hierarchy of subcenters, linked by the most developed subway network in the world. Rather than relying on excessive rural to urban land conversion and then suffering from the detrimental urban sprawl that resulted, Japan based its urban growth on internal intensification through well-balanced spatial planning policies and a balance between micro-processes and larger-scale structuring interventions.

By preserving and reinforcing fine-grain and local connectivity, Japan has avoided the destruction wrought by the collapse of the centuries-old social structure in China. Japanese society supports both social resilience and vibrant economic activity. By providing an appropriate framework for investment at the district, city, and national scales, Japan has produced well-balanced cities with high degrees of connectivity at the district, city, and national scales. Its numerous medium-scale projects and investments have avoided the large-scale dependence that China suffers from and contributed to the emergence of livable, low-carbon, and successful cities.

Source: World Bank 2016b.

FIGURE 6.5A
Integrated urban planning and regulation promote density

Bogota, Colombia

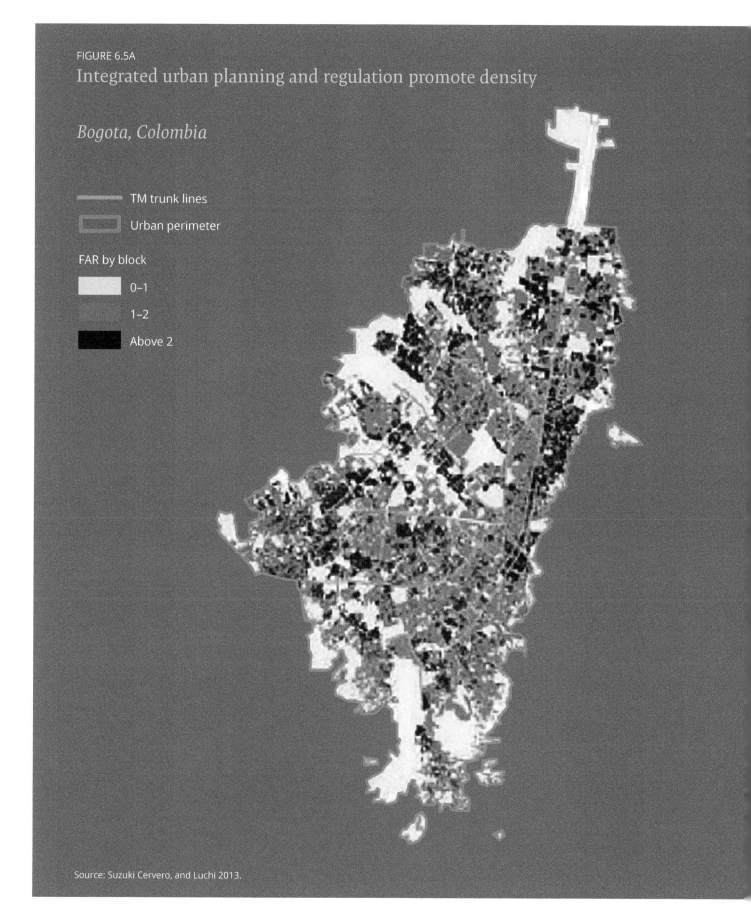

Source: Suzuki Cervero, and Luchi 2013.

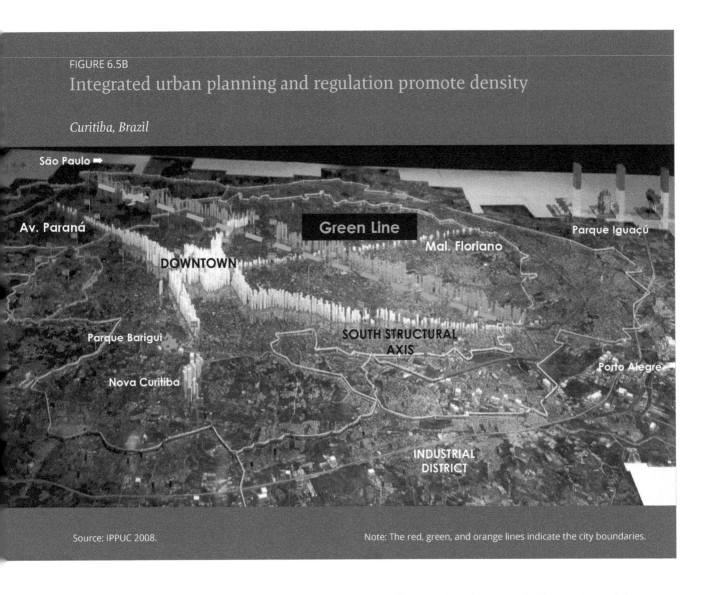

FIGURE 6.5B

Integrated urban planning and regulation promote density

Curitiba, Brazil

Source: IPPUC 2008.

Note: The red, green, and orange lines indicate the city boundaries.

In contrast, transportation in many cities has been motivated by the unique objective of improving mobility. In these cases, the opportunity of pro¬moting sustainable patterns of urban growth in the long run is lost. For instance, in Bogota, land use regulation has not been coordinated with TransMilenio corridors. The city maintains a low floor area ratio (0–2) throughout the city, except within the central business district and a few other selected spots (see figure 6.5a) (Suzuki, Cervero, and Luchi 2013). These cities lose the opportunity to achieve less fragmented, livable cities.

Roads, densification, and land use change in four East African cities

As part of this research project, a study of roads in four East African cities — Addis Ababa, Dar es Salaam, Kigali, and Nairobi — examined the extent to which the timing and spatial incidence of public investment drives population densification and private investment in housing and industrial structures

(Felkner, Lall, and Lee 2016). The study used data from very high-resolution satellite images to measure road investment using remote-sensing classification methods at a very high spatial resolution. It then used econometric techniques that measure roads and urban structure over time — including differences-in-differences with propensity score matching — to estimate the quantitative associations between road investment, land use changes, economic productivity, and population density.

The results quantify the full extent of the road network in each city for five categories of roads: three-lane paved roads, two-lane paved roads, two-lane paved roads with paved service lanes, one-lane paved roads, and unpaved roads. Also quantified is the full extent of road investment and road changes over 2003–13 (figure 6.6). The spatial resolution of the data enabled the authors to identify precisely where road investment was made in each city for each type of road and to spatially quantify the level of that investment.

FIGURE 6.6

Percentage of area devoted to paved and unpaved roads in four East African cities, 2001 and 2013

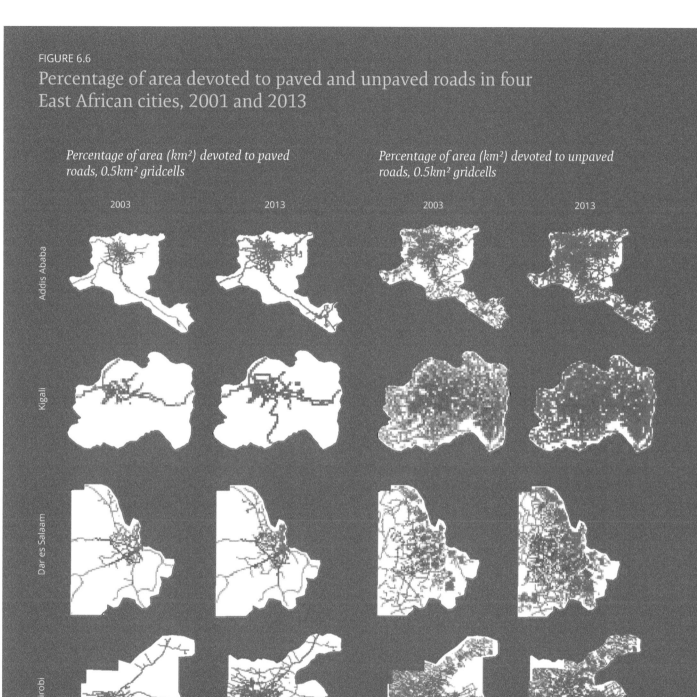

Percentage of area (km²) devoted to paved roads, 0.5km² gridcells

Percentage of area (km²) devoted to unpaved roads, 0.5km² gridcells

2003 2013 2003 2013

Addis Ababa

Kigali

Dar es Salaam

Nairobi

Total area:				
0%	0.01%–1.053%	2.022%–2.457%	4.223%–7.512%	
	1.053%–2.022%	2.457%–4.223%	7.512%–364.486%	

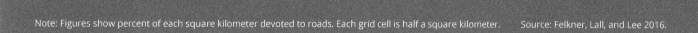

Note: Figures show percent of each square kilometer devoted to roads. Each grid cell is half a square kilometer.   Source: Felkner, Lall, and Lee 2016.

African cities generally have low levels of road investment (chapter 2): In a representative sample of 30 global cities on the proportion of land area devoted to roads (UN Habitat 2013), Kigali ranked 19th, Addis Ababa 24th, and Nairobi 27th. Yet these four cities saw heavy road investment over 2003–13, measured in terms of total road length and total area devoted to roads. The area for roads increased 54 percent in Nairobi, doubled in Dar es Salaam, trebled in Kigali, and almost quintupled in Addis Ababa. Total road length almost doubled in Dar es Salaam (increasing by 98 percent, from 1,771 kilometers to 3,498 kilometers) and rose by 78 percent in Addis Ababa. It grew more modestly in Nairobi (23 percent) and Kigali (19 percent).

The study finds that paved road investment was positively and significantly associated with population density growth; growth in economic activity, as proxied by night light radiance; and industrial land use growth.

- **Road investment and population density**. Paved road investment is associated with a 37 percent increase in population density for all cities pooled. It is associated with a 17 percent increase in Kigali and a 34.4 percent increase in Nairobi. Most of the estimated associations are strongest within 1–2 kilometers of the road investments. The bulk of the paved road investment impact appears to come from one-lane paved roads, less from two-lane paved roads with paved service lanes.

- **Road investment and economic activity as proxied by night light radiance**. Paved road investment is associated with an increase in economic activity (as proxied by night light radiance) of 24 percent in Kigali and 13 percent in Nairobi. As with population density, the magnitude of the estimated coefficients tends to be highest within 1–2 kilometers of the locations of the investment. These results held across multiple robustness checks. (Results for Addis Ababa are questionable, because of likely errors in the city's night light data related to the linear interannual calibration process.)

- **Road investment and industrial land use**. Paved road investment is associated with a 31 percent growth in industrial land use, a result that holds across robustness checks. Two- and three-lane paved road investments have stronger associations with industrial land use growth than one-lane paved roads. Paved road investment corresponded to a 74 percent increase in industrial land use in Addis Ababa, an 83 percent increase in Dar Es Salaam, and a 325.4 percent in Kigali. The results for Nairobi were negative and significant.

- **Road investment and formal residential land use**. Results are inconclusive. When estimated for all cities pooled, paved road investment is associated with a significant decrease in formal residential land use growth. Results are negative for Dar es Salaam and Nairobi but positive for Kigali. The results are positive for Addis Ababa for unpaved roads.

Citywide economic benefits of road improvements in Kampala

The research findings reported above show the spatially localized benefits of urban road improvements. There are also broader citywide economic benefits of transportation improvements. In recent research on road improvements in Kampala, Bernard, Bird, and Venables (2016) examine the potential benefits of improving the northern bypass around the city, aimed at improving connectivity between the west and east of the city (map 6.1) and upgrading the existing road network to facilitate movements within the city.

The direct beneficiaries of these improvements are workers using motorized transport, whose transportation costs decrease. Other residents also benefit, because lower transportation prices reduce the cost of living, at least in the short term, because over time, people relocate: The better-off locate farther from their jobs as commuting times decrease, reducing pressure on land close to the city center and allowing poorer people to settle close to their jobs. Low-skilled informal workers may actually benefit more than high-income workers, depending on the strength of agglomeration effects. If these effects are strong enough in the informal sector, as they were in Colombia (Duranton 2016), the relocation and increased clustering engendered by the transportation improvement will boost productivity in the nontradable sector (in which most low-skilled workers are employed). The resulting increase in wages in that sector might surpass the wage effect for high-skilled workers.

The long-term effect of the bypass on urban welfare is eight times it short-term impact; the long-term effect of upgrading the road network is three times as great. Transportation investments not only decrease the aggregate commuting time of users of motorized and nonmotorized transport, they also make easier for firms and households to relocate and have agglomeration effects on the city. If households and firms can relocate, both projects lower the cost of living by 19 percent for high-income households and 6 percent for low-skilled workers. With stronger scale economies in the informal sector and increasing returns to scale, the difference between low- and

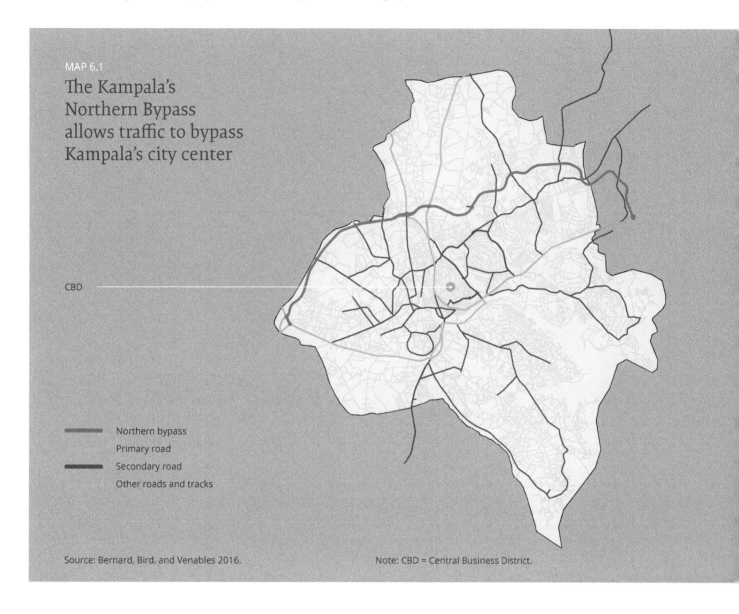

MAP 6.1

The Kampala's Northern Bypass allows traffic to bypass Kampala's city center

CBD

— Northern bypass
    Primary road
— Secondary road
    Other roads and tracks

Source: Bernard, Bird, and Venables 2016.

Note: CBD = Central Business District.

high-skilled workers decreases, with a reduction in the cost of living of 3 percent and 9 percent, respectively. These investments' long-term effects on urban welfare are much higher than their short-term impacts: those from the construction of the bypass eight times, those from upgrading the road network, three times.

This research shows that the benefits of changes in the urban landscape, such as investment in transportation infrastructure, take time to emerge. Firms and households respond to these changes gradually. In the long term, planning policies should support relocation in response to change of connectivity for the full benefits of investments to be realized.

Providing public goods and services for livability

Many African cities provide low access to public services and amenities. In expanding public services such as schooling, health, water, and sanitation, planners must consider that these services are subject to economies of scale and specialization. It is often less costly to provide a given level of per capita service for a dense urban population than for a dispersed rural population (box 6.3; see also chapter 1). Being less costly, the optimal level of provision will likely be higher, so cities can provide better education, health, and other services than rural areas.

BOX 6.3

Providing water to the poor in African cities

The experience of some African cities shows that access to safe water can be widely provided to the poorest households. A forthcoming World Bank report studies how five African cities — Dakar (Senegal), Durban (South Africa), Kampala (Uganda), Nyeri (Kenya), and Ouagadougou (Burkina Faso) — have provided reliable service to poor people in challenging environments (World Bank 2016). It concludes that these cities have improved access for the poor primarily through effectively managed utilities, which recover all operating costs and some capital costs while scoring well on other measures of efficiency and cost-effectiveness.

Five lessons emerge from the report:

1. **Successful reforms need local leadership**. All reforms were started and implemented by local leaders. Outsiders assisted only with knowledge and financial support. The start of successful reforms displayed three mutually reinforcing conditions: (a) a catalytic event or space for reform, (b) a skilled technical leader motivated to improve service, and (c) a relatively stable political leader who supported and protected the reform. These conditions are inherent to a particular context and cannot be manufactured, created, or effectively driven by outsiders.

2. **Utilities that serve the poor well** involve the community. In Durban, eThekwini Water established a consultative committee with low-income communities. The committee became engaged and supportive when the utility addressed requests to increase the free basic water allowance. The utility leader who drove eThekwini's turnaround credits the continued renewal of his contract by the elected city council to eThekwini's success in serving poor communities. Uganda's National Water and Sewerage Commission noted that serving poor communities creates a powerful ally, saying "In Kampala, the poor vote." Its leadership reports that the "Water for All" campaign has won support from both poor communities and the government.

3. **Independent structures are helpful but not sufficient for effective service provision**. Formal structures, such as independent boards and regulators, are not sufficient to ensure effective service provision, because they are not immune to predation or capture. However, these structures can be useful for bolstering professional corporate cultures and coordinating supportive relationships with external stakeholders. Affermage and related contracts in Senegal provide clear rules that are costly to change. Provided the utility keeps doing a good job, the contracts support success. The Office National de l'Eau et de l'Assainisement (ONEA) in Burkina Faso is publicly owned and operated. Its performance contract with the government is supervised by a multistakeholder committee comprising representatives of customers, NGOs, and the donors who finance the sector. The committee monitors performance of both the utility and the government under the contract on the basis of independently audited financial and technical reports. Such designs embed accountability to external stakeholders in formal structures that can also help mobilize support against predation.

Because the gains from enhanced urban service provision accrue to urban households, they offer an extra incentive for migration. As migration eventually leads rural and urban living standards to converge, the gain in well-being from urban public services will tend to moderate urban wages. Urban workers face some costs that are higher than for rural workers — such as housing and commuting — and so need higher wages to compensate for them (see chapter 3). Better urban services will counter these effects, helping the city break into markets for internationally traded goods.

Recent research shows that access to basic services increases steadily with population density (Gollin, Kirchberger, and Lagakos 2016; for differences in access to particular services.[30] Rural and urban are thus not binary but a continuum: Moving to more densely populated areas can improve one's living standards. Many obstacles could prevent a rural family from moving to a city; fewer would prevent households in a small town from moving to a larger one.

4. Efficiency needs to improve — it's not just a matter of getting more outside financing. These turnarounds required hundreds of millions of dollars of investment in networks and production facilities. Betweeen 2006 and 2015, the utilities serving the five case study cities increased the number of water connections by an average of 93 percent (box figure 6.3.1). They financed these improvements partly by improving their efficiency, so that they could increase their operating cash flows to raise and repay loans for infrastructure investment. Some borrow commercially, but most rely mainly on development bank lending, taking advantage of credit enhancement offered by their national governments.

5. Different approaches are necessary to make access affordable for the poorest households. These cities implemented increasing block tariff structures and used cross-subsidies between commercial/industrial and residential customers to guarantee affordable access by the poorest households. Where informal land tenure does not allow service provision, or the pattern of settlement or topography makes conventional network designs infeasible, they improvised new technical and institutional arrangements, including working with small providers to deliver services where the utility is restricted by capacity or mandate (as in Ouagadougou). This option is proving handy for a wider range of utilities.

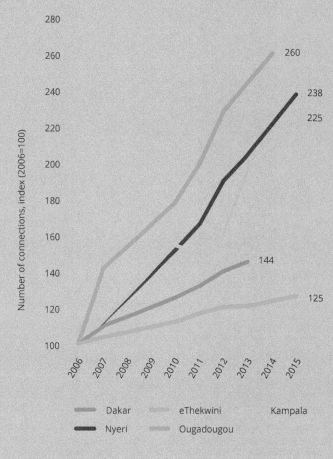

Source: World Bank 2016a.

Why has such migration from smaller to larger urban areas not been observed? It may be that too little information is information for a detailed study of migration in Africa; most data are on rural-to-urban migration. Other possible explanations include the fact that denser areas have a limited absorptive capacity; government policies are working to prevent slum proliferation; and migration is limited by unclear land titling, risk aversion, and poor information (Gollin, Kirchberger, and Lagakos 2016; De Brauw, Mueller, and Lee 2014).

Depending on the country and the service, migrants can be better off or worse off than other residents (figure 6.7). Differing urban management policies might explain these differences in access to services.

FIGURE 6.7

Access to electricity by newly arrived migrants and other residents in the Democratic Republic of Congo, Ghana, Nigeria, and Sierra Leone

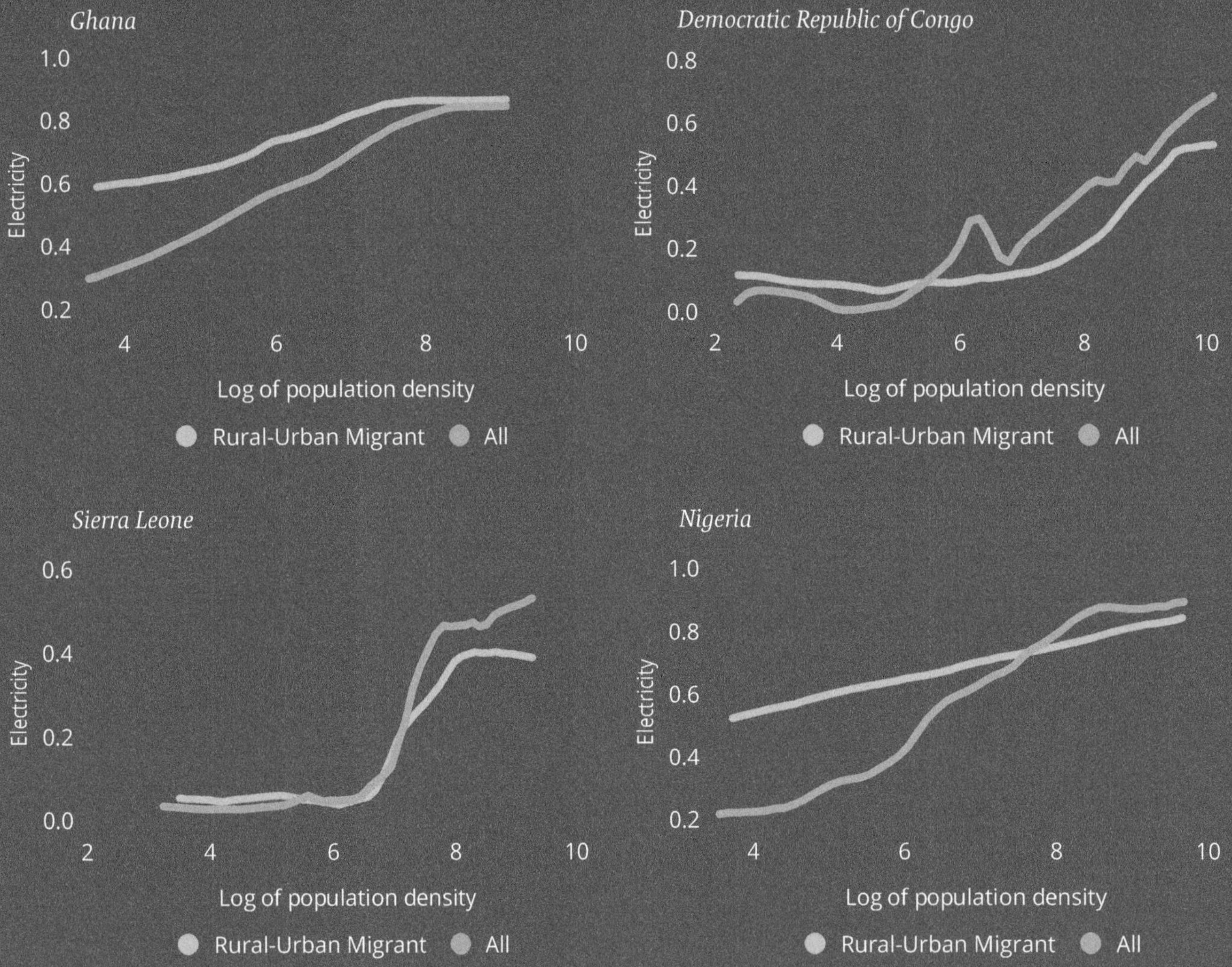

Source: Gollin, Kirchberger, and Lagakos 2016.

Financing lumpy urban infrastructure investments

Public authorities should seize the opportunity of residential density to build highly productive infrastructure and public services. That effort will require building revenue systems to finance provision. The capital costs of public infrastructure must be incurred far in advance of the productivity and livability benefits. The large capital outlays required can be daunting. They are likely to far exceed the budget of any city government (figure 6.8).

Because cities with good connectivity generate large gains in productivity for their inhabitants, they offer many potential tax points. Transactions within the city could be subject to a sales tax, and households (or firms) could be made subject to a local income (or business) tax. But the least distorting form of taxation may be appreciation in urban land values. As the city becomes more productive, in order to benefit from the enhanced productivity that it enables, firms and households must locate to it. As this happens, the value of land parcels appreciates, usually with the level of connectivity. This appreciation capitalizes the additional productivity provided by locating on that parcel.

Land-based financing can thus be an attractive option for infrastructure investment. It takes different forms at different stages of a city's evolution (figure 6.9). Such financing has clear advantages in principle. First, if the infrastructure is worth providing, the appreciation in land values that it generates must exceed the cost of provision, most likely by a wide margin. Second, as the appreciation in land values is an economic rent rather than a payment to a factor of production — that is, it does not depend on the effort of the land or its owner — taxing that rent does not distort productive behavior. Appreciation does not require the tax point to be a land transaction, in which there is considerable scope for falsifying the transaction to evade taxes. An alternative is an annual tax based on a market estimate of the average value of land in the area.

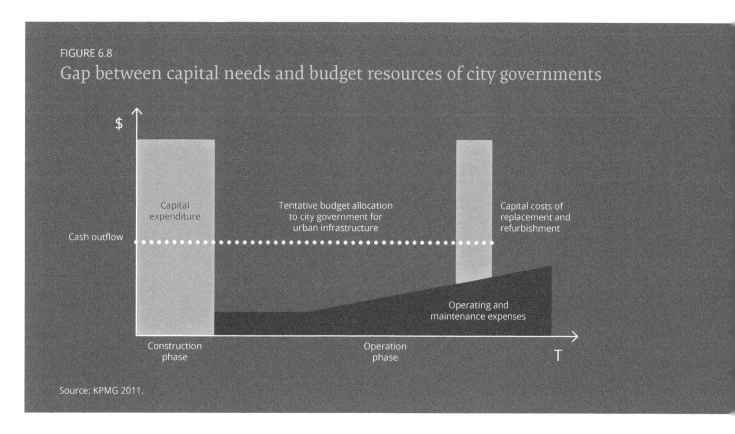

FIGURE 6.8
Gap between capital needs and budget resources of city governments

Source: KPMG 2011.

FIGURE 6.9

Land-based financing instruments and city evolution

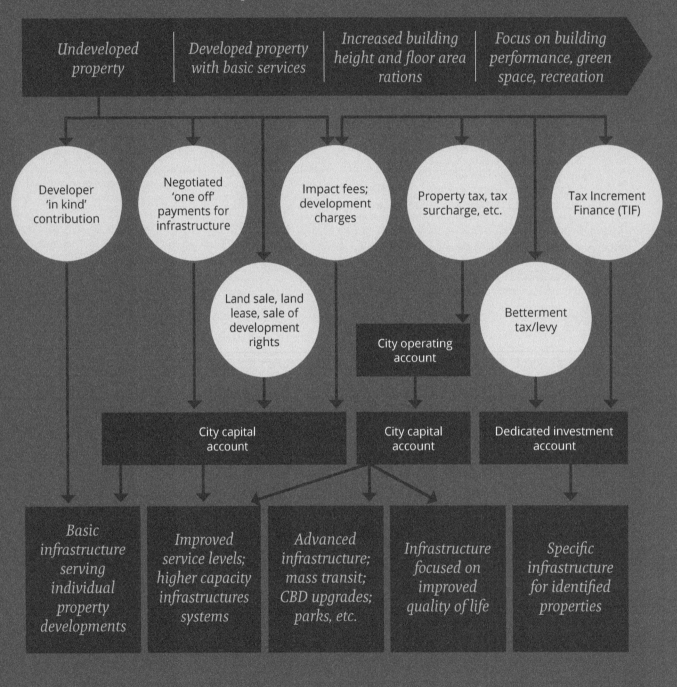

Source: African Centre for Cities 2015.   Note: CBD = Central Business District.

156

African cities are generally poorly positioned to finance their infrastructure needs through typical channels such as grants, transfers, own-source revenue, or borrowing. Land-based financing holds great potential to contribute to infrastructure financing — as long as some conditions are met:

- Demand for property.

- An effective supply of developable land, land rights, property finance, and a working real estate sector.

- A sound regulatory and policy framework, with good legal backing.

- The financial and technical capacity to implement and monitor land-based financing instruments.

Most African cities do not yet meet these preconditions; they should work toward meeting them, with the goal of leveraging land values to fund much needed infrastructure projects. A study of Ethiopia, Kenya, and Zimbabwe and a scan of 28 large property development projects in Africa finds only very little land-based financing (African Centre for Cities 2015). Of the three countries, Ethiopia has generated the most significant volume through the land-lease system. Kenya and Zimbabwe have legislation in place but are underperforming or ineffective in ring-fencing the proceeds for infrastructure.

Where land-based financing instruments are in place in Africa, the modality is largely limited to in-kind contributions, such as installation by developers of the secondary infrastructure connections and, at times, bulk infrastructure required for particular projects. This infrastructure may not be optimally located or not well coordinated enough to form an integrated infrastructure network. These land-based financing instruments also tend to benefit middle- and high-income groups, who are the main consumers of such development projects. In many cases, the local government subsidizes them in an attempt to boost local economic development.

A better form of land-based financing may be the development charge, a one-off payment made by a developer when land use changes are approved or new developments begin. It is matched by a complementary policy and governance framework, as well as by implementation capacity.

If cities in Sub-Saharan Africa remain crowded, disconnected, and costly, they can be neither kind to their residents nor productive. These cities are still being built. Before it is too late, they can ensure that they are not locked into inefficient and unsustainable patterns of urbanization. Given the high sunk costs and enduring nature of infrastructure, any approach to urban development that lacks early planning and coordination will burden future generations with cleaning up the mess — a terribly inefficient strategy.

To inspire higher expectations, cities in Africa need better institutions. It is up to local and national authorities to undertake the institutional reforms needed for effective planning and coordination that will increase urban economic density and productivity and spur Africa's belated structural transformation. Institutional structures must lead, not lag, urban infrastructure. If they do, the region's cities will become not only better connected and more efficient but also kinder to their inhabitants, whose skills will be critical to economic growth and development. Only when this happens will the doors of African cities stand open to the world.

References

African Centre for Cities. 2015. *Urban Infrastructure in Sub-Saharan Africa: Harnessing Land Values, Housing and Transport*. University of Cape Town, South Africa.

Banerjee, S., A. Diallo, V. Foster, and Q. Wodon. 2009. "Trends in Household Coverage of Modern Infrastructure Services in Africa." Policy Research Working Paper 4880, World Bank, Washington, DC.

Banerjee, S. G., and E. Morella, 2011. *Africa's Water and Sanitation Infrastructure: Access, Affordability, and Alternatives*. Washington, DC: World Bank.

Bernard, L., J. Bird, and A. J. Venables, 2016. "Transport in a Congested City: A Computable Equilibrium Model Applied to Kampala City." Draft, March 29, University of Oxford.

Cervero, R. 2013. "Linking Urban Transport and Land Use in Developing Countries." *Journal of Transport and Land Use* 6 (1): 7–24.

Collier, Paul. 2016. "African Urbanization: An Analytic Policy Guide." Paper presented at the Fourth Tokyo International Conference of African Development, "Land Use Planning and Spatial Development for Smart Growth in African Cities," Tokyo.

de Brauw, A., V. Mueller, and H. L. Lee. 2014. "The Role of Rural–Urban Migration in the Structural Transformation of Sub-Saharan Africa." *World Development* 63, 33–42.

Duranton, G. 2016. "Agglomeration Effects in Colombia." *Journal of Regional Science* 56 (2): 210–38

EMBARQ. 2013. *Social, Environmental and Economic Impacts of BRT Systems. Bus Rapid Transit Case Studies from around the World*. Washington, DC.

Felkner, J. S., S. V. Lall, and H. Lee. 2016. "Synchronizing Public and Private Investment in Cities: Evidence from Addis Ababa, Dar es Salaam, Kigali, and Nairobi." April 22, World Bank, Washington, DC.

Foster, V., and C. Briceño-Garmendia, eds. 2010. *Africa's Infrastructure. A Time for Transformation*. Agence Française de Développement and the World Bank, Paris and Washington, DC.

Fujita, M., and H. Ogawa. 1982. "Multiple Equilibria and Structural Transition of Non-Monocentric Urban Configurations." *Regional Science and Urban Economics* 12 (2): 161–96.

Gakenheimer, R. 1999. "Urban mobility in the Developing World." *Transportation Research Part A* 33 (7–8): 671–89.

Glaeser, E. 2011. *Triumph of the City: How Our Greatest Invention Makes Us Richer, Smarter, Greener, Healthier, and Happier*. London: MacMillan.

Glaeser, E. L., and J. E. Kohlhase. 2004. "Cities, Regions and the Decline of Transport Costs." *Papers in Regional Science* 83 (1): 197–228.

Gollin, Douglas, Martina Kirchberger, and David Lagakos. 2016. "Living Standards across Space: Evidence from Sub-Saharan Africa." March 31. Available at https://collaboration.worldbank.org/docs/DOC-20505.

Grover Goswami, A. G., and S. V. Lall. 2016. "Jobs in the City: Explaining Urban Spatial Structure in Kampala." Policy Research Working Paper 7655, World Bank, Washington, DC.

Guerra, E., and R. Cervero. 2011. "Cost of a Ride: The Effects of Densities on Fixed-Guideway Transit Ridership and Capital Costs." *Journal of the American Planning Association* 77 (3): 267–90.

Hallegatte, S. 2009. "Strategies to Adapt to an Uncertain Climate Change." *Global Environmental Change* 19 (2): 240–47.

Hidalgo, D., P. Custodio, and P. Graftieaux. 2007. "A Critical Look at Major Bus Improvements in Latin America and Asia: Case Studies of Hitches, Hic-ups, and Areas for Improvement; Synthesis of Lessons Learned." World Bank, Washington, DC.

Hidalgo, D., and T. Yepes. 2004. "Are Bus Rapid Transit Systems Effective in Poverty Reduction? Experience of Bogota's Transmilenio and Lessons for Other Cities." Paper presented at the Transportation Research 84th Annual Board Meeting, January 9–13, 2005, Washington, DC.

IPPUC (Instituto de Pesquisa e Planejamento Urbano de Curitiba). 2008. *Curitiba: Integrated Urban Planning. Urban Planning and Regeneration: Key to Tackling Climate Change*. Presented in Dundee, March 18th, 2008. IPPUC: Curitiba, Brazil.

ITDP 2007. *Bus Rapid Transit Planning Guide*. New-York: Institute for Transportation and Development Policy.

KPMG. 2011. *Financing the growth of your city*. Singapore, Singapore: KPMG.

Liu, F. 2005. "Interrupted Development. Failure in Urban Development and Housing Markets." Paper presented to the Federal Reserve Board–George Washington University Seminar in Real Estate and Urban Economics, Washington, DC.

Lucas, R. E., and E. Rossi-Hansberg. 2002. "On the Internal Structure of Cities." *Econometrica* 70 (4): 1445–76.

Owen, A. D., and G. D. A. Phillips. 1987. "The Characteristics of Railway Passenger Demand: An Econometric Investigation." *Journal of Transport Economics and Policy* 231–53.

Peltier-Thiberge, N. 2015. "Lagos' Bus Rapid Transit System: Decongesting and Depolluting Mega Cities." World Bank Transport for Development Blog. December 8. Available at http://blogs.worldbank.org/transport/lagos-bus-rapid-transit-system-decongesting-and-depolluting-mega-cities-0.

Perdomo, J. A., H. Castañeda, and J. C. Mendieta. 2010. "Evaluación de impacto de las Fases I y II del sistema de transporte masivo TransMilenio sobre el tiempo total de desplazamiento de los usuarios del transporte público tradicional en Bogotá." Documentos CEDE 2010-11, Universidad de los Andes, Bogotá, Colombia.

Regan, T., Nigmatulina, D., Baruah, N., Rausch, F., and Michaels, G. 2015. "Sites and Services and Slum Upgrading in Tanzania." Paper presented at the Spatial Development of African Cities Workshop, World Bank, December 16–17.

Srinivasan, S., and C. R. Bhat. 2005. "Modeling Household Interactions in Daily In-Home and Out-of-Home Maintenance Activity Participation." *Transportation* 32 (5): 523–44.

Suzuki, H., R. Cervero, and K. Luchi. 2013. *Transforming Cities with Transit. Transit and Land-Use Integration for Sustainable Urban Development*. Urban Development Series. Washington, DC: World Bank.

UN-Habitat. 2013. "The Relevance of Street Patterns and Public Space in Urban Areas." UN Habitat Working Paper.

UNICEF (United Nations Children's Fund), and WHO (World Health Organization). 2012. *Progress on Drinking Water and Sanitation*. 2012 Update. New York.

World Bank. 2015. "Take the Bus: It's Faster than Your Car." December 2, Washington, DC. http://www.worldbank.org/en/news/feature/2015/12/02/take-the-bus-its-faster-than-your-car.

———. 2016a. *Providing Water to Poor People in African Cities Effectively: Lessons from Utility Reforms*. Washington, DC: World Bank.

———. 2016b. Vietnam 2035 : Toward Prosperity, Creativity, Equity, and Democracy. Washington, DC: World Bank.

About the contributors

Somik Vinay Lall

Somik Vinay Lall is the World Bank's Global Lead on Territorial Development Solutions and its Lead Economist for Urban Development in Africa. He heads a World Bank global research program on urbanization and spatial development and founded the Bank's urbanization reviews program. He is an expert on development policy related to urban and territorial competitiveness, agglomeration and clusters, infrastructure, and impact evaluation, with more than 18 years' experience in Asia, Africa, and Latin America. He was a core member of the team that wrote the World Development Report 2009: Reshaping Economic Geography; a senior economic counselor to the Indian prime minister's National Transport Development Policy Committee; and the lead author of the World Bank's flagship report on urbanization Planning, Connecting, and Financing Cities Now. His work focuses on "place-shaping policies" around cities, clusters, and corridors and the functioning of factor and product markets. He has published dozens of articles in peer-reviewed journals.

J. Vernon Henderson

J. Vernon Henderson is the School Professor of Economic Geography at the London School of Economics. His research focuses on urbanization in developing countries. He is a co-principal investigator on a major ongoing research project on urbanization policy in Africa and globally. He has published dozens of articles in peer-reviewed journals. He is the co-editor of the Journal of Urban Economics and the Handbook of Regional and Urban Economics and serves on several editorial boards. He is the founder and a past president of the Urban Economics Association.

Anthony J. Venables

Anthony J. Venables is Professor of Economics at Oxford University where he directs a programme of research on urbanisation in developing countries and the Oxford Centre for the Analysis of Resource Rich Economies. He is a Fellow of the Econometric Society and of the Regional Science Association, and is a Fellow and Council member of the British Academy. Former positions include chief economist at the UK Department for International Development, professor at the London School of Economics, research manager of the trade group in the World Bank, and advisor to the UK Treasury. He has published extensively in the areas of international trade and spatial economics, including work on trade and imperfect competition, economic integration, multinational firms, economic geography, and natural resources. Publications include The spatial economy; cities, regions and international trade, with M. Fujita and P. Krugman (MIT press, 1999), and Multinationals in the World Economy with G. Barba Navaretti (Princeton 2004).

Juliana Aguilar

Juliana Aguilar is an economist, consultant in the Social, Urban, Rural and Resilience Global Practice at the World Bank, where she works on the link between urban form and urban development and on urban studies in Mozambique and the Democratic Republic of Congo. She holds a master's degree in economics from the Universidad de los Andes (in Colombia).

Ana Aguilera

Ana Aguilera works as an Urban Development Specialist at the World Bank Group. Her work focuses on improving city management with an emphasis on urban economics and spatial development. She has studied the relationship between urban morphology, productivity and access to basic services in cities. Her work also comprises survey management and design to measure living standards and socioeconomic indicators. In 2014 she was awarded with the Youth Innovation Fund for her work using Big Data to understand mobility patterns in cities. Ana graduated as an Economist from Universidad Católica Andrés Bello in Caracas, and holds a MSc. in Public Policy from The University of Chicago.

Sarah Antos

Sarah Antos is an urban geographer at the World Bank who has worked extensively with spatial data in the field of international development. In particular her work as focused on remote sensing and the classification of high resolution imagery. Before joining the World Bank, she worked at the World Health Organization and US's Office of Foreign Disaster Assistance, where she used satellite imagery and survey data to improve disaster recovery efforts. She holds a bachelor's and master's degree in Geography from The George Washington University.

Paolo Avner

Paolo Avner is an urban economist in the Social, Urban, Rural and Resilience Global Practice of the World Bank. His current work focuses on the impacts of land use regulations and transport systems on the spatial development of developing country cities. Prior to joining the Bank, Paolo worked in France as a research engineer in LEPII in order to integrate the urban dimension into the worldwide energy prospective model POLES. He then joined the Center for International Research in Environment and Development (Paris) and collaborated to the development of an applied land use - transport interaction model (NEDUM 2D). His work specifically focused on the ability of public policies and investments to curb greenhouse gas emissions from urban transport while limiting the costs of these policies for urban residents. Paolo has graduated from La Sorbonne University and from University Paris X - Nanterre as an economist and is currently finishing his PhD at École des Hautes Etudes en Sciences Sociales, Paris.

Olivia D'Aoust

Olivia D'Aoust is an Urban Economist in the Social, Urban, Rural and Resilience Global Practice at the World Bank, where she works on urban development in Africa, particularly the drivers of and impediments to cities' productivity and livability. She is involved in projects in the Democratic Republic of Congo, Ethiopia, South Africa, South Sudan, and Uganda. She holds a PhD in economics from the Université libre de Bruxelles and a master's degree in demography from the Université catholique de Louvain.

Chyi-Yun Huang

Chyi-Yun Huang is an urban specialist at the World Bank with more than 10 years' experience in integrated urban planning and design, city management, and sustainable development. She is currently leading or contributing technical expertise to various operations and analytical studies in Ethiopia, South Africa, Tanzania, and Uganda. Before joining the Bank, as a Young Professional, she was an executive planner with Singapore's national planning agency. She holds an MSc in urban planning from Columbia University and a BA in architecture from the National University of Singapore and is a LEED accredited professional.

Patricia (Tracy) Jones

Patricia (Tracy) Jones is a project manager and researcher for the Urbanization in Developing Economies Project. Her research focuses on economic development in Sub-Saharan Africa, particularly the interplay between history, institutions, and long-run growth. She holds a DPhil in economics from the University of Oxford.

Nancy Lozano-Gracia

Nancy Lozano-Gracia is a senior economist in the Urban, Rural and Social Global Practice at the World Bank. She was one of the main authors of Planning, Connecting, and Financing Cities—Now! She provides diagnostic tools and a policy framework for policy makers to manage the challenges brought about by urbanization and has led work using innovative data collection methods such as satellite imagery, new survey designs, and Big Data approaches to improve the understanding of urban challenges. She holds a PhD in applied economics from University of Illinois in Urbana-Champaign.

Shohei Nakamura

Shohei Nakamura is an economist in the Poverty and Equity Global Practice of the World Bank, where he specializes in urban poverty and spatial inequality. Before joining the Bank, he was a visiting fellow at Harvard's Graduate School of Design. He holds a PhD in urban and regional planning from the University of Michigan.

Notes

1   This study uses urban footprints rather than administrative areas to define urban areas, because countries define urban in different ways.

3   The six cities are Mogadishu (Somalia); Kananga, Tshikapa, Kinshasa, and Bakavu (Democratic Republic of Congo); and Dakar (Senegal).

7   National population density is computed based on data from WorldPop (http://www.worldpop.org.uk). It is used to derive measures of local population density matching the living standards indicators.

10 The analysis is based on nominal wages, as in Bacolod, Blum, and Strange (2009). They claim that firms do not care about the cost of living.

11 The answers to all questions are ordinal and therefore violate the assumptions about the use of standard methods when performing factor analysis, which are based on Pearson's correlation matrix. The polychoric correlation matrix was therefore used (Kolenikov and Angeles 2009).

13 Lower exposure means that at a certain distance (usually 10 kilometers), people can potentially interact with fewer people than they do in other cities.

14 Higher fragmentation near the city center shows that density values vary widely in this area. Henderson and Nigmatulina (2016) argue that African cities' terrain is highly rugged, suggesting that there could be less usable land near the city center.

15 This report conceptualizes better connectivity as a driver of more specialized allocation of land in either commercial or residential use, causing households and firms to cluster (see Fujita and Ogawa 1982; Lucas and Rossi-Hansberg 2002). Other views exist on the effect of a decline in commuting costs. Better connectivity can incentivize workers, especially the rich, to move to the suburbs (Alonso 1964; Muth 1969; Mills 1972). Besides pushing workers out from the city center, improved connectivity pushes manufacturing firms farther out, to the urban periphery (where land and labor are cheaper) while keeping services (which require less space and benefit more from localized agglomeration spillovers) downtown. See Baum-Snow (2007) for the United States and Baum-Snow and others (2016) for China.

16 See Gobillon, Selod, and Zenou (2007) for a detailed review of theoretical explanations for and empirical evidence of spatial mismatch.

17 An average that weighs employment accessibility throughout urban areas by the number of people residing in each location is arguably a more accurate depiction of accessibility in cities. Such figures were not used here because they were not available for London. Table 2.1 provides a more complete picture of Nairobi.

18 Conversely, car accessibility is very high in the United States—very few metropolitan areas have less than 100 percent average accessibility to employment within an hour (Levinson 2013)—and public transit accessibility is much lower. The city in the United States with the highest average employment accessibility via public transit is Salt Lake City, with only 25.4 percent of jobs reachable within 60 minutes (Owen and Levinson 2014). In many cities the average is far less: Only 2.2 percent of jobs in Riverside, California and 2.8 percent in Atlanta, Georgia are accessible by public transit within 60 minutes. These numbers reflect the shaping of American cities by cars and roads, which decentralize both people and jobs. In such contexts, efforts to fully connect workers and firms through transit are unlikely to succeed.

19 The nine African cities are Abidjan, Dakar, Douala, Harare, Johannesburg, Lagos, Lusaka, Nairobi, and Pretoria.

20 See Nakamura and others (2016) for details.

21 The World Bank Enterprise Survey data are based on a standardized questionnaire, which makes them comparable across countries. The sample is stratified by firm size and geographic location, which means that the data are representative at the city level for many countries. The analysis is restricted to manufacturing firms based in the largest city in a country. As the data include only firms with five or more employees interviewed, they are unlikely to be representative of the average African firm, but they may be representative of firms that are likely to expand into export markets. More than 10,000 firms in 67 cities, including 16 cities in Africa, were analyzed. Urban nominal wages were converted using 2010 exchange rates.

22 The definition of tradables used is broad, including, for example, all manufacturing, transportation, and financial intermediation, and the data include only firms with at least five employees.

23 For example, a naive export value for an IPod is $150, but its domestic value added in China is $4 (Linden and others 2007).

24 Two contrasting paths for the development of urban mobility appear in the experiences of China and Japan (World Bank 2015f). More details are provided in box 6.2.

25 International experience suggests that strong institutions are a precondition for successful implementation of all instruments for tapping land value increases to finance infrastructure. They include institutions that assign and protect property rights, institutions that enable independent valuation and public dissemination of land values across uses, and a strong legal framework supported by a healthy judicial system to handle disputes and oversee the process. But as land-based instruments are considered for financing infrastructure, their risks must be recognized. These risks include the cyclicality of real estate markets; incentives for corruption over land transactions; and the "transformation" of local authorities into real estate developers, favoring profits not welfare.

26 A subsequent version of the paper is in Henderson, Reagan, and Venables (2016).

27 These indicators are based on the Institutional Profiles Databases (which include a land tenure component), produced by the Agence française de développement (AFD) and the French Finance Ministry based on the set of indicators developed by Lavigne-Delville and others 2009. The data used rely on Picarreli (2015), who conducted additional desk research to eliminate inconsistent observations that would bias the results. The retained indicators are deemed sufficiently consistent to provide an accurate picture of urban land tenure security.

28 Other countries, including Mauritius, Nigeria, South Africa, and Zimbabwe, have higher ratios.

29 BRT is a bus system that dedicates road lanes exclusively for buses. The system uses bus stations, allowing pas-sengers to pay before boarding, similar to metros and light rail systems. BRTS have proven to be cheaper and faster to build than other transit systems. Building a heavy rail system can cost 10 times as much as building a BRT system. Though less expensive than heavy rail, light rail can still cost four times as much as BRT. In addition, installing a BRT can take just two years; building an underground metro can take a decade (Suzuki, Cervero, and Luchi 2013).

30 The exception is what Edward Glaeser calls "demons of density," which eliminate the positive effect at the high end of the distribution (Glaeser 2011).